Transportation and Logistics
One Man's Story

by

Jack C. Fuson
Lieutenant General
U.S. Army, Retired

MILITARY INSTRUCTION

Center of Military History
United States Army
Washington, D.C., 1994

Foreword

This volume, which depicts the fortunes of a U.S. Army logistician in a time of upheaval and deals with problems of moving troops and supplies to far theaters of war, may be read as a personal tract for the times as well as history. For thirty-five years of service, in a career of firsthand experience fighting in the Pacific and Asia and high staff responsibility in Europe and Washington, Jack C. Fuson grappled with fundamental issues of transportation and logistics and amassed a lifetime of knowledge in managing the arteries of war. Some of those issues have been prefigured in the two companion studies in the special logistics series of which this volume is a part: General Carter B. Magruder's incisive account of logistic support planning for an overseas theater of operations, *Recurring Logistical Problems As I Have Observed Them*, and Lt. Gen. Joseph M. Heiser's intimate story of the complex challenges facing a communications zone in peace and war, *A Soldier Supporting Soldiers*.

In this work the focus shifts to transportation, to the practical art of moving armies, in particular to those operations which have recurred in the wars of this century, when great magnitude and urgency have tested the military's resources. For there is a maxim in strategy and logistics—no less true today than in New Guinea, Korea, and Vietnam when General Fuson learned his craft—that success usually goes to the side with the capability to feed in the troops and goods at the superior rate. All through the pages that follow, General Fuson presents vivid examples of the impact of military transportation on the prosecution of war.

Anyone at all concerned with logistic effectiveness and the requirements for mobility in an era of contingency missions will find much in this book to contemplate. Equally important is General Fuson's stark reminder that logistics is the true limitation on strategy and tactics.

JEFFREY J. CLARKE
Chief Historian
Acting Chief of Military History

About the Author

Jack C. Fuson served as a logistics consultant to the General Accounting Office, having retired from the Army with the rank of lieutenant general in 1977. His Army career of over thirty years, during which he served in three major wars, concentrated in the areas of transportation and logistics. His major assignments included international logistics project officer for the U.S. Joint Chiefs of Staff, Director of Transportation for the U.S. Army, and Assistant Deputy Chief of Staff for Logistics (Personnel, Doctrine, and Systems). He was also the Senior Logistician for the U.S. Army, Pacific, and the Military Assistance Command, Vietnam. After he served as commander, Fort Eustis, Virginia, General Fuson's career culminated in his assignment as Deputy Chief of Staff for Logistics, U.S. Army.

General Fuson received a bachelor of science degree in military studies from the University of Maryland. He also graduated from the Industrial College of the Armed Forces, the Armed Forces Staff College, and the U.S. Army Command and General Staff College. He has lectured at the Command and General Staff College, the National War College, the Armed Forces Staff College, and Association of the U.S. Army symposiums. He has also written various articles for *Army Logistician*.

Preface

My purpose in writing this book has been to highlight several logistic problems which kept recurring during my thirty-five years of service in the United States Army.

The first problem stems from the Army's organization for logistics. Since World War II, no one commander has been in charge of the total system. This creates problems at the operating level. The postwar dissolution of the Army Service Forces only made the system more unwieldy.

The second problem is the lack of in-transit asset visibility: transportation personnel do not know the contents of supply containers nor can they track containers in transit. As a result they cannot deliver shipments to the intended customer with the documentation he requires to validate the transaction. During the Vietnam War, shipments of repair parts and components that lost their identity in transit were returned to the supply depot in Okinawa. There, highly paid specialists opened the boxes and identified the contents. They then closed the boxes and sent them back to the theater accompanied by new manifests. The concept of *inventory in motion*, which Lt. Gen. Joseph Heiser, Jr., ably described in *A Soldier Supporting Soldiers*, requires 100 percent intransit asset visibility to provide the kinds of benefits inherent to it.

The third problem is the failure to understand the concepts of transportation management, traffic management, and movement control. Their accurate use is vital during time of war and essential to the cooperation necessary between the military and the civilian economy in both peace and war.

The fourth problem is the lack of any Army organization and doctrine for amphibious support operations. Such operations were very successfully developed during World War II and should be considered.

The fifth problem concerns the lack of emphasis on retrograde planning. Such planning is always overshadowed by operational and logistical planning for forward movement.

An additional and very critical problem is the lack of adequate support personnel, especially for transportation and supply, during the initial stages of an operation. These personnel must accompany the early echelons, so that supplies and equipment arriving in the objective area can be properly handled. Unfortunately, these personnel are usually brought forward only after major support problems occur.

This happened even during Operations DESERT SHIELD and DESERT STORM!

In addition to these recurring logistics problems—some that have also been emphasized by Generals Magruder and Heiser, authors of the first two books in this series—I wish to weave into my account some emphasis on leadership. I have included a memorable 1918 article on the subject by Maj. C. A. Bach. Important principles like this are imperishable.

I would like to thank Col. Thomas W. Sweeney, director of the U.S. Army Military History Institute at Carlisle Barracks, Pennsylvania; Dr. Jeffrey J. Clarke, chief historian of the U.S. Army Center of Military History; and my editor, Theodore F. Watts, and Ms. Karen Moyes at the Logistics Management Institute. I would also like to thank Ms. Diane Donovan, editor, and Ms. Beth MacKenzie, visual information specialist, both from the Center of Military History.

In addition, I would like to acknowledge the help that Lt. Gen. Joseph Heiser, Maj. Gen. John Murray, and Maj. Gen. Raymond C. Conroy provided by reading the final manuscript as well as the valuable reviews my son John Warren and my daughter Jennie made of the early drafts.

Despite the magnificent work of these individuals, all interpretations and conclusions remain my own as well as any errors or omissions that may be discovered.

JACK C. FUSON

Contents

Illustrations

Figures

Maps

Photographs

Illustrations courtesy of Lt. Gen. Jack C. Fuson (USA, Retired), the U.S. Army Transportation Museum, or from the files of the Department of Defense.

Transportation and Logistics
One Man's Story

Prologue

As I review the course of my life, from my earliest memories through each of the various stages that I have gone through to arrive at where I am today, I find some logical progressions between stages but also much that resulted from luck and circumstances beyond my control. Unlike those who say how they would like to relive their lives so they could change events and improve their pasts, I have no such feelings. I would not like the risk in trying it again. I would be afraid of not doing as well as I have.

I was born on 23 November 1920 in St. Joseph, Missouri, to parents who had been raised in the small southern Illinois town of Wakefield. My father was a medical doctor, an internist who specialized in heart disease. My mother was a housewife and remained one throughout her life. My father, one of ten children—five boys and five girls—had been raised on a small, ninety-acre farm in Wakefield.

All the children worked on the farm until they were old enough to secure an additional job teaching in grade school. As soon as the boys could acquire enough money to enter college, they did. They would work one year, then attend summer school or attend school part time until they had completed their coursework. As was common practice in those days, the girls would work at home until they were old enough to marry and start their own families. Of five sons, my father and one other became medical doctors, another was an outstanding organic chemist, author, and medical school professor at Illinois University, while two brothers remained school teachers and farmers.

My mother, also born and raised in Wakefield, had one older brother. Her father, Peter Warren, started a country store and mill in Wakefield and became a part-time local banker to fill the need for such services in Wakefield. He extended credit to farmers so they could buy the feed and equipment to farm. After the fall harvest, the loans would be repaid with interest. It was just this simple in the late nineteenth century. Eventually my grandfather moved to nearby Newton, Illinois, a larger town of 10,000, to start a regular bank. This Newton bank still exists and I have considerable interest in it.

My father graduated from the medical school at Washington University in St. Louis, Missouri, in 1915. He interned at Barnes Hospital, part of the Washington University Medical School. When the United States entered World War I in 1917, Barnes Hospital organized one of the first field hospital units and my father joined it. The hospital unit and my father went to France that year to provide medical support to the British and French armies for the rest of the war; they returned to St. Louis in 1919. My mother remained in Wakefield during the war with my older brother, born just before my father went to France in 1917. When my father returned from France, he accepted an offer to join a physician practicing in St. Joseph, Missouri, thus beginning a medical career that lasted for fifty years.

My older brother John Warren and I grew up and attended school in St. Joseph, a town of about 50,000. For his senior year, my folks sent John to the Missouri Military Academy (MMA) in Mexico, Missouri, a fad at the time. They sent me there the very next year and I remained for all four years of high school. The MMA spanned the eight years of grade school as well as high school. The first superintendents and part owners, Col. Charles Stribbling and his son, Charles Jr., established the MMA as one of the outstanding military schools in the country. As I look back on my career in the Army, I must credit a lot of my success to my training at this academy. Although I didn't realize it at the time, I learned many lessons there, which I carried with me throughout my life, such as leadership, discipline, integrity, patriotism, and the importance of training.

Before I graduated from the academy in 1939, I had considered applying to West Point because I had been told that I could obtain an appointment. My father would have no part of it; he wanted me to follow in his footsteps and become a doctor. He had wanted my brother to attend medical school as well, but John had decided to become a lawyer. (My brother died after an operation for a stomach ulcer in 1944 while I was overseas during World War II. He was only twenty-six.)

After my brother rejected medicine for law, my father insisted that I study medicine rather than attend West Point. I enrolled in pre-medicine at Washington University in St. Louis, in the fall of 1939, after military school; I remained there until shortly after Pearl Harbor. At Washington University I also joined the ROTC program and soon found myself being used as a basic military instructor for the other freshmen. I was better prepared than many of the cadet and noncommissioned officers at the university.

My four years at MMA, plus an ROTC summer camp, qualified me to receive a commission as a second lieutenant of infantry upon reaching the age of twenty-one. I turned twenty-one on 23 November 1941 and, shortly after Pearl Harbor, received a letter from the War Department requesting my intentions about accepting the commission. Like most young men at the time, I wanted to enter the Army as soon as possible, so I replied immediately and soon received orders to report to Jefferson Barracks in St. Louis, Missouri, to be sworn in as a second lieutenant of infantry. The War Department also informed me that I would receive orders to proceed to Fort Benning, Georgia, to attend the Officers' Basic Course.

In addition to enthusiasm for my patriotic duty, I had other concerns on my mind. In the summer of 1939 I met Miss Georgia Bahnsen, a young lady from Americus, Georgia, who was attending the St. Louis Institute of Music that summer on the Washington University campus. We became very good friends that summer. In the fall she returned to Georgia Southwestern College in Americus. We corresponded during the winter and when Georgia returned to Washington University the following summer, we resumed our relationship.

Late in the summer of 1940, I visited her in Americus. Although her family was very cordial, her friends would hardly speak to me. It is hard to realize now that strong southern feelings against northerners persisted in 1940. (Latent distrust of northerners could have been rekindled in Georgia by the opening of *Gone with the Wind* that year.) Despite such hardships, we continued to correspond regularly during the fall semester.

We were not considering marriage until after graduation. But the sudden attack at Pearl Harbor and my orders to enter the Army caused us to change our minds and marry at once. During the Christmas recess of 1941, my folks accompanied me to Americus, Georgia, for our wedding on 27 December 1941. We both came back to St. Louis and moved into a small apartment while I finished the semester.

Shortly after I returned to school, my orders were changed to report to a newly organized Engineer Amphibious Command at Camp Edwards, Massachusetts, instead of Fort Benning. This was quite a shock because we were looking forward to being stationed at Columbus, Georgia, only a few miles from my wife's home. She had planned to live at her parents' home while I was in school. I also wondered why an infantry officer with only ROTC training and no engineering training was being assigned to an engineer command. It was also unsettling not to find anyone who had ever heard of the Engineer Amphibious Command. Only later did I learn that the entire basic infantry class to which I was assigned had been shifted to the Engineer Amphibious Command because of the desperate need for personnel.

CHAPTER 1

The New Amphibious Army

I reported to the brand new Engineer Amphibious Command (EAC) at Camp Edwards on 16 May 1942. The camp was still in a state of confusion. Assigned bachelor officer's quarters accommodations and told where I could eat and where I should report daily for further instructions, I soon met other young officers in the same state. We wondered where we were and what was expected of us. I vividly recall that on the second or third day, several of us scanned the bulletin board and discovered a notice to meet in formation at 0900 the next day in front of the orderly room. Several hundred officers and enlisted men lined up as directed.

The senior officer and commander of the newly formed EAC, accompanied by his small staff, arrived to take charge. The commanding officer was Col. (later Lt. Gen.) Daniel C. Noce. Almost immediately, I recognized him as the commander of the ROTC camp that I attended at Fort Leavenworth, Kansas, during the summer between my junior and senior years at Missouri Military Academy. He did not recognize me and I made no attempt to identify myself.

Colonel Noce announced that the group would divide into two engineer amphibious regiments—the 591st and the 592d. The 591st would probably go to Europe and the 592d to the Pacific. He told us to choose a regiment and to line up in the one we preferred. My group of friends lined up with the 592d bound for the Pacific. The next bulletin board notice divided the two regiments into a regimental headquarters company and three battalions of four companies each. Initially, the regiment seemed very disorganized, but this condition existed everywhere as the services expanded during those months after Pearl Harbor.

For our amphibious group, the Army was creating an organization and structure where nothing had existed before. The fact that we were at war with both Germany and Japan, one who used *Blitzkrieg* warfare and the other capable of sneak attacks, challenged our military planners. One of the major problems confronting the high command was how to reach the enemy most effectively. We could have the best trained and equipped Army in the world, but unless it could be transported into the enemy's stronghold, it would not be effective. Developing the Army's own amphibious capability was one solution.

The Army planners wanted to be able to move troops and supplies over short distances between a friendly "near shore" and an enemy-held "far shore" in their own landing craft. After the combat forces landed, the Army amphibious boats would continue to move additional units, supplies, and equipment from the near shore to the far shore as long as needed. When it became possible for deep-draft ships to resupply the far shore area, the Army amphibious units would remain in the combat area to discharge supplies into their own landing craft and then move ashore and discharge the supplies over the beach. These supplies would then be moved into beach supply dumps, established and operated by the Army amphibious units, or would be sent directly to the combat unit service support areas. This resupply process would continue until Army service support units relieved the amphibious units. The Army's amphibious shore units had to be capable of establishing all the necessary shore facilities such as landing beaches, exit roads, supply dumps, and antiaircraft and beach defense positions.

The Marine Corps and the Navy had an amphibious capability just as they do today, but their supply of landing forces and landing craft was limited. At the peak of World War II, the marines had only six amphibious divisions. The Army required an amphibious capability for approximately ninety divisions. Also, the Marine Corps amphibious mission differed from that of the Army. The marines were trained and equipped to land, establish a beachhead, stay there for some thirty to forty days, then reboard Navy ships and move on. The Navy remained in the combat area to support the marines on their beachhead.

The Army needed units to perform the same amphibious operations provided by the Marine Corps, but it needed the troops to operate for much longer periods of time. After landing at the target area, the Army then had to move in and establish a line of communication to sustain combat operations as far inland as necessary. The Army's mission included large-scale installations such as airfields, hospitals, and supply depots.

The Army also accomplished amphibious landings by moving combat troops and combat support units over long distances on Navy attack ships. The Army amphibious units with their engineer shore parties and landing craft would remain to operate the follow-on beach and supply operations. Follow-on shipping would arrive without discharge capability. The amphibious units would unload the ships, move cargo ashore in their landing craft and move the cargo over the beach to shore dumps for pick-up by the combat support units. The operations in New Guinea in the Southwest Pacific in 1943 and 1944 were classic examples of this situation.

Within several months after the attack upon Pearl Harbor, the War Department had formed the Engineer Amphibious Command to organize and train Army personnel to operate landing craft and establish beachheads. Although security restrictions prohibited widespread news that such new units existed, civilian boating groups and military personnel with marine experience soon learned about it. In fact, the Army recruiting service advertised in the newspapers and distributed pamphlets in the coastal areas to attract men into this new Army organization.

While classed as an engineering unit, the EAC drew personnel from all branches of the Army, as well as officers from the Navy, the Coast Guard, the Marine Corps, and the Coast and Geodetic Survey. Personnel from the Coast and Geodetic Survey were assigned as instructors in their specialties. Seamen from the Merchant Marine, masters from vessels, and amateur yachtsmen from up and down the East Coast became members of the landing craft units.

Many of the officers who ended up in the boat battalions, although college graduates and members of power boat squadrons, had no military experience or training. It was to have some members of these units with military experience that those of us from the infantry had been assigned to the EAC. That is how this midwesterner far from either great ocean became part of this seagoing organization. I was initially assigned as a battalion adjutant while the command was being organized and records were being accumulated.

I will never forget my first payday. After almost six weeks at Camp Edwards, we were finally told we would get paid. As one of the four adjutants from our regiment, I reported to the finance office where we picked up rosters for each company and our bags of money. We then spent an entire twenty-four hours going from company to company, lining up the men in alphabetical order, and paying each one in cash.

The two regiments were reorganized into the 1st and 2d Engineer Amphibious Brigades (EABs). The 1st EAB consisted of the 591st, the 541st, and the 531st Engineer Amphibious Regiments; and the 2d EAB comprised the 532d, 542d, and 592d regiments. There were also some separate brigade troops. Later, two additional brigades of comparable size were formed.

As quickly as possible, officers and enlisted men were assigned to these units according to their skills. I was assigned to the first regiment of the second brigade, the 532d Engineer Amphibious Regiment, commanded by a Regular Army engineer officer, Lt. Col. Donald C. Hawkins. We moved immediately to a wooded area and established our campsite on the banks of Cape Cod in Cotuit, Massachusetts. Small recreational piers in the area were expanded as fast as possible to berth our boats. Our first boats were mostly small pleasure craft donated by patriotic citizens. Boat construction varied and they were powered by many different engines, mainly gasoline with a few diesel. The Navy had provided one small 36-foot landing craft.

The initial training plan was misdirected—landing craft and shore support units were organized and trained separately. The EAC went through several reorganizations before it arrived at what was considered the best approach. After some experimentation it was decided that dividing the landing craft and shore party units into separate regiments was an error and that a better mix was a regiment consisting of landing craft and shore party engineers capable of supporting one Army division. Each regiment was soon reorganized into one boat battalion and one shore battalion.

As soon as these units had been assembled and basic training had been completed, we began mission training. At first it was a case of the blind leading the blind. Most of the landing craft available to the boat battalions for moving personnel were landing craft personnel (LCP) and landing craft, personnel ramp (LCP[R]). We also had a few landing craft vehicles (LCV) with larger ramps for moving small vehicles. Some used gasoline and some used diesel. We had very few larger crafts, like the landing craft mechanized (LCM) that would later become our standard landing craft. The LCM was fifty feet long with a much wider bow ramp and was much more seaworthy than the smaller, 36-foot LCP. The two 670-horsepower Gray marine diesel engines that powered them are still the standard landing craft engines.

We trained with both the 45th and the 36th Divisions. In the early evening, just after dark, we would pick up the infantry units on one beach and move them several miles to land them on another beach. After some maneuvering, we would retrieve the infantry units and return them to their home beach. We repeated this all-night operation almost every night throughout the summer and the fall of 1942. Initially we moved squads, then platoons, then companies, then battalions, and finally one entire regimental combat team.

The shore battalions were first divided into near shore and far shore companies. In these practice landings, they would load and unload the boats and set up shore installations on the presumed enemy beaches. An advance party would land and place lighted markers to direct the follow-on main landings. We developed and improved this technique as we trained.

In the original concept, a near shore company was trained in the proper methods of loading boats; it remained on the near shore and continued to reload the follow-on craft. The far shore company would establish the beachhead in enemy territory, then build landing ramps for vehicles, clear the beach of obstacles and mines, construct exits from the beach proper, locate and build initial supply and vehicle dump areas, mark the beach, and assist the landing force with many similar jobs. In addition to unloading boats and ships, the far shore company established defensive positions.

We soon realized that both the near shore and the far shore missions should be accomplished by the same shore company. Thus the same shore company would load out the combat units and then land in the objective area ahead of the combat units to accomplish the far shore missions. During actual combat operations later, the shore companies, as well as the boat companies, demonstrated their ability to fight as infantry in order to protect and hold their beachheads.

For several months the EAC had searched for a more suitable year-round training base in the Gulf of Mexico because winter training was not possible on Cape Cod. In the fall of 1942, the command departed the Cape. The 1st EAB moved south to train with combat units preparing for landing operations in North Africa. The regiments of the 1st Brigade each contained three boat battalions but no shore units.

The follow-on EABs, the 2d, the 3d, and the 4th, were to be deployed to the Pacific with both organic boat and shore units as well as several support units. The 2d EAB was supported by the following units: the 262d Medical Battalion, the 287th Signal Company, the 162d Ordnance Maintenance Company, a quartermaster headquarters and headquarters company, the 3498th Ordnance Medium Maintenance Company, the 189th Quartermaster Gas Supply Company, a support battery, a medical detachment, the 2d Engineer Amphibious Brigade Band, and later the 5204th Amphibious Truck Company.

Our shore battalions consisted of a headquarters, headquarters company, and Companies D, E, and F. They were well organized and had been fairly well trained as engineers before they arrived at Camp Edwards, Massachusetts. As a combat engineer battalion, they were equipped with the normal construction equipment, but they were issued some additional bulldozers and cranes to be used on the beach. They required training in the other shore party functions.

The boat battalion was not as well prepared. Because we didn't know what type landing craft and command and control craft we would have, we did not know how best to organize for operations. First, we were told that each standard boat company, A, B, and C, would be assigned fifty 36-foot landing craft. One landing craft mechanized, the 50-foot landing craft, would be assigned to the boat battalion headquarters and headquarters company. Each boat company would have an organizational maintenance and supply capability. The level of maintenance to be performed at company or battalion level had not yet been determined.

After our last large training maneuver with the 36th Division at Martha's Vineyard, we were told that our brigade, the 2d, would move to a year-round training base some sixty miles south of Tallahassee, Florida, close to Carrabelle on the northern Gulf Coast. Everyone imagined our new home would be a paradise with palm trees and white sandy beaches. What a surprise awaited us.

Most of us traveled all the way down by train on crowded day coaches. The entire move took some three days. Some of the landing craft made the trip under their own power using the inland waterways, which provided excellent training, but most of the craft moved by rail, as did most of our other equipment.

Carrabelle did have a few palm trees, but it was mostly a swamp with the biggest flies and mosquitos we would see until New Guinea. The cantonment-type camp we had been told was there had not been built. For the following few weeks, we repeated the rough, hard work of building another campsite.

As soon as the camp became livable, we started training on the shallow beaches and the sandy reefs of the Gulf of Mexico. The first training directive issued by the Engineer Command called for the 2d EAB to remain at Carrabelle until April 1943 to train infantry units for amphibious operations. The Army ground forces had established an amphibious training center next to the brigade's area, so everyone settled down for a great winter in Florida.

Back at camp, the boat maintenance company set up shop and prepared our few boats for training. At the same time, a tentative training program was being prepared for the combined amphibious operations.

Then came the next big surprise—all plans were canceled. The brigade received orders to move immediately to Fort Ord, California, and to stage for shipment on the first available transport to the Pacific theater for actual landing operations. We turned our boats over to an advance detachment of the 3d Brigade which would replace us at Camp Carrabelle. We began packing up for our next train ride. It was distressing to the few families who had arrived there to be immediately shipped back home. Although we had no idea how long we would be at Fort Ord, it didn't look as though it would be long enough to justify moving our families to the West Coast. It is difficult today to realize the differences in cross-country travel between the 1940s and the 1990s.

We began the move from Camp Carrabelle to Fort Ord during the first few days of November 1942. We required nine troop trains plus additional freight trains for our equipment. Each troop train included a mess car in which the troops ate on a scheduled basis. Every day the trains would stop so that the troops could unload and exercise on the platforms. The trains had pullman cars with berths for sleeping. Although not up to peacetime standards, the cars were comfortable. Most of the men found the trip enjoyable. We all saw countryside that we had never seen before. (We didn't really appreciate the comfort of these trains until a few months later when we were moving north from Townsville to Cairns in Australia.)

Fort Ord is located in one of the most picturesque parts of California. It was a great place compared with Camp Cotuit or Camp Carrabelle. We were housed in steam-heated barracks, along paved roads, with surfaced drill fields and excellent bivouac areas. Nearby were movie theaters, a post exchange, a laundry service, and excellent rifle ranges.

We conducted a little landing craft training using old Navy landing boats in Monterey Bay, a perfect place for surf training. As you move from north to south in the bay, the intensity of surf increases, which enabled us to experience landing in calm water in the north to absolutely impossible surf in the south. We had not had this kind of training either on Cape Cod or in Carrabelle.

We also accomplished a great deal of field training—extended order drills and the like—because Fort Ord has so many excellent training facilities. We devoted most of our time to obtaining new equipment and supplies and preparing for overseas movement. This was a new experience for everyone.

We also had to take overseas physicals and update our personnel records. After the physicals, we lost several hundred men and required replacements. My most serious loss from the physicals was my company's first sergeant, a veteran of World War I. He had been my most able, competent, and trusted assistant in addition to being a very excellent teacher. He was considered too old to go overseas. Having to leave the company just before it went overseas broke the old fellow's heart.

By this time, I was the company commander of the combined Regimental and Battalion Headquarters and Headquarters Company. Because the larger craft had been assigned to one headquarters company, it was decided to consolidate the two headquarters and headquarters companies. I commanded nine officers, all of whom had recently been commissioned directly from civilian life because of their boat experience. Although they didn't know much about the military, they were skilled with boats and navigation. It didn't seem to matter that all nine were older than I.

In addition to the field training, most of our boat personnel attended a five-week course in antiaircraft gunnery. This was very important because our craft would all have .50-caliber antiaircraft machine guns mounted on board. This was our live fire training. We also received extensive aircraft identification training to learn the difference between American and Japanese aircraft.

In late December, we received orders to ship our equipment to the port of embarkation (POE) in San Francisco. In late January 1943, we received final orders to move our units to the POE, where the entire 532d Regiment boarded the SS *Noordam* and set sail.

As I shuttled from Massachusetts to Florida and from Florida to California, my wife Georgia also began her long association with the U.S. Army. Like all Army wives, her support was vital then and would continue to be in the years ahead. Army wives, in fact, constitute a special breed whose contributions to service life are far more vital—and often far more onerous—than outsiders could ever know.

We had initially decided that Georgia would not accompany me to Camp Edwards because there were just too many unknowns. Before my departure, we met Ruth Kelley whose husband, Dr. Jules Kelley, was the superintendent of the Barnstable County Hospital on Cape Cod, near Camp Edwards. When Ruth learned about our problem, she insisted that Georgia accompany me to Edwards and stay with her and her husband until we could find a place of our own. They practically adopted Georgia, and she remained their guest until, with Ruth's help, she located a small house we could afford. I saw very little of the Kelleys or Georgia after that. Only later did I become acquainted with the difficulties of finding a house that we could afford on my $30-a-month second lieutenant's salary.

Florida turned out to be more convenient for both of us since my wife's hometown, Americus, was relatively close to Carrabelle. She had returned home by the time we moved there and drove the family car down to the nearest town, Sopchoppy, Florida. In that very small village, she found a small house to rent that consisted of an under-sized living room, one bedroom separated from it by an old sheet, and a tiny kitchen with a small kerosene stove. The water pump was on the back porch. There was no inside plumbing, but we had a privy. We moved in and were much better off than anyone else in our regiment. A few days later my battalion commander, Maj. Oscar W. Traber, from Nackadish, Louisiana, moved his wife and her maid in with us until they could find a place to live. It was close living, to say the least.

As we moved from Carrabelle to Fort Ord, our family situation became better. After realizing that my unit was to remain there for several months of additional training, I decided Georgia could join me. It turned out to have been a sound decision. Soon after Georgia arrived, she and two other wives whom we had known on Cape Cod found an excellent three-bedroom house which we could afford in Carmel, California. The three couples moved in and had a wonderful final months in scenic Carmel. We spent many nights at home—something that had not been possible on Cape Cod or at Camp Carrabelle. We both cherished this time as we prepared ourselves for the inevitable separation and our unknown future.

CHAPTER 2

From New Guinea to the Philippines

Our loading out on the SS *Noordam*/was rapid and uneventful, except for one mystery. The last night before sailing, we saw a barge tie up alongside the outboard side of the *Noordam*, from which three vehicles were craned aboard. Because they were well covered, we had no idea of what they were. We later discovered that these were the first amphibious trucks to be deployed, which accounted for the secrecy. We also learned that soon after we were underway, all the regiments had been outfitted with an amphibious truck company.

The development of these amphibious vehicles, called DUKWs, was unusual—they were developed, tested, and procured in ninety days. They had been conceived by Rod Steves, a boat designer, and Dick Kerr, the transportation specialist for the Arabian-American Oil Company. Several years later, I had the pleasure of meeting and working with these very talented men. In fact, Dick Kerr was my principal adviser when I was project officer for the development of the plastic DUKWs, a product that was never completed.

Dick Kerr and Rod Steves were among that handful of experts that General Frank S. Besson called upon to develop new equipment and new technology during his career. General Besson was probably the most innovative person I have ever known. He was responsible for much of my success in the Army along with Maj. Gen. Rush B. Lincoln and Lt. Gen. Joseph M. Heiser, Jr., both of whom I will speak about later.

Our trip to Australia was long and monotonous. A Japanese submarine threat persisted in the aftermath of the Japanese defeat in the Battle of the Coral Sea, fought in May 1942. This caused us as a single ship not in convoy to travel a zig-zag course very far to the south. It took us thirty days to reach Australia. Because we were a crowded troop ship, conditions were cramped.

While enroute, we made one stop for two nights in Wellington, New Zealand. We were allowed shore leave, which improved morale.

A few days later we landed in Townsville, Australia, and learned that because of the stevedore strike, we would have to unload our own ship. We could not imagine that a country in danger of Japanese invasion would permit such an important segment of the work force to strike. We found out later that dock strikes occurred frequently. With the help of the ship's crew, we discharged the troops and the accompanying gear onto trains and started our movement north to Cairns, Australia—a trip which turned out to be an amazing experience.

The narrow-gauge Aussie train seemed more like our stage coaches of the West fifty years earlier. It was old, slow, dusty, and terribly uncomfortable. It travelled so slowly that the troops frequently jumped off and walked alongside for exercise. In fact, as train commander I encouraged this under supervision. My company of about 250 strong occupied the entire train.

Our route north followed most of the seacoast part of the province of Queensland and we saw lots and lots of sugarcane and felt lots of hot and sticky weather. About half way up the coast, one of the heaviest rainstorms I had ever experienced stopped the train at a small town named Babinda. The train conductor informed me that both the bridge ahead of us and the one behind us had been washed out. There was no way to proceed or return and he didn't know how many days it would take to rebuild the bridges. Because there was no kitchen car on our train, we had been issued only enough combat rations to last us on the trip to Cairns.

I now faced the problem of feeding my company once the combat rations ran out. After a conference with my company officers and senior noncommissioned officers, I left the train and visited the mayor of Babinda. He was extremely cooperative and helped arrange meals at the four restaurants in town. The willing and friendly Australians and their mayor helped me develop a plan to feed the troops. I would sign for all the meals and forward the chits to the proper Army authorities for payment. I never found out if the payments had been made.

I explained the arrangement to the troops at a company meeting. I also told them they were free to go to town if they wished. I specified the restaurant to which each squad and platoon had been assigned and how reimbursement was to be made. I also explained to them how nice the city fathers had been and called upon each man to act courteously. I told the troops that I expected each man to return for company formation each day. The ringing of the train bell would signal the formation. I also assigned shore patrols to each area in Babinda. I told them that when the bridge had been repaired and the train was ready to resume its trip north, I would again ring the bell and I expected each man to report back to the train immediately. Because I had a well-disciplined company, I expected no trouble. The bridge ahead was repaired after two days, so we reassembled for our trip north.

I called a company formation to tell the troops how proud I was of their conduct in Babinda. No trouble occurred and they returned for formation on time. Some were helped by others; no one was injured but some were very drunk. I received no complaints from the village. I have always wanted to return to Babinda but have never been able, even though I have visited Australia in recent years. Babinda is remote and very difficult to reach. The trains have not improved much and the roads are even worse now than in 1943.

As soon as we arrived in Cairns, we moved to our next home, Trinity Beach. It is sixteen miles north of Cairns and thirty-five to forty miles south of Port Douglas. This area was excellent for an amphibious unit. Trinity Beach is typical of the northern coast of Queensland with a wide, white sandy beach that shelves gradually. It is great for landing water craft and is an excellent training site for amphibious operations. The Great Barrier Reef was a challenge because we had no navigational charts. The beach itself is backed up by good soil running some two miles inland before hitting a very steep mountainous slope covered with all types of jungle. This mountain jungle area rises several thousand feet before arriving at the tableland, a very fertile area, relatively flat and clear for several miles until it turns into the Australian back country desert.

The tableland became the permanent home for three Australian Imperial Forces (AIF) divisions after their return from North Africa. We built our campsite at the foot of the mountain at the edge of the jungle. While waiting to receive our boats, we used the jungle as a training area to prepare for New Guinea.

We expected to be issued boats as soon as we arrived at Trinity Beach. The 411th Base Shop, part of our 2d EAB, had arrived in Australia in early December, accompanied by our new boats in knockdown form. Unfortunately, when the base shop arrived in Cairns to take over the promised assembly plant, they found only an old saw mill that had not been converted. Its owners were still holding out for more money. In early February 1943, when this problem had been settled, the 411th, assisted by our engineers, immediately began to build an assembly plant.

Finally, in early April, the first new landing craft came off the line. It was a 36-foot landing craft vehicle personnel (LCVP), designed and built by the Higgins Boat Company of New Orleans, Louisiana. It had a wide bow ramp and was powered by the standard 670-horsepower Gray marine diesel engine. Very soon the 411th was assembling seven of these landing craft every day. As they came off the line, they were slowly issued to our boat companies until each had the fifty landing craft it had been authorized.

Our 532d regiment was the only regiment of the brigade in the area. The other two were located at Rock Hampton, Australia, several miles south near Townsville. We were to be stationed on the northern coast of Australia just below New Guinea because the beaches offered excellent amphibious training conditions and the terrain directly behind us was excellent for jungle training. We were scheduled to train with the 9th Australian Division, one of the units returning from North Africa and stationed on the high tableland beyond the jungle. In North Africa, they had been known as the "Rats of Tobruk" because they stopped Rommel at Tobruk. The 9th had been in constant combat in North Africa for nearly three years and were legendary combat soldiers. We learned from their experience.

The upcoming campaign would rely on amphibious landings. The initial battles to be fought in New Guinea to stop the Japanese had to be fought on land from Port Moresby, over the Owen Stanley Mountain Range, to the eastern and northern coasts of New Guinea. The Japanese navy still posed a threat in the Coral Sea and along the northern coast of New Guinea. In early 1943, the Allies lacked an amphibious capability in the southwest Pacific theater.

Soon after the Australian 9th Division had moved into their campsite on the tableland, our two staffs began planning for combined amphibious training. As we introduced the 9th to amphibious operations, they trained us in combat skills. Our troop amphibious experience had been very limited—mostly that which we had received many, many months earlier off Cape Cod. The few months we worked off Trinity Beach with the 9th Division provided invaluable training. In addition to having had combat experience, the Australians were great to work with. The men were all originally from the Sidney area but, after three years in North Africa, had been given only seven days leave in Sidney before being moved north to the tableland. We heard much about this injustice as the months progressed, but such was the urgency everywhere. Large numbers of Japanese were still in the area and were capable of invading Australia.

Early in July, the War Department renamed the 2d Brigade the 2d Engineer Special Brigade and named the regiments engineer boat and shore regiments. The word *amphibian* was dropped without explanation.

When I look back on the Army's frightening lack of preparedness at the beginning of World War II, I hope this condition will not occur again. In 1941 we had not planned on an island-hopping campaign ranging across the Pacific Ocean. Most units like ours had no organization, no doctrine, no equipment, and certainly no experience in the field to which they had been assigned. Our training on Cape Cod had been limited to picking up units of the 36th Division, moving them by boat to another beach and then back to home beach, all on the same evening.

The shore party knew it would assist the combat unit to load and unload, develop the far shore beach, and build roads and supply dumps, but never had the opportunity to actually practice this. Many questions remained unanswered: Which supplies would accompany the troops? Which would follow on? What, if any, documents were needed? And how could we ever maintain asset visibility for the vast amount of supplies passing through our hands?

Moving troops on and off the 36-foot landing craft was simple, but how to load and discharge a deep draft follow-on ship was much more difficult. Unfortunately, this lesson had to be learned much later during actual combat. During most of our training off Trinity Beach, we used the small 36-foot LCVP. We did not see any LCMs or larger navy landing craft such as the landing ship tank (LST) and the landing ships dock (LSD) until just before we left for New Guinea. We still had no navigation or control boats and were still very short of landing craft and lacked much of the equipment for the boat and shore battalions. Nevertheless, in early August 1943 we were ordered to New Guinea along with the 9th Division.

The new regimental commander, Col. J. J. F. Stiner, made me responsible for loading our regiment aboard a ship scheduled to arrive at Cairns Harbor. I contacted the port authority and learned that it was a C1MAV1, a small, four-hatched, deep-draft ship that had just docked. I went aboard and discussed our plans with the captain and the first mate, warning them that I had never loaded a ship. As soon as I returned to camp, we started moving to the port. Without the help of the ship's first mate, I would never have been able to load the ship. After loading we moved north to Morobe, New Guinea, a small village a few miles south of Nassau Bay and north of Buna. (*See Map 1.*) Buna had just been taken by combined elements of the 41st U.S. Infantry Division and the 7th Australian Division.

We unloaded our ship (moored in the river near Morobe) onto local barges as well as a few of our landing craft. Our regiment then established a campsite alongside this river, with part of the 9th Division nearby. Loading and unloading this ship provided more on-the-job learning.

As soon as we were ashore and had established our camp, we began moving elements of the 9th Division up the coast to join the Nassau Bay Salamaua operation. In cooperation with the 9th Division's support troops, we moved the troops and then their equipment and supplies. We did not have enough boats to make the move in one trip. All our movement had to be made at night because of Japanese aircraft and shore detachments along the way. Our only escorts were a couple of Navy PT boats from a squadron located on the Morobe River. Unknown to us, one of the officers assigned to this PT squadron was Lt. John F. Kennedy.

The Salamaua operation expanded day by day as we encountered and drove back more Japanese. Every night our boats carried up more troops, artillery, ammunition, tractors, jeeps, and supplies. The shore party established and conducted loading operations near the 9th Division around Morobe and on the far shore. Every return trip brought back wounded and sick troops, returning troops, and mail.

Our boats would often have to cut back their motors to land quietly in the dark within fifty yards of Japanese machine gunners. If the firing became too intense, our boats would pull off and quietly anchor offshore until the firing could be stopped. They would then return to the beach and finish unloading. They made several trips each night if time permitted. Gradually, over one hundred boats were obtained to support the Salamaua campaign. Salamaua finally fell on 12 September 1943.

Lack of navigational charts made operating our boats along the New Guinea coast very difficult. These waters had never been charted. Because of our proximity to the equator, we could predict neither the time of a tide nor its depth. As we moved north, however, we slowly charted the area.

As soon as we moved to New Guinea, the 2d Brigade was able to attach useful brigade support units to the regiment. Company B of the 562d Engineer Boat Maintenance Battalion was attached to our boat battalion for direct maintenance support for our boats as we operated north. This company did an amazing job for the next year or so.

Although we encountered extensive action while supporting the Australian 9th Division during its assault on Salamaua, our first large operation was the Lae landing. (It was from Lae, New Guinea, that Amelia Earhart began her tragic flight toward Howland Island on 2 July 1937.) Our headquarters was located at Morobe but, to support the 9th Division operations, we scattered small boat and shore detachments up and down the coast from Milne Bay to Salamaua.

After receiving orders to make the Lae landing, the regiment reassembled at Morobe as fast as possible. We would have a rehearsal with the 9th Division and the Navy in the Milne Bay area. Our units moved down to participate. At the time, we had only a few 50-foot LCMs and relied mostly on the 36-foot LCVPs. Therefore, we could move only one regiment of the 9th Division at a time. The landing plan called for the Navy to move the remainder of the 9th in their larger LST and landing craft tank (LCT).

After the rehearsal in Milne Bay, we reassembled at Morobe and prepared for the landing at Lae. After loading one regiment of the 9th Division at Morobe on 3 September, we moved out to join the Navy convoy for the 75-mile move up the coast. We landed the next morning at daybreak. Just before the troops hit the beach, the Japanese began firing heavily, but the escort ships that the Navy had placed on both flanks soon silenced them.

SOUTHWEST PACIFIC THEATER
1942–1945

Miles

0   1000

CHINA

Okinawa

FORMOSA

MARIANA ISLANDS

LUZON

PHILIPPINES

Guam

MINDANAO

Truk

PALAU ISLANDS

CAROLINE ISLANDS

BORNEO

CELEBES

Admiralty Is

BISMARCK ARCHIPELAGO

NEW GUINEA

NETHERLANDS INDIES

PAPUA

Lae

Morobe

CORAL SEA

Cairns

Townsville

AUSTRALIA

120°

140°

Map 1

The Lae operation comprised two beach landings some eighteen miles east of Lae and an airborne drop of the 503d Parachute Regiment into the Markham Valley at Nadzab, an old airstrip. The three forces were to converge on Lae.

Our shore party landed rapidly on Red Beach and began its work. As we were followed by the 20th Brigade, 9th Australian Division, with all of their equipment and supplies, the beachhead began to grow. Although we did not see the Japanese air force during the day, they did attack the beach area and its newly established installations every night. During these attacks, our boats would disperse offshore to present small isolated targets. As a result, the Japanese generally ignored them. After unloading, most of the boats would return immediately to Morobe to pick up another load, but around twenty boats remained in the beach area to support the troops as they moved down the coast to Lae.

The terrible jungle terrain, heavy rain and mud made the shore roads impassable. We used the landing craft to supply the 9th Division's advance by water. We moved troops, guns, ammunition, supplies, and equipment down the coast from Red Beach where we had landed the Australians. As the operation expanded, we brought more boats up to assist in this coastal support operation. Lae was captured on 15 September 1943.

General Douglas MacArthur, figuring that a quick landing at Finschhafen, New Guinea, would catch the enemy by surprise, ordered an attack there for 22 September. Having only four days to prepare for this next operation, we moved out with our Australian brigade, the 20th of the 9th, and successfully landed north of Finschhafen on Scarlet Beach. During this landing, we moved our boat and shore elements with our own landing craft while the Navy moved the 9th Division on LSTs and LCTs. We made the initial landing, established the beachhead, and installed beach markers to guide the Navy ships to the proper beaches.

For the first time, the Navy launched a very heavy bombardment before the landing, which silenced some but not all of the Japanese positions. Our shore party personnel landed without much resistance, but the first two waves of the 9th suffered quite a few casualties until the Japanese pillboxes were destroyed. Again, after landing north of the village of Finschhafen, the infantry moved south along the coast with the support of our boats. Because of nightly visits by Japanese aircraft, our boats had to anchor offshore in very rough waters. The Japanese considered the shore installations more lucrative targets and seldom bombed the landing craft.

The 9th met more and more resistance as it moved on Finschhafen, making it necessary to reinforce the 20th Brigade with additional troops and artillery. By early October, we had established regular supply lines between Lae and Scarlet Beach near Finschhafen, bringing up troops, supplies, and equipment and returning personnel to Lae.

After the fall of Finschhafen, we assembled our regiment, including our boats, in the Finschhafen harbor. It was the first time since leaving Lae that our boats had been able to reassemble as a unit for protection, maintenance, and rest.

The 9th Division's next mission was to push toward Sio. The coast from Finschhafen northwest to Sio was much different from the southern coastline from Lae to Finschhafen. The few beaches were always small and rocky and the shoreline was just as rough and rocky as the coast of Maine, but our boat personnel met the challenge.

Sio was the last mission for the 9th Division before returning to Australia for rest and rehabilitation. They had been in combat for several months and had endured heavy casualties and lost much equipment. We were sorry to see them go, but they had certainly earned a rest.

After Sio most of our LCVPs were replaced by LCMs, which greatly expanded our carrying capacity. We also received an LCM equipped with four twin .50-caliber machine guns mounted in Martin turrets, a 37-mm. gun, two 20-mm. guns, and a rocket launcher. This "flack boat" had been designed by our brigade ordnance officer, Lt. Col. Elmer Volgenau, and built by our 162d Brigade Ordnance Maintenance Company. The added fire power allowed the boat battalion to protect our convoys from enemy aircraft and shore batteries. From then on, this flack boat was used on every mission and established quite a reputation for itself.

Our next operation was planned against Hollandia, New Guinea. As the Japanese had evacuated southern New Guinea, they had moved to the north coast at Wewak and had apparently decided to make a major stand there. General MacArthur therefore decided to bypass Wewak (350 miles from Sio) and land at Hollandia, 700 miles away. This operation, vastly larger than anything we had previously taken part in, covered a much greater distance. The number of troops, landing craft, warships, and carrier-based planes involved exceeded anything we had ever seen before. Because of the great distances, we had to take along enough supplies and equipment for thirty days. Once we had established the beachheads, there could be no nightly runs back to supply bases as we had been doing.

The Hollandia operation consisted of landings by two divisions: the 41st U.S. Infantry Division was to land at Humboldt Bay just south of Hollandia and the 24th U.S. Infantry Division just north of Hollandia at Tanahmerah Bay. Our regiment, the 532d Engineer Boat and Shore Regiment, would support the 41st, with whom we had previously worked in Nassau Bay. Our sister regiment, the 542d, was to support the 24th. We had a full scale rehearsal landing over Red Beach, where we had landed for the Lae campaign, while the 542d Regiment rehearsed with the 24th Division offshore at Goodenough Island.

For the first time we would travel to the combat area on Navy ships. The LCVPs were carried in the davits aboard the LSTs while our LCMs were to be moved by an LSD, a new type of ship we saw for the first time. We were really impressed. The three huge LSDs in our flotilla could carry LCMs or barges fully loaded with tanks or trucks. Because of their bulky loads, the only personnel on the LSD were the ship's crew and our boat crews. It was a luxury for the boat crews to travel without a ship full of infantry men. From then on, we all wanted to travel to the landing area aboard LSDs until we ran into Japanese kamikazes in the Philippines. Then we all wanted to ride on the smallest possible ship.

For the first time we observed the thunderous barrage of naval gunfire with strafing and bombing from carrier aircraft, an awesome show. As soon as the preparatory fire ended, our landing craft began landing troops and equipment across four beaches on Humboldt Bay in the Hollandia area. The Japanese that had survived our pre-landing barrage had apparently taken off for the hills and left everything behind. Not only were the beaches covered with personal gear but worse, with stacks and stacks of Japanese equipment and supplies.

Our intelligence had chosen less than satisfactory places to come ashore. Although the beaches provided excellent landing areas, they were very narrow and led to almost impenetrable mango swamps several hundred yards deep. As a result, hundreds and hundreds of troops were pouring ashore followed by thousands of tons of supplies, tanks, trucks, and equipment, with no place to go. Our shore engineers had a challenging task. I bivouacked my company close to the edge of the swamp, just behind the stacks of Japanese supplies, and prepared defensive positions. We could hear gunfire everywhere but, as it turned out later, it was all from our own troops. There were no Japanese around, but friendly fire is never friendly under such conditions.

As soon as we had established our position, we began to assist the shore battalion to clean up the landing area. Despite the terribly congested beach, all the Navy ships were unloaded and left before dark. The first day and night were quiet: no Japanese aircraft appeared. The Japanese were also quiet on the second day, but we could hear the firing of a lot of small arms of undetermined origin. One always assumed that one was the target. Early during the second night, the red alert sounded. We could hear a dive bomber and we all went to the foxholes. Antiaircraft fire from the shore and from ships offshore filled the sky. All at once we heard a whoop, whoop, whoop, when a bomb hit a gasoline dump very close to our position on our beach. The flames spread quickly to most of the other supply dumps and worst of all, they spread to the ammunition dump.

Because of the piles of abandoned Japanese supplies and equipment and the additional thirty-day supply for the 41st Division, we faced terribly congested conditions on this narrow beach. We couldn't disperse our supplies and equipment so we had to stack and concentrate them. This violated good policy and placed everything in danger of being destroyed by fire and explosions.

Our regimental executive officer, Lt. Col. Del Brocket, who had been with the regiment under three regimental commanders, organized us on the beach area. We rolled gasoline barrels to the right and left to cut a wide, clear strip from the water through the area. Bulldozers pushed all types of supplies into the water. We organized human chains to pass supplies from one man to the next until they reached the safety zone. Everyone worked to save what he could. Suddenly the fire reached the main ammunition dump, sending explosions and flames everywhere. The supplies burned all night and continued for several days, destroying nearly all of the 41st Division task force's thirty-day stockage.

Everyone worked through the explosions and the fires and, fortunately, casualties were light. Observers on ships offshore could not believe their eyes, they told us later. It was apparently a sight to see. With great efficiency, our boats evacuated casualties from the burning beach to offshore ships for medical attention.

It took several more days to clear the beach. Since it would take several weeks to receive resupply, the 41st Division task force had to share food and supplies with the other Sixth Army troops. This meant that supplies for everyone were very thin for some time, but eventually the resupply ships arrived from Australia.

Although the Hollandia landing at Humboldt Bay was a disaster, the terrain surrounding Hollandia was a very large valley that was mostly free of jungle—not typical of New Guinea. The Sixth Army, under Lt. Gen. Walter Krueger, moved its headquarters into the valley followed by the Eighth Army, commanded by Lt. Gen. Robert Eichelberger. After our 2d Brigade moved all of its units into the area, we were back together again for the first time since Cape Cod. Base section troops were phased in and assumed logistical responsibilities. We continued to support Base B, as it was called, and gradually were relieved of our boat and shore responsibilities so we could begin reorganizing, re-equipping, and refurbishing all our equipment for the next operation. This was the first opportunity the regiment had to regroup since landing in Morobe in early August 1943.

To recapitulate, Morobe, our first stop in New Guinea, had been home for regimental headquarters. Meanwhile, most of the elements of the boat battalion and the shore battalion had been scattered up and down the coast. While some units had been supporting the 9th Australian Division in its new locations and other units were preparing for future training exercises around Milne Bay at the eastern tip of New Guinea, still other units were preparing to support the Nassau Bay operation north of Morobe.

After Nassau Bay, the regiment reassembled to make the Lae landings on 4 September. During the rest of the month, most of the regiment reassembled in the Lae area while boat and shore units supported the 9th Division as it moved down the coast for the final assault on Lae itself, north on Huon Gulf. Immediately after Lae had been captured, the regiment reassembled to assist the 9th Division in preparing for the Finschhafen landings north of Lae on 22 September 1943.

Following the successful Finschhafen operation, the regiment had continued to support the 9th Division as it moved up the New Guinea coast to capture Sio and eliminate the remaining Japanese in that area, until the unit returned to Australia in mid-January 1944. For the next three months, from January through April, the regiment supported the Finschhafen area and then the 41st U.S. Division for the Hollandia operation. We operated in the Hollandia area until October 1944, when we moved out for the Leyte operation in the Philippines.

Although it has not been included in the official records of the Hollandia operation, our 532d Engineer Boat and Shore Regiment managed to get into serious trouble at Hollandia. As the first unit to land, we took charge of the enormous supply dumps that the Japanese had abandoned. Our supply personnel were very surprised and pleased to discover a large cache of Japanese beer which they immediately began to issue in daily rations to our regimental units. When the Sixth Army headquarters found out, they ordered the beer to be turned over to their headquarters and General Krueger severely reprimanded our regimental commander. It proved too good to be true.

While the Sixth Army moved up the New Guinea coast, other South Pacific forces captured the offshore islands from New Britain and Saidor to the Admiralties. After Hollandia and the Admiralties had been secured, the area command decided that it was not necessary to clear the Japanese out of the rest of Dutch New Guinea, rather, it was time to return to the Philippines.

Before starting the Leyte operation, I changed jobs. My executive officer, Lt. Ralph Waite, took over command of the headquarters and headquarters company, and I was reassigned as the intelligence officer (S2) of the regiment and was soon promoted to major. For the Leyte landings in the Philippines, we moved under X Corps control in order to support the 24th U.S. Infantry Division. The X Corps, with two assault divisions, was to land on the northern coast of Leyte in the area of Tacloban and Palo. That was about all we knew about the landing plan until we loaded aboard ship and departed from Hollandia. Security was very tight.

Although most of the attack force was loaded aboard ships by the base at Hollandia, we loaded our own boats and equipment aboard an LSD and the LSTs to which we had been assigned. The Sixth Army Service Command coordinated the ship loading. The plan called for the Sixth Army Service Command to take over from us and from the 592d about thirty days after D-day in the landing area on Leyte. We would thus be free for the next operation. Plans also specified that the cargo ships be loaded for selective discharge, based upon the conditions found in the landing area. We also were told that the Leyte operation, under the Sixth Army, would include other landings on Leyte to the south.

The first day out, we learned more about the island of Leyte and our landing area. The surprise assault would encounter little or no resistance from the Japanese. With the purpose of liberating the Filipinos from the Japanese, we were told to avoid shooting Filipinos. We were part of an enormous convoy, but didn't really realize its size until we arrived off the coast of Leyte on D-day minus three or four. Fortunately, we met no resistance enroute.

As our convoy moved into Leyte Gulf early on D-day, 20 October 1944, the Navy bombardment began in the dark. I have never in my life seen such a display of firepower from battleships, cruisers, and destroyers. An entire fleet seemed to have opened up on Leyte. During the bombardment, we began unloading our landing craft and launching our gunboats and control boats from the LSDs and LSTs. About half the landing craft were ours and half belonged to the Navy.

We found out that before the operation, the Army and Navy had a contest over whose landing craft were to dominate the D-day landings. The Navy commanders insisted that all the landing craft be Navy with none from the Army. The Army leaders insisted that the Navy provide only life boats for the return trip from the beach. The Army leaders pointed out that Army boats would have to make the D-day assault and remain after the Navy departed. The Army had to have its boats there to continue follow-on support. This conflict apparently reached the Joint Chiefs of Staff before it was decided that the Army boats would participate in the D-day landing. This decision established the doctrine for future operations.

The 24th Division that we supported landed on Red Beach in the Palo area. The 1st Cavalry, supported by the 592d Engineer Boat and

Shore Regiment, landed to the north in the Tacloban area. We heard that we could expect excellent landing beaches backed up by excellent terrain, but we found just the opposite. I landed with the regimental commander and his staff in our control boat, between the second and third waves, in the Palo area. The initial landings went unopposed, but soon after that all hell broke lose.

As I walked up the beach to establish our regimental command post, I was hit by an artillery or mortar shell. I was not seriously injured, but my left side received a lot of shrapnel which covered me with blood from head to foot. After my fellow officers evacuated me to a Navy hospital ship, they thought they would never see me again.

When the medics had cleaned me up, they found nothing really serious, but a broken left eardrum and lots of shallow wounds up and down my left side. The most serious problem was a piece of shrapnel embedded at the base of my tongue. Removal of this shrapnel required a painful, three-hour operation because they were not able to deaden the nerves all the way to the base of my tongue. They were afraid that they might cut my jugular vein, so they worked very slowly. Fortunately, it was successful. After a couple of weeks in a general hospital at Hollandia, I returned to my regiment about the middle of November.

I had witnessed only the beginning of the Leyte landings. After my return, I heard the gory details about the landings and their problems. The beach was not a good place to land. They could not use LSTs because of the shallow water offshore. The Tacloban area beaches were better, but they were so busy and the area was so narrow and congested that they could not handle the LSTs reassigned from Palo beach. Portable causeways were brought in to land and unload our LSTs on D-day plus two or three. Such causeways had been planned for, and three or four sections were required at each landing site. Because the beach at Palo was backed up by swamp and mud, it was nearly impossible to build roads to move equipment and men off the beach. The landing was made during the rainy season, which meant terrible weather and impassible terrain.

It appeared that intelligence had made a large error. During planning for the landing, General MacArthur's engineer had raised an argument against landing on Leyte during the rainy season. The main purpose of these landings was to free Leyte and build airstrips there to support the larger invasion of Luzon. MacArthur overruled the engineer and forced the operation during the wrong season. In 1944, the rainy season was much worse than usual at Leyte; two typhoons hit the island in addition to the rain. The World War II Army histories cover this argument in detail.[1]

---

[1] Robert Ross Smith, *Triumph in the Philippines* (Washington, D.C.: U.S. Army Center of Military History, 1991).

Soon after I returned to the regiment, we were told that we would move around to the island of Mindoro, on the west side of the Philippines group, to build airstrips there to support the Luzon operation. The Mindoro operation had been planned for much later but had to be moved forward because of the airstrip problem.

In addition to the beach and poor terrain on the mainland, unloading our supply ships at Leyte had also been a problem. Although the base at Hollandia had been told to load the ships for selective discharge to make all parts of the cargo available, the Sixth Army Service Command at Hollandia had not done so. Apparently, the 6th Army Group had not observed the loadings performed by the base command closely enough. They had not been loaded for selective discharge, they had not been loaded with enough dunnage to brace the cargo, and the cargo had not been secured adequately. At Leyte, they needed steel matting for beach ramps and the Tacloban airstrip immediately. The matting had been loaded first, at the bottom of the ships, and then completely covered by vehicles and break bulk cargo. Had they loaded the ships for selective discharge, they could have unloaded the matting first. Instead, the entire ship's cargo had to be off-loaded to make the matting accessible. The Army learned a very important lesson the hard way.

Our regimental commander, Colonel Stiner, had become sick in Hollandia and was replaced by Col. Alexander Murray Nielson, also an engineer.

During the discharge operations, the Navy furnished transport beach parties who did an excellent job assisting our shore parties on the beach. These Navy transport beach parties provided much the same type service to Marine Corps landings as the engineer shore parties did for Army landings.

During this same period, the great sea battle of Leyte Gulf was underway, but our forces did not hear about the battle for many days and did not understand its scope or importance. It was a very important turning point for our operations in the Philippines and in the Pacific theater.

We next moved against the Philippine island of Mindoro, about the size of Leyte, but with a much smaller population, located only twelve miles south of Luzon. Its inhabitants were scattered along the coastal regions. There were no Army divisions available for the Mindoro operation, so General Krueger, the Sixth Army commander and overall commander of the operation, created a separate task force called the Western Visayan Task Force (named after the Visayan Sea).

He placed the task force under the command of Brig. Gen. William C. Dunckel. Its principal combat components were the 19th Infantry Regimental Combat Team of the 24th Division and the separate 503d

Parachute Regiment with whom we had worked in Australia and again at Lae, New Guinea. Also included was the 3d Battalion of the 21st Infantry of the 24th Division plus an antiaircraft group and the 532d Engineer Boat and Shore Regiment. Initially, they planned to drop the 503d Parachute Regiment into Mindoro, but the runways on Leyte could not accommodate the troop carrier aircraft required to lift the 503d.

Since the primary mission of landing on Mindoro was to build airfields, the task force included a large number of airfield engineers: four U.S. Army engineer battalions, a Royal Australian work squadron and, of course, other service troops to unload the LSTs. General Krueger had assigned as service troops 1,200 infantrymen from a newly arrived division that had not yet entered combat in the Philippines. This billet was very unpopular with the infantrymen, but they pitched in and helped our shore party personnel very well.

As I recall, we assigned a labor detail of seventy-five men to each LST. In those days we loaded about 400 tons of break bulk cargo in the stern of the LST on the bottom deck and loaded the forward area with tanks and vehicles. We unloaded the break bulk cargo by hand because we did not have forklifts or pallets. We moved the cargo out to the bow of the LST by hand and either loaded it onto trucks for movement to dumps or stacked it on the beach until trucks were available.

The total force included about 12,000 combat troops, 6,000 service troops, and approximately 9,500 Allied airmen. The aircraft were scheduled to arrive by D-day plus five, when the first airstrip was to have been completed.

The task force departed from the east coast of Leyte on 12 December 1944 and headed south for the Surigao Strait, between Leyte and Mindanao, and through the Sulu Sea to Mindoro. A good sized Navy escort fleet accompanied us. This was the first time our naval forces had entered the South China Sea which, until recently, the Japanese fleet had completely controlled.

We sailed unmolested until the afternoon of 13 December. That day we saw our first Japanese kamikaze. He came up unchallenged, flying low over the water, and crashed into our flagship, the cruiser USS *Nashville*. We all saw the explosion in which over 130 men were killed outright, including several key commanders and staff officers.

The task force commander, General Dunckel, and the convoy commander, Rear Adm. Arthur Struble, were wounded and badly burned. However, they quickly transferred to another ship to continue. At meetings I noticed that General Dunckel was covered with bandages for some time. I am sure his burns were serious.

The *Nashville* was able to return to Leyte. Later in the day, another kamikaze hit a destroyer which also had to return to Leyte. We saw

Japanese aircraft frequently from the time we reached Mindoro. Often we saw kamikazes that were impossible to defend against and caused a tremendous amount of damage.

We landed near the southern tip of Mindoro opposite the small sugar plantation village of San José, following the usual naval bombardment, on 15 December. We landed on Blue Beach to the north and White Beach to the south, separated by about a half a mile of less favorable terrain. Both were excellent, with gradual shelving and good water, and both backed up to excellent terrain. The shore party immediately began organizing the beaches and supervising unloading of the LSTs and landing ships medium (LSMs). The 1,200 infantrymen provided very valuable manual labor. We established beach dumps and immediately reconnoitered the entire area.

Because there were no trained service troops, the 532d operated the base which included a small, narrow-gauge railroad. We found some experienced railroaders in our shore battalion and this detachment moved into the rail yard and found four old locomotives and some 300 freight cars. They were also met by Filipinos delighted to see Americans. They had operated the railroad before the Japanese arrived and they told us they had sabotaged the engines so that the Japanese could never use the railroad. Our crews and the Filipinos together got the line operating in a few days. From then on, our railroad became a very effective form of land transportation.

During the landings, we encountered no enemy opposition. The few Japanese troops on the island left for the mountains which covered Mindoro. The 19th and the 503d were able to move out and secure all their objectives by the end of D-day.

Airfield construction units had priority discharge over the beaches to move their equipment and supplies. By the end of D-day, the engineers were ready to begin construction of a landing strip. The engineers found the old San José airstrip impossible to improve; they located a suitable area and, by D-day plus one, were fast at work.

In addition to building and repairing new roads to clear the beaches and to establish a line of communication, our engineers had to direct the repair and operation of all the utilities in San José. They received enthusiastic assistance from the Filipino residents.

For the first time, we also had to take over a complete operation of a port. Our commander served as the cargo control officer and was responsible to chart the waters, direct incoming ships to anchorage, schedule ship departures, unload and transfer cargo, and perform all other functions of a port. Responsible for the defense of the entire beach area, we established defensive positions on both flanks, to the rear and to the front. This was in addition to our main job of discharging the initial ships and unloading the follow-on resupply ships.

By the end of D-day, most of the Navy escort vessels had dispersed or returned to Leyte because the Japanese still controlled the South China Sea. This left us very much exposed. Eight of the first ten Liberty ships bringing resupply had been hit by kamikazes and were lost or put out of commission. The kamikaze problem was so serious that we began bringing ship crews ashore at night and bivouacking them in our area.

The initial resupply convoy, containing two ammunition ships, arrived about D-day plus ten. One had been destroyed enroute. The second arrived offshore and was ordered to anchor about ten miles out. I went aboard to direct the ammo ship to its anchorage and told the ship's captain that the current procedure was to take crews ashore at night. This delighted the captain, who said he could not wait to get ashore. I said I would return at 1700 hours to take him and his crew ashore.

As I returned to the beach I saw a kamikaze come in low and hit the ammo ship amidships. There followed the greatest explosion I had ever seen: it looked like an atomic bomb. As the mushroom cloud rose up to the sky, the tremendous wave created by the explosion picked up our LCM and moved us about 150 yards up onto the beach. It also swept all of the equipment and supplies off the beach and deposited them inland. Although many people consider me too conservative in handling ammunition, that experience taught me to be very cautious about berthing and working ammo ships.

During this period, our boat crews accomplished many extremely dangerous rescue operations. They located and rescued crews of downed aircraft, they attempted to find survivors from ships hit by kamikaze pilots, they landed and resupplied U.S. patrols on Mindoro and neighboring islands, and they refloated several PT boats damaged during fights with the Japanese.

Because of inadequate water transportation during the initial move from Leyte to Mindoro, our LCMs and control boats had to be towed by LSTs, LCMs, Liberty ships or other ships. The crews on our control boats and LCMs lived aboard their boats most of the time. Several crews lived aboard their boats for over two years, showing how adaptable soldiers can be. Most built elaborate quarters on the sterns of the LCMs.

Homemade wine was available on every boat. Each boat had been issued two 5-gallon wooden casks for storing water which, when augmented with the dried fruit from jungle rations, became fermentation vats. Soon the natural chemical process produced wine. Every visitor to a boat was expected to sample this homemade wine. Most of it was awful.

From 15 December 1944 until January 1945, when the landings on Luzon were made, San José took continuous poundings from

Japanese aircraft. Their main targets were ships in the stream during the day and the airfield construction at night. Enemy air was not our only problem. At about 1800 hours on 26 December, we were alerted that a Japanese naval force, consisting of two cruisers and several destroyers, was on its way to Mindoro and would arrive about 2000 hours.

When they first sighted the force, the Air Corps immediately reinforced the aircraft at Mindoro, bringing in as many as the airstrip could hold. The U.S. Navy had only a few PT boats in the area. Immediately, all the aircraft and the PT boats moved out to engage the enemy. We increased our defensive positions on shore and prepared for a possible beach landing. We were alerted to the fact that some Japanese troop ships had also been observed behind the combat ships.

By 2330, the Japanese task force had moved to a position right off our beach and began shelling the two airfields. A few shells hit the beach but caused no great damage. All available aircraft began to attack the Japanese task force. It was like an extra-large 4th of July spectacle with white and red tracer streams everywhere.

When all the shelling began, we noticed a lack of activity at the battery of 90-mm. antiaircraft guns located on our beach. Since I was responsible for the beach defense, Colonel Nielson sent me to the battery to find out what was wrong. The battery commander told me that they could not fire at a surface ship; they could only fire up at an airplane. They lacked a horizontal aiming capability and could not lower the gun tubes enough to fire horizontally. I asked him to lay the guns down as far as possible, sight over the barrels, and fire them toward the ships like rifles. Even if it didn't do any damage, it would probably distract the Japanese from the punishment they were giving our aircraft. The captain and I did just that. In no time, the 90-mm. guns were firing toward the Japanese task force, which apparently did distract them and raised the morale of our gun crews.

The attacks by our aircraft were very successful, but at a high cost in aircraft and pilots. Just after midnight the Japanese task force retreated, without attempting a beach landing. It was later reported that three destroyers and a heavy cruiser had been badly damaged. Each time I observed our Army and Navy aircraft and the Navy PT boats engaged in combat, I became more respectful of their courage and effectiveness.

Soon after the departure of the Japanese task force, we secured most of our troops for the night. There were lots of stories and discussions the following day, but it was mainly back to work. During the next month, our boat battalion engaged in several tactical operations up and down the coast of Mindoro and to other islands. Our regiment also conducted several offshore reconnaissance missions. In March, I took four of my men to reconnoiter the beaches and enemy strength on Lubang Island because the high command was considering a landing there. Lubang is off the north coast of Mindoro toward the island of Luzon.

About midnight, two PT boats dropped us off near Lubang, about a mile off its southern coast. We arranged with the boat commanders to pick us up again two nights later at the same time and place. We went ashore in two often-used rubber rafts. On the beach, we deflated our rafts and hid them in the brush. After daybreak, we moved out to a predesignated location to meet a Filipino scout. He was apparently a soldier who had remained on Lubang after the Japanese arrived and had stayed in touch with Allied intelligence. He had lookouts stationed all over the islands and was very helpful.

The scout became our guide. He told us that there was a unit of Japanese soldiers camped at the far end of the island. They were thought to be fearful of their position and seldom left their camp. He said he had them under constant observation and knew all their movements. He took us into his village and we met the village chiefs, who treated us like real heroes. They fed us and assisted us in all of our missions.

I had assigned each of my men a certain area to reconnoiter and map. I returned to the beach, pumped up one of the rubber rafts, and spent most of the two days there making a complete survey of the beach area and the area behind the beach. I reconnoitered and mapped the shoreline during the day and charted the water in the evenings to determine the best areas for ships to anchor and discharge the landing parties and their equipment and supplies. I also wanted to discover the best beaches for landing craft to land the troops and their equipment and to find useful exit paths from the beach to the island targets. We selected a perfect area for the landing force to use.

At the designated time, we returned to our rafts, moved out to our rendezvous, boarded the PT boats, and returned to our base at Mindoro. It had been a very simple and uneventful mission highlighted by our unexpected meeting with the Filipinos. I always wanted to return to Lubang after the war, but was never able.

We did not encounter any enemy fire, but another of our task forces, landing troops on Lubang a short time later to clear the island, encountered very heavy resistance. I was not present.

In March 1945, Colonel Nielson, our regimental commander, was reassigned to an engineering job on Luzon. Lt. Col. Robert Casper, who had been the 2d Brigade executive officer, replaced him. Initially, Colonel Casper had been our shore battalion commander and had trained on Cape Cod. Casper had remained with the brigade for the entire period.

Mindoro remained our regimental home for almost a year—longer than any other place we stayed during the war. During this period many of us were given forty-five days leave back to the States, which was certainly welcome. Because my mother was very ill, I was one of those granted leave.

While on Mindoro, we had placed detachments on nearly all the other islands. This required running daily resupply missions as part of a clean-up operation within the larger Operation VICTOR. When the Sixth Army had been assigned the Luzon invasion, the Eighth Army, under the command of General Eichelberger, had been assigned Operation VICTOR with the mission to clear the Japanese from all the southern Philippine Islands, the Visayan group, which consisted of Palawan, Cebu, Panay, and many smaller islands. The 542d participated in the landing on Palawan Island.

Our regiment remained on Mindoro until June or July 1945, when we were told to reassemble our units from all over the Visayan Islands and move to Panay to be attached to the 40th U.S. Infantry Division. We would assist the 40th Division in amphibious training and plan our next operation. As our unit with full gear boarded the LST for Panay, Maj. Robert Butch, one of our regimental staff officers, was followed up the ramp by his pet chicken Mildred on the way to her first landing. Unfortunately, no one photographed the event.

We moved to Panay, established a campsite near the 40th, and began to help them prepare their equipment and supplies for loading aboard Navy combat transports. Having come ashore on Panay after the island had been cleared, the 40th Division had never participated in a combat landing.

Our regiment was very careful to tell them how to load for selective unloading, having learned that lesson a couple times before. We told them of the importance of overseeing the base command when base personnel loaded their initial resupply shipping, even though it was not their official responsibility.

On the first day or so in August, we learned of our next operation. The 40th Division would become part of the XXIV Corps then located on Okinawa. The corps would make landings on the southern coast of Japan for Operation OLYMPIC. Our regiment was to land and support the 40th Division. The 592d, the 542d, and one regiment from the 4th Engineer Special Brigade would take part in D-day landings as part of a four-division landing operation under the Sixth Army.

We were also assigned a second mission. Before we landed on Japan on D-day, we were to land some Marine Corps radar vans on five small islands just off Kyushu, on D-day minus five and D-day minus four, in time to rejoin the 40th for the main invasion. The radar vans would establish a radar screen for the landing forces. During operations on Okinawa, Navy destroyers had been used for the radar screen, but this proved disastrous because kamikazes had been able to sink several destroyers, which eliminated the radar.

Because I was the S3 (operations and training officer), the S2 (intelligence) of the regiment and I were heavily involved in planning the landings. A study of the available maps and charts showed that these little islands were uninhabited but very mountainous, with sheer cliffs coming down to the sea. We could find no suitable beaches on the islands. We could not figure out how to land these heavy, small-wheeled radar vans to accomplish the mission. Nevertheless we loaded the vans and their Marine Corps personnel on the assault ships, along with the 40th Division, and prepared to join the big OLYMPIC operation.

Just before we sailed, we heard that bombs had been dropped on Hiroshima and Nagasaki. We did not understand what had happened, but we soon learned of the Japanese surrender. There would be no combat landings on Japan!

By 1945 our LCM crews had lived, eaten, and worked aboard their own vessels for almost three years. They had performed excellently under very serious and dangerous conditions, including absorbing many battle casualties. Although many had been recognized with decorations, I'm sure many had been overlooked.

Our shore battalion personnel had also done an impressive job loading and unloading ships and boats and supervising the stevedore companies and service units with whom they worked. Many times they had been called upon to defend beach areas, and they had performed extensive construction and utility work for the whole period.

As I assess our war experience, I realize that we did not devote enough time and effort to proper documentation and labeling of cargo units. We moved the cargo from ship to shore and into a dump area. It was then up to the supply personnel to sort it out, to segregate the items by class, and to separate items within each class. This is a very difficult job when the cargo is coming in faster than you can check it and accurate documentation does not come with it. Again, rations, POL, construction materiel—basic supplies—are not a problem. The kind of cargo that causes problems is repair parts. Such items are requested by part number or serial number. Parts identification, or asset visibility, which had not been a problem during our landings in New Guinea or the Philippines, became difficult when we got to Mindoro.

During the early combat landing with the combat divisions, the division's support personnel maintained their own asset visibility throughout the process. They turned the boxes or equipment over to us and we loaded them. At the destination, we discharged the items and returned them to the same division support personnel. Since they had marked their boxes, they knew the contents of each. When resupply in quantities began arriving at Mindoro, for example, we had been relieved by the base personnel.

Then the problem of asset visibility increased dramatically. I cannot say what kind of job base personnel performed because records are difficult to find. The Army did not have one standard system for marking like the defense system has today. Each technical service followed its own system religiously.

CHAPTER 3

Postwar Korea

I soon learned that I was to join the 40th Division G3 (assistant chief of staff, operations) and fly to Okinawa to meet with the XXIV Corps commander and staff to receive further orders.

The division G3 and I spent one day on Okinawa being briefed and preparing plans. We learned that we would not return to the United States as we first had heard. The point system to be used for discharging troops had been announced and most of our regiment had many, many more points than needed to return to the States. We had been overseas in combat for almost three years. The troops were not happy about not going home, but were glad that we did not have to land in Japan. We all knew that the invasion would have been a very bloody operation.

We were told the XXIV Corps, with the 6th, 7th, and 40th Divisions, was heading for occupation duty in Korea. The landings were to take place through Inchon, Korea. The 532d would land the three divisions at Inchon, take over the port, establish a corps supply and storage area behind the port, and support the operation until a base section could be brought in and established.

We returned to Panay, where our units remained on board ships, and sailed immediately for Korea. We briefed our staffs, prepared detailed plans, and began briefing all the units aboard.

I accompanied the regimental staff, along with both battalion commanders, their staff and a part of the boat battalion, as we moved by LSD from Panay to Inchon. During the trip, we reviewed the situation based on the limited information available. The sudden end to the war and our shift to Korea for occupation duty had not been included in anyone's planning book. In Okinawa we had not been able to obtain maps or charts of Inchon or even of the channel leading up to the port. It was another case of the blind leading the blind, but at least this time we were not planning to be shot at.

After we arrived off Inchon, several of us went ashore to find out how to enter the harbor. We could not believe what we found: the tide variation at Inchon was thirty feet, second only to the Bay of Fundy. Few navigators had ever experienced anything like a 30-foot tide. The tide went out at between six or seven knots, faster than the speed of our landing craft. We also discovered that there was no tidal basin we could use. A small tidal basin had existed many years before, but it had not been maintained and didn't have gates or a mechanism to operate them.

We did use the basin for unloading landing craft and barges, however. The shore end of the basin was adequate for landing and discharging both the Navy LSTs and our LCMs. The sides were adequate for discharging barges. We loaded the landing craft and barges from ships off shore and brought them into the basin at high tide. Our LCMs could be discharged rapidly, so they could move back out to the deep water as the tide receded, to be loaded again for the next tide. The LSTs and barges, however, would land in the basin at high tide and remain on the mud to be unloaded during low tide. Some six hours later at the next high tide, they would move back out to deep water. We also had a few additional landing areas available for landing craft and barges to discharge their cargos in the same fashion as in the basin.

Today, the port of Inchon is enclosed by a sea wall with gates, through which ships enter and leave the port. The port at Inchon has become as modern a facility as you will find anywhere in the world—I saw it just before the 1988 Olympic games.

In 1945, however, most of the facilities in Korea were inadequate. The Japanese, during their fifty years of occupation, had done little or nothing to maintain transportation or utilities anywhere in Korea. The Japanese had treated the Korean people terribly. No Koreans had been permitted to hold any type of supervisory job; all were relegated to day labor jobs. They had not even been permitted to teach their own language at the few schools that remained. They were truly demoralized.

Operating in New Guinea and the Philippines had prepared us for the primitive port facilities in Korea. The steep and rocky terrain immediately behind the port was not suitable for use as a supply dump. We established our supply dumps at an old storage depot area between Inchon and Seoul. This later became Ascom City, a major supply installation in Korea. Although the Japanese had left a lot of supplies and equipment there, we emptied the depot without any trouble.

We found a couple of treasures housed in these warehouses. The Japanese had filled one warehouse with British Parker double-barreled shotguns. A Parker shotgun is still one of the finest in the world. We immediately took these over and later issued them to each company and battalion in the task force for recreational shooting. We also uncovered many cases of Japanese shotgun shells which we also issued to the troops. Unfortunately, more than half were no good. It was irritating to pull the trigger at the plentiful quail and duck, only to hear a click.

We faced serious cargo problems. Many ships arbitrarily sent to Inchon laid off the coast waiting to be unloaded. Like all of the ships in the Pacific, they had been loaded for some other mission, not for Inchon, and certainly not to support occupation troops. We couldn't unload the ships because we couldn't handle this many vessels and we didn't have any place to put the cargo. The corps support group that worked with us would study the cargo manifests. If they found usable cargo, they would pass the word to us and we would find it on the ship and bring it to our offshore anchorage.

Assigned as port commander from the first day in Inchon, I had to organize the personnel and equipment to support the three divisions of the XXIV Corps task force with three classes of supply: Class I, food; Class III, petroleum, oils, and lubricants; and Class IV, construction materiel. Meeting this requirement posed little or no problem. I discharged all of this as we found it. Disposition of other supplies, especially repair parts and components, was more difficult.

When we found out that someone needed certain spare parts, we checked the manifest to see what ship contained them. We then boarded the ship and started digging. Even if the ship's manifest was fairly accurate and specified in which hold and at which level the box was stored, it was a terrible waste of time. But the ships were just anchored there waiting because the war was over.

Very soon after we left, a transportation medium port unit took over and was ordered to discharge all the ships completely or to reroute them to some other destination. Piecemeal unloading was stopped.

My port command had many other problems moving supplies and equipment to the three divisions. For example, because the ships had all been loaded for operations in the hot Pacific, there weren't any winter clothing or stoves aboard. We occupied Korea in the fall and the weather soon turned cold. In those days, we couldn't fly in high-priority items, such as winter clothing, as we would today. We had to wait for winter clothing, stoves, and firewood to arrive by ship from the States.

At one time, there had been lots of wood in mountainous Korea, but during the fifty-year Japanese occupation, the Koreans had pretty well stripped their mountains of trees. We all suffered pretty severely for the several months of the Korean winter until clothing arrived. The troops lined their khakis and fatigues with newspapers or straw mats to keep warm.

I had several other problems. Because we did not have enough stevedore companies or quartermaster companies to handle all the cargo, I was forced to use whatever personnel and equipment I could find. Some Korean and Japanese stevedores were available, but their mutual hostility required that they form separate work groups. Because the few Army quartermaster port units I commanded also disliked the Japanese, we worked the gangs separately. I therefore organized the stevedores into three ethnic groups: Koreans, Japanese, and Americans.

We also had a shortage of trucks to clear the port. We found some Korean trucks that we put to work with our quartermaster truck companies. Learning that a Japanese truck company was available, I told the Japanese company commander to bring his vehicles to the port the next morning. I then noticed that about half the trucks were towing the other half. I had told the Japanese commander to bring all his trucks, and he did. I had forgotten to tell him to bring only the ones that were operable. I had to learn to be more precise when dealing with Asians.

We established a separate ammunition operation just south of the port proper. Our DUKW company moved the ammo from ship to shore and then inland to an ammo storage area. The DUKWs could operate around the seashore across the reefs without concern for the swift tides. This technique was used later during the Korean War, and it is still used in Inchon today. The DUKWs, the barges, and the Navy LSTs and LSMs were most helpful, but our LCMs performed the heaviest ship-to-shore work in Inchon as they had in New Guinea and in the Philippines.

Although we had problems with the primitive Inchon port, the corps commander and his staff had many more. The corps commander, Lt. Gen. John R. Hodge, and a small staff had landed at Tempo Airfield on 4 September, just four days before we landed with the three divisions at Inchon. The staff had little preparation for Inchon. As soon as the troops arrived and established camps, the job of receiving the surrendering Japanese began. Although I did not observe this, I understand it was difficult.

Taking over all of the functions and jobs previously held by the Japanese and running Korea was a bigger problem. General Hodge knew that the Japanese had prevented the Koreans from getting any management experience for fifty years, so he decided he had to keep key Japanese personnel to run the country. When he could bring in U.S. troops or civilians to assume leadership responsibilities, he would drop the Japanese. At the same time he planned to train the Koreans to take over these jobs, but this plan was not acceptable to the Koreans. Although they lacked training, the Koreans insisted on taking over their country directly from the Japanese.

At the time no Korean party or group was ready to take over and run the government. Industry and commerce had ceased; public utilities and services hardly existed. The Korean economy was in a shambles. The turbulent and tense political atmosphere complicated all of these problems. More than seventy political parties had been formed since the Japanese defeat and the arrival of the American troops. The Korean situation was becoming more complicated because the Russians and the Chinese were also applying political pressure.

To placate the Koreans, General Hodge relieved and replaced all the Japanese. Soon, thousands of Koreans held key jobs. Hodge also brought in as many advisers in these fields as our government could provide at the time. Compared to his problems, we were in pretty good shape at the port because we took over all functions when we came in and continued to operate the port as if it had been another landing.

We left the port this way when we turned it over to a transportation corps port command early in February 1946. Our command rotated back to the States as a unit, just as we had shipped out as a unit some three years before. Although we had many replacements, many of us had been together throughout the war and continued this relationship after the war.

CHAPTER 4

A Career in the Army

Although the entire regiment moved back to the United States as a unit on board the same ship, when we arrived at the Seattle port of embarkation in March 1946, we were handled as individuals. It's difficult to imagine the number of servicemen returning from overseas ready to be processed out of the service all at the same time. The Army was being dismantled as quickly as possible.

After our records had been turned over to the processing center in Tacoma, Washington, we were assigned to barracks and mess facilities and told to do what we pleased until our orders had been prepared and transportation provided to send us home. We had to report to headquarters every day to check on our orders.

After we hit port, we called home and tried to answer the questions about when we would be home. We then went into Tacoma to start celebrating. After a while we received change of station orders and thirty days leave, following which we were to report to the processing station closest to home, in my case Fort Leonard Wood, Missouri. After spending part of my leave at my parents' home in St. Joseph, Missouri, and part of the time at my wife's home in Americus, Georgia, my wife and I returned to Fort Leonard Wood. I was told to report to the processing point daily for further instructions.

In the meantime, we found a small room to rent in Joplin, Missouri, and began living once again. Several of my midwestern friends from the regiment reported to Leonard Wood the same time as I did. We got together daily with our wives, most of whom had met each other at Cape Cod or Fort Ord before we went overseas. Needless to say, this was a wonderful way to kill time. Very soon, we were told to report to camp.

After arriving at Leonard Wood, we had been warned that we would each have to decide whether to remain in the service or be separated. Everyone had discussed this decision a lot during those first few days. Most of us from the regiment decided to remain in the Army for at least the immediate future. Those staying in soon received orders to return to the 2d Engineer Special Brigade, now stationed at Camp San Luis Obispo, California. This was close to

Morro Bay, where we had been stationed for a short time before shipping out in 1942.

At my request, I was once again assigned to the 532d Engineer Boat and Shore Regiment. While I was reporting in, my wife was busy finding a place to live. She rented a small house on Morro Bay, California, very close to Camp San Luis Obispo. I was still a major and was assigned to the 532d Boat Battalion as the executive officer. I would soon see many familiar faces. We were to be stationed at San Luis Obispo; however, our boat-operating and maintenance facilities were to be located at a site still to be built on Morro Bay. In the summer of 1946 it was still an unspoiled bay.

Soon after settling at our new camp, the battalion commander, the area engineer, and I looked around Morro Bay to find a training site. (The battalion commander, Lt. Col. Albert Gasper, had also led our unit at Inchon.) Neither the boat battalion nor the shore battalion had equipment of any kind. Apparently, the chief of engineers had submitted requisitions for all the necessary TO&E gear, but we could not trace them. It probably had something to do with the drastic postwar reduction in the Army's size.

I was soon told to report to Brig. Gen. David A. D. Ogden, the brigade commander. Only our 2d Brigade was to remain on active duty. The 3d and 4th Brigades were being deactivated. Brig. Gen. William F. Heavey, who had commanded our brigade throughout the war, was retiring. General Ogden, who had commanded the 3d Brigade throughout the war, became the 2d Brigade commander. I didn't know Ogden except by reputation, but I soon learned to respect him. He later became the Inspector General of the Army and retired as a lieutenant general.

When I reported to General Ogden, he outlined the problems he was having finding out the status of our equipment requisitions. He asked me to go to Washington as brigade liaison officer to expedite acquisition of the equipment. I was to report to the Office of the Chief of Engineers and remain there until we got the equipment. His office would be in touch.

On 4 March 1946, my wife and I drove back to Washington, stopping for one night in St. Joseph, Missouri. Fortunately, my mother had given us a car. In 1946, it was almost impossible to find an automobile—new or used—since automobiles had been out of production for four years. We rented a room in Chevy Chase, Maryland.

I reported to the Office of the Chief of Engineers, located in the New War Building, now part of the State Department building. Although most of the War Department headquarters was in the newly constructed Pentagon, the chief of engineers had remained in the New War Building even though the space could not house his entire staff.

The Supply Division was located in temporary building T–5 at Fort McNair, the present site of the Industrial College.

I reported to T–5, was assigned office space, and met the people with whom I would work. This began several difficult weeks. The Supply Division was very helpful, but was having problems with all engineer units stationed in the States. As it turned out, General Ogden was very wise to place a liaison officer in Washington. He needed someone to personally contact the sources of equipment. I dealt with the Engineer Supply Division, the Army Service Forces supply staff, and most of the equipment manufacturers.

After a few weeks, I got our equipment and supplies moving to San Luis Obispo and was ordered back to our home station. Washington was a difficult assignment, but a very important one in which I learned a great deal about supply procedures. In the meantime, the brigade moved back to Fort Ord, California, because San Luis Obispo was to be closed. We did not have adequate training or living facilities at San Luis Obispo and nothing at Morro Bay. The construction of an amphibious base there would have been very expensive.

Georgia and I returned to California and rejoined the brigade at Fort Ord. We were fortunate to have been assigned excellent quarters at the Presidio of Monterey. This was the first time we had occupied government quarters.

Soon after I rejoined my boat battalion of the 532d, General Ogden called me for another special assignment. The War Department had given the Sixth Army, to which we were assigned, the job of locating a permanent amphibious training base for the Army on the West Coast. As the brigade's representative, I reported to Sixth Army headquarters at the Presidio and joined a small group of five other officers headed up by the Sixth Army engineer, Brig. Gen. Garrison H. Davidson, a former All-American football player at West Point.

We spent several weeks surveying the entire West Coast, from Alaska to San Diego, to locate areas adequate for amphibious training. We attempted to find the ideal location for beach and surf training, backing up on enough land for shore training of combat troops. The most interesting and beautiful part of the trip was a reconnaissance up the inland waterway from Vancouver to Prince Rupert, Alaska, and back. Toward the end of our survey, General Davidson was replaced by the Sixth Army chief of staff, Maj. Gen. Frank D. Merrill of the famous "Merrill's Marauders." He lived up to his reputation and we enjoyed his company for the trip.

We found several adequate areas and reported all this information at the conclusion of our survey. The War Department approved our recommendation to locate the main headquarters and base at

Fort Warden, a small Army post on the northwest coast of the Olympic Peninsula. This old historical post, close to Port Townsend, was about to be closed again. We also located several islands in the sound that could be used for landing and training areas. Several months later, the 2d Engineer Brigade moved from Fort Ord to Fort Warden.

After completing the reconnaissance, I was again assigned a special job as combat liaison officer. The 532d Engineer Boat and Shore Regiment was to participate in joint amphibious training exercises with the Navy, the Marine Corps, and the 2d U.S. Infantry Division stationed at Fort Lewis, Washington. General Ogden asked the regimental commander to assign me as combat liaison officer between the 2d Engineer Special Brigade and the other forces. I was put on temporary duty at Fort Lewis for sixty days to assist the 2d Division in planning for the joint exercises at Camp Pendleton.

Before leaving for the operation, key people from the regiment also joined me at Fort Lewis. We all loaded aboard ship with the 2d Division and moved out for San Diego. The remainder of our regiment, including our boats, was picked up off Fort Ord as the convoy sailed to San Diego. The landings were to be conducted over the Marine Corps facilities at Camp Pendleton, California.

About the time I returned to the brigade, the Army began the first postwar Regular Army integration program designed to increase the number of Regular Army officers, since the Army had very few at the time. Many of us applied for Regular Army commissions and were told to choose three branches in order of priority. My first choice was engineers, but one of the requirements for Regular Army commission in the Corps of Engineers was a college degree in engineering which, of course, I did not have. In fact, I had no degree whatsoever, having left college in the middle of my junior year.

The brigade executive officer, Col. Draper F. Henry, suggested that I make the Transportation Corps my first choice because this newly developed corps was to perform work very similar to that performed by the engineer special brigades during World War II. I followed his advice and received a Regular Army commission in the Quartermaster Corps/Transportation Corps during the first integration program in July 1946. Before Congress authorized a permanent, separate Transportation Corps, all personnel were assigned to the Quartermaster Corps and then detailed to the Transportation Corps.

As soon as the brigade learned about my selection, General Ogden reassigned me as the post transportation officer at Fort Ord, with temporary duty to the brigade until completion of the joint training exercise. Ogden then told the War Department what he had done and requested that I be left at Fort Ord. This was not approved and I soon received orders to report back to the Transportation Center at Fort Eustis, Virginia, as soon as the exercise was completed.

At the time, the Army and the other services were demobilizing. Personnel of all ranks were being released from the Army or, in some cases, being retained at a reduced rank. We knew of many colonels, lieutenant colonels, and majors who were reduced to enlisted ranks if they chose to remain until retirement age. Obviously difficult for the officer, this was especially difficult for the wives. Many installations were being closed, equipment being declared surplus, and of course, budgets being slashed drastically. It was a trying period.

In early January 1947, we packed up and moved back to the Transportation Training Center at Fort Eustis to attend the First Officers' Advanced Course. My wife and I packed up the car and started back across the country with our two-week-old baby for our third trip within nine months. In those days, traveling across the country in an automobile was not easy. There were very few motels then, so the traveler had to rely on rather run-down city hotels, difficult to get in and out of, or the more primitive tourist cabins. The age of the interstate highway was still several years in the future. We decided that my wife and our new baby would remain in St. Joseph with my parents while I went on to Fort Eustis.

In 1947, Fort Eustis was as unattractive as any place I had ever seen. It had been an Italian prisoner of war camp during the war. Most of the wooden barracks were rebuilt World War I and II units that had been painted black and surrounded with a high barbed wire fence. There was not a single tree on the main post.

I reported in and was assigned a bachelor officers' quarters. Since the First Officers' Advanced Course would not start until fall, I was assigned to the First Officers' Basic Course. Most of the students were not the first and second lieutenants for which the course had been designed, but were captains and majors who had been in World War II for several years. Most of us had never been in the Transportation Corps. After I completed the three-month course, the Transportation School assigned me as an instructor and I ended up teaching the First Officers' Advanced Course rather than enrolling in it as a student.

When I arrived at Fort Eustis in January 1947, the school was just getting organized after having moved from Mississippi where it had been during the war. Very few members of the staff and faculty had been assigned yet. It was the school commandant, Lt. Col. (later Maj. Gen.) Rush B. Lincoln, who decided that I should attend the short course and then join the school faculty to teach the advanced course. Lincoln, who had attained the rank of full colonel by the end of the war, had been downgraded like so many other young colonels. A very good friend and adviser, he is one of the three officers to whom I credit the success of my career.

Soon after arriving at Fort Eustis, I began looking for a place to live. I rented a small, one-bedroom apartment in the only decent apartment building complex in the Newport News area. I was told I could work my way up to a larger unit. As soon as a larger apartment became available, my wife and baby joined me by train. In those days, trains provided the only efficient cross-country transportation. Having little or no furniture, we borrowed some temporary items from the post until we could buy our own. The Army takes care of its own and does so very well.

I was initially assigned to the Marine Branch of the Transportation School and taught Marine Port and Amphibious Operations. We had to design our own courses and write our own classroom material with very little help. Our supervisors had been newly assigned as well and were just getting their own feet on the ground. It is difficult now to recall conditions in the Army in those early days just after World War II.

The Transportation Corps had been organized during the war and had no approved TO&Es yet. No written doctrine had been prepared. I spent about half of my three years at the school in the Marine Branch and the other half in the Movements Branch. At that time, the school had two teaching departments: a Transportation Department (consisting of a Movements Branch, a Highway Branch, a Marine Branch, and a Rail Branch) and a Military Arts Department which taught general military subjects such as operations, intelligence, logistics, and personnel.

During the basic course, I was introduced for the first time to transportation management, movement control, and traffic management. As I taught my marine subjects, I became more and more interested in the subjects taught in the Movements Branch and I devoted a great deal of time studying them. Also during this period, I heard Colonel Lincoln talk about his World War II experience in movement control at the very top level of government.

Colonel Lincoln had been one of ten engineer officers whom Maj. Gen. Charles P. Gross, the first chief of transportation, had taken with him when he was assigned the job on the Army staff. Lincoln had graduated first in the West Point Class of 1932 and, like most of the top graduates, chose the Engineer Branch. During World War II, while working for the Transportation Branch of the Army staff's Logistics Division, Lincoln became the Army's main movement control man.

During the war, President Roosevelt met every six months or so with Churchill and Stalin, accompanied by their principal military advisers and staffs. President Roosevelt took General Marshall,

Admiral King, and General Arnold with him. The Combined Military Transportation Committee, made up of the transportation chiefs from each country, also attended the meetings.

At the conclusion of each top-level meeting, the plan of action for the next few months (for example, to take Europe first and the Pacific second and how to do it) was turned over to the Combined Military Transportation Committee on the last night so the committee could decide if the plans were feasible. As the U.S. action officer on the committee, Colonel Lincoln would work all night with the other members of the committee to validate the plan and to finalize the Joint Military Transportation Movement Plans and Programs. This had to be done before approval of the overall plan. This was movement control at the top level.

Of the four branches in the Transportation Department of the school, the Movement Branch had the most written doctrine and supporting reference material. While preparing for the Normandy invasion, the U.S. Command in Europe had adopted the British Army's Q-movement system, which was very well established, well documented, and very effective. The Q-movement representative, a principal member of the British staff, is always well respected by the British Army. Because the managers of our communication zone (COMZ), established in Europe during the invasion, adopted this system to control movements throughout the war, it was adopted Army-wide.

Transportation is one key to effective combat operations. The movement of troops into battle and their support and resupply are obviously vital to military victory. In the British Q-system, all participants in the operation must determine their transportation requirements and submit them to the transportation manager so that transportation can be allocated properly in accordance with command decisions. In peacetime, when transportation is available units can obtain sufficient transportation if they have the money. In time of emergency or war, transportation is always limited and it must be totally controlled.

Even in war, however, it is difficult to force users to determine their transportation needs quickly. At the national level only the top commander has the authority to allocate transportation to all sectors of the military and, in the case of total war, to the civilian economy as well. This had been true in World War II. Lt. Gen. John C. H. Lee, a strict disciplinarian, commanded the COMZ. He believed in the Q-system and required all U.S. forces in Europe to follow it. If one had not submitted his requirements for transportation in advance, he didn't get transportation except in an extreme emergency. General Eisenhower apparently supported General Lee.

During my second year at Fort Eustis, Nell Monroe Fuson, our second child, was born. I spent my last year at Eustis learning and teaching transportation management and movement control. After completing my three years duty on the staff and faculty, I got the opportunity to attend the Transportation Officers' Advanced Course 4. I initially thought that I didn't need it because I had been teaching the advanced course for three years. My superiors thought differently and credit for attending such a course is more important than teaching it.

As I progressed through the nine months of the course, I began to appreciate why I was enrolled. I learned a great deal when we reached the various military arts subjects, which were essential to my future Army career. The course also prepared me for the next and most important career course, the Command and General Staff College at Fort Leavenworth, Kansas.

After the Korean War broke out in 1950, more and more forces went to Korea. Our class at Fort Eustis knew that following graduation in the spring of 1951, most of us would also be assigned there. Our class included officers with World War II experience in all fields, including some transportation at the junior grade level. When Maj. Richard Biggs and I, both at the top of our class, were assigned to the Office of the Chief of Transportation in Washington, D.C., instead of Korea, we were very much surprised.

Georgia and I again began the predictable chore of looking for a place to live near Washington. With two young children and a third on the way, we gave up on apartments. Very few were large enough to accommodate us. Finally Georgia found a small house which we could afford in the Braddock Heights area of Alexandria, Virginia, not far from the Pentagon and my office in Tempo Building 7. Tempo 7, a huge run-down temporary office building from World War II, located on the site of the parking lots for Washington National Airport, housed most of the Army's Technical Services.

Our third child, named Jack Carter Fuson, Jr., was born on 23 August 1951 at DeWitt Army Hospital, Fort Belvoir, Virginia.

I reported to the chief of transportation and was assigned to the Terminal Division. This division had staff supervision over all ports and water operations and managed the U.S. Army Transport Command. Since World War II, the chief of transportation had been responsible for the management of all troop and cargo transport ships, a tremendous job. This function was later turned over to the Navy and became the Military Sea Transportation Service.

I worked as the chief of the Planning Branch of the division for the next one and one-half years as a newly promoted lieutenant colonel. In addition to planning various marine operations in Korea, Maj. James D. ("Dunny") Dunn and I developed TO&Es for all the marine units: port units, harbor craft units, landing craft units, and so forth. We produced the first official Transportation Corps authorized organizational tables. We used our World War II experience and the information I had picked up teaching at Fort Eustis to prepare these documents. As I observed units based on these tables operating in Korea and Vietnam, their accuracy amazed me.

We also supported the "distant early warning" (DEW) defense line, which the United States and Canada were establishing against Russian bombers coming over the North Pole. This job required establishing communications, ports, and antiaircraft stations on a line in northern Canada, Alaska, and Greenland. The construction and support of these stations had to be provided mostly by water, which existed only during one or two months of the year when the ice had melted. I made several trips to our major commands and support areas in Goose Bay, Newfoundland, and Thule, Greenland. Fortunately, we never had to use the DEW line, even though we devoted a tremendous effort to build and support it.

CHAPTER 5

War in Korea

Following World War II, the Army and Navy had been dismantled so rapidly and had discharged their trained personnel so fast that by June 1950, when the Korean War began, both services lacked experienced personnel. This affected the Army Transportation Corps acutely. The Army leadership has always had the opinion that because established commercial transportation existed, plenty of transportation experience also existed. They did not think it necessary to maintain transportation experts on active duty in the Army.

The first group demobilized after World War II, the Transportation Corps was also the first group to experience a shortage when the Korean War started. Consequently, it was the first to be called back to active duty. The very few experienced transportation personnel available at the beginning of the Korean War had been moved to their various billets overseas and in the continental United States. By 1952 and 1953, most of our experienced transportation personnel had already served their tours in Korea and had returned to the States.

The major port supporting the movement of materiel was Pusan on the southern coast of Korea. (*See Map 2.*) After MacArthur's counteroffensive, the port of Inchon was used to its limited capacity. Most of the men, equipment, and materiel entered the country through Pusan and the nearby minor ports of Kunsan, Masan, Ulsan, and Suyon. From Pusan, supplies to support the Eighth Army were moved forward by coastal water transportation, by the country's rather limited rail system, and by highway. This rail line had not been operational during the occupation in 1946.

Pusan Port quickly became a bottleneck as usually happens during wartime. The chief of transportation assigned Col. Ralph Garretson, his executive officer, to go to Korea to assume command of the port of Pusan and relieve the traffic jam. I was one of the four officers Colonel Garretson selected to accompany him. An opportunity to put into practice the principles I had been learning and teaching at Fort Eustis was an exciting prospect.

Soon after receiving orders for Korea, Colonel Garretson and his four officers, Lt. Col. Buck Bratcher, Lt. Col. Richard Biggs, Lt. Col.

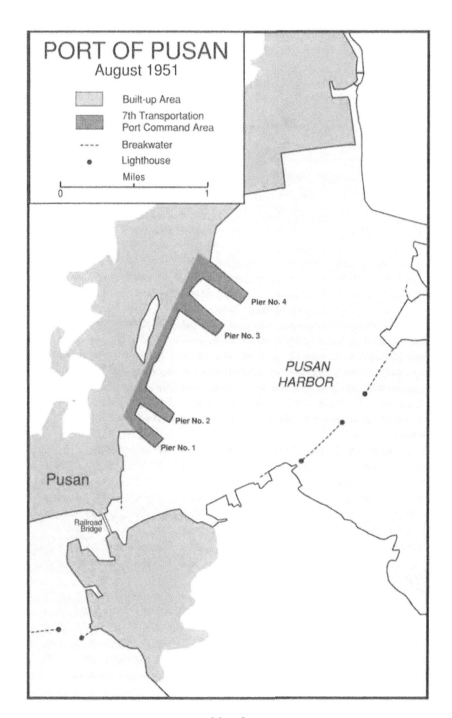

PORT OF PUSAN
August 1951

Built-up Area
7th Transportation
Port Command Area
- - - - Breakwater
• Lighthouse
Miles
0   1

Pier No. 4

Pier No. 3

PUSAN
HARBOR

Pier No. 2

Pier No. 1

Pusan

Railroad
Bridge

Map 2

John Youens, and I departed for Pusan. We stopped for briefings at
the San Francisco port of embarkation and at the Headquarters, U.S.
Army, Pacific, in Hawaii, then went on to Korea.

Very soon after we arrived in Pusan, Garretson made assignments for the four of us. Biggs took over command at the port of
Kunsan and Bratcher became chief of the Terminal Operations
Division at Pusan proper. His job was to discharge and backload all
the arriving ships and to clear the cargo from the dock to its first
destination. Youens commanded one of the truck battalions supporting the main port at Pusan. I commanded the main ammunition port
at Ulsan, Korea. An accident at Ulsan had just blown away about
half of the port.

I first directed the rebuilding of the port and its ammunition discharge facilities. The Army Corps of Engineers performed the work in
a very satisfactory manner. Even after repair, this port had very limited capabilities. Because it had no piers, we unloaded ships onto
barges in the stream, then moved the barges ashore using our small
tugs. From the barges we transferred the ammunition directly to rail,
when railcars were available. When they were not, we stacked the
ammunition on the beach. We tried to limit beach storage to dumps
less than 20,000 tons for safety reasons. This was sometimes difficult
because our highest priority job, as always, was to discharge deep-
draft ships so they could return for another shipment. Eventually, we
could unload 15,000 to 20,000 short tons a day.

The method we used to move the ammunition across the beach
and onto the railcars, or to the beach dump area, was new to me.
Korean stick gangs carried handmade sticks, supported across the
shoulders of two men, from which the ammo was suspended. A load
of up to 500 pounds could be carried on a stick supported on two
men's shoulders. For heavier loads, such as a 1000-pound Air Force
bomb, two gangs were used. One two-man gang slung the front of
the load between them, and the other two men supported the rear of
the load. These stick gangs had been carrying heavy loads this way
all their working lives. One could recognize a stick gang member by
the indentation or groove the stick had worn into his back.

These amazing teams could carry heavy loads from the barge up
into the railcar or to the beach all day long. They moved with a regular
and steady cadence as if they were marching to music. As I got to
know these stick gangs, I would occasionally take over from one of
the men and help with the unloading. Getting into the right cadence
was the most difficult part, but I soon learned how to do it. Every time
I joined in, the gang would get excited and clap in approval. I became
very familiar with all of the gangs and learned to communicate with
them without learning the language very well. I enjoyed getting to

know them and working with the Koreans during my wartime tour as I had during our occupation after World War II.

I commanded one port company and supervised the Korean stevedores aboard ship and on the beach. The port company made an excellent team. I most respected the two NCO ordnance safety inspectors from the Ordnance Corps and an enlisted Coast Guard Safety Inspector adviser. The Coast Guard inspector monitored ship operations and the ordnance inspectors watched the stevedore operation aboard ship and over the beach. They were on the job constantly and knew their jobs well. I became completely dependent upon them for advice. My experience with ammunition ships in the Philippines during World War II taught me a lesson I would never forget.

Once we had a problem in Ulsan that I was afraid might lead to an explosion like the one we had in Mindoro. We were receiving fire bombs for the Air Force by the shipload. The bombs looked like two 55-gallon drums fitted together end to end. If the two sections became separated the slightest bit, they would start smoking. We found this out the hard way. One day the stevedore crew reported that as soon as they opened the hatch, they saw smoke coming out. I ordered the stevedore crew ashore immediately and the ship's crew followed.

When I asked for ten volunteers, the Army and Coast Guard ordnance inspectors raised their hands along with many of my port company personnel. We boarded the ship and began unloading the bombs very carefully until we found the one smoker and took that rascal out as fast, and as carefully, as we could. We put it on one of our control boats, took it to sea, and dumped it overboard. It was a relief to have solved the problem safely, and it reinforced my respect for ammunition. I obtained decorations for all the volunteers.

The nearby little town of Ulsan was full of young girls. The usual VD and social problems occurred among our soldiers as they always do. I made it a point to become friends with the town mayor, the chief of police, and the main city doctor. By working with these three leaders, I kept trouble and VD to a minimum. We provided the penicillin for the doctor to treat any girls with VD and we had an excellent cooperative relationship.

During 1952 and early 1953, the Allied forces attempted to inflict as much damage as possible on the North Korean and Chinese forces. General James A. Van Fleet, in command of the Eighth Army since April 1951, really believed in artillery fire. He insisted on firing nearly 10,000 rounds of artillery a day, which became known as the "Van Fleet Day of Fire." The Ulsan port became the main source of ammunition for Van Fleet's artillery. We had to work around the clock to move all the necessary ammo through our port onto railcars where it could be distributed to the various Eighth Army ammunition supply points. The Third Military Railroad Service (MRS), together with the Korean National Railroad, operated the South Korean rail in a professional manner.

The Third MRS consisted of a headquarters, two operating battalions, and a shop battalion. These units came to Korea from our training command at Fort Eustis, but now they were Regular Army troops. They had originally been reserve rail units from our major railroad companies who had been called to active duty during World War II. These rail units had been developed and supported by railways and came to the Army as experienced men. They had worked for United States and Allied forces all over the world. Their accomplishments in Europe, Iran, and Japan were well known.

During the Korean War, personnel could spend twelve months on duty in Korea and then rotate back to the States or could extend to eighteen months before rotating. Both Colonels Bratcher and Youens rotated back after their one-year tour. Colonel Biggs and I chose to extend for the eighteen months. When Bratcher rotated, Colonel Garretson moved me back to Pusan and gave me the Terminal Service Division, a job I had wanted very much. I overlapped with Bratcher for about a month and learned a great deal from him. He had worked in a similar capacity at the New York port of embarkation for several years and was very experienced with commercial stevedoring. My only experience had been ship-to-shore over-the-beach during World War II.

When we came to Pusan port, we had a few experienced transportation officers and enlisted men in top jobs and very few experienced men below that level. When I took over the Terminal Operations Division, I had a few experienced lieutenant colonels, majors, and captains, but I also had many inexperienced second and first lieutenants. Instead of being able to assign a lieutenant colonel or a major as a pier superintendent to work four or five ships, I had to place a young lieutenant in charge. He was assisted by even less experienced second lieutenants and NCOs. I had no alternative, but I soon found out that even without experience, all of my team was doing a great job.

Our stevedores, all Korean nationals, were well trained in technical stevedore operations. If a new type operation was required, one which the Korean stevedores had not yet experienced, the ship crew would soon fill us in. I soon learned that in most cases, if you have the courage to give these difficult jobs to young, well-educated, aggressive people, they soon learn the satisfaction that comes from job accomplishment. From then on, you won't be able to hold them back. In many cases, for the first time in their lives they will have an opportunity to take responsibility and to realize their own capabilities. It

matures them immediately. Years later, many of these young lieutenants and captains told me how much they appreciated the opportunity I gave them to learn of their abilities so early in life. In civilian
life, such opportunities are rare.

We had three types of personnel: U.S. military (officers, NCOs,
and enlisted men), Korean nationals, and Japanese subcontractor personnel. The members of our 7th Transportation Port Command provided most of the port supervision. We had a few Transportation
Terminal Service companies, which provided stevedore supervision
and acted as cargo checkers. Large numbers of direct-hire Korean
civilian stevedores and laborers assisted in the warehouse open storage areas and performed all other types of labor. Japanese contractors
provided most of our harbor craft and inland and coastal ships. These
included the heavy-lift crane, the flattop barges, the tugs, and hundreds of small, covered cargo lighters on which the operators and their
families lived. Japanese contractors also provided and maintained our
materiel handling equipment (MHE) which, in those days, consisted
mainly of small warehouse forklifts and tractors.

U.S. military truck companies of the 48th Transportation Group
provided most of our port clearance truck transportation. All of the
port and supporting labor performed very well. We had no major labor
problems except pilferage. To control pilfering, a Military Police unit
provided shipboard and shoreside security. This police unit was augmented by combat units in the area when available. The very serious
pilferage problem required extra troops.

My boss, the director of port operations, also a very experienced
man, had entered the Army from commercial port operations during
World War II and had worked in most of our ports of embarkation
during and since the war. Familiar with all types of port operations, he
was a very fine teacher. I learned more about port operations during
these six months than any other time during my thirty-five years of
active duty.

Colonel Bratcher had one major misunderstanding of our responsibilities in Army Transportation: he failed to maintain 100 percent
item identification all the time an item was in Army transportation's
hands. He theorized that since the customer ordered the items, we
should give them to him and let him worry about identifying them. I
soon learned that we were doing something wrong.

The major Technical Service depots for Korea, located in the
Pusan area, received all the incoming Technical Service cargo. They
processed the cargo for movement to Eighth Army and COMZ units,
or they stocked it in their depots in Pusan for future use. Although we
shipped a great deal of cargo directly forward to the combat zone, it
was mostly Class I (food), Class III (POL), Class V (ammo), and

vehicles of all kinds. We moved most of the difficult to handle items, such as components and repair parts, to a Technical Service depot first. We handled over a million tons of cargo a month through the port and its outposts. We unloaded 18 to 20 ships alongside our piers and another 10 to 15 carrying bulk cargo in the stream. Nearly all the depots were on the water or close by the port.

We could move cargo by barge, truck, or rail, but we mostly used barge and truck. The largest Technical Service depot was Ordnance Base Depot (OBD) No. 1, located on the water about a mile away from the main port. We moved a lot of the extensive ordnance cargo by water. Ordnance items included tanks, all types of vehicles, tires, tracks, guns, and many other "end items." The biggest and most difficult cargo were the thousands of boxes of components and repair parts.

With each shipment, we usually received adequate documentation that described all the items in detail, providing the part number, requisition number, and destination. The ship's manifest generally arrived before the ship, but not always. Even if the documentation arrived in theater, it would not necessarily be forwarded to the port. Each box was marked with a color code for each Technical Service: red was for Ordnance, green for Quartermaster, and so forth.

No one can imagine the amount of wartime cargo shipped out and received in overseas ports, nor the speed in which it arrives unless you actually witness it. The port and beach cargo handlers have to rapidly move the cargo through the port to its first destination. There is never enough storage space to store cargo in the port. It must move on. Keeping a port clear of ships and cargo is always the port's biggest problem. Generally, it is not the port's capacity to move cargo that causes the problem, but the first destination's capacity to receive the cargo, to check and inventory it, and to prepare it to move on.

All the while, the Technical Services depot personnel must maintain 100 percent asset visibility (100 percent content identification), especially if transportation could not provide the receiving customer with the necessary documentation. Without the documentation, the customer cannot immediately identify the item or send it to its alternate destination.

The receiving supply installation's problems usually increase because of a lack of supply personnel. Obtaining adequate logistics personnel in the theater has always been a major problem. The combat commander understandably wants his combat troops first. Consequently, commanders do not add space for support troops in their order of battle until support problems get out of hand. They notice this phenomenon when a shortage develops and equipment for the combat troops does not reach the front. Then the supply support personnel problem becomes a crisis.

Only at the crisis level do the commanders worry about support troops. This was our problem in Pusan during the Korean War. It occurred later in Vietnam during the 1960s. It occurred again, I am told, during Operation DESERT SHIELD in the Persian Gulf.

Since 1951, the United Nations had been negotiating with North Korea for a peace treaty. The Allies knew that once a treaty had been signed, the United States would no longer be able to support the South Korean forces with combat supplies. To beat the deadline, we were moving as much equipment and supplies into the theater as possible. We were following the in-transit identification system that the Technical Services used to identify cargo in addition to its accompanying documentation.

Many transportation operators had the habit of identifying cargo for movement to its destination by color coding alone. This was not adequate. When the transportation operators picked up the item for shipment at its point of origin, they received documentation that identified the item completely. They should have provided the customer at its destination with the same detailed information. We were remiss at the port of Pusan, also. We tended to move the boxes with red corners to OBD–1 without regard for their contents. We also packed the shipping documentation in boxes just like the cargo, leaving it to the customer to sort. This procedure lost the identity of the item.

The receiving Ordnance depot had to sort all the boxes and attempt to match the parts to the documentation to trace which part corresponded with which requisition. At the speed we pushed cargo into OBD–1, it was impossible for them to keep up. The depot could not even unload our trucks and barges as fast as we moved them in and it certainly could not match the cargo with its documentation.

The director of operations would order me to unload our trucks and barges at the depot so we could unload the endless stream of ships and clear the cargo off our docks. I would send cranes and crews to the depots to unload our trucks and barges. We ignored identification in our rush to move out the incoming cargo. We stacked it all up until the mounds of ordnance parts and equipment got to be so high that the depot could no longer operate. Everyone knew that we had enough cargo in the depot to support the Allied and Korean forces for at least ninety days, but there was no way to sort out items and issue them to the customer in an orderly manner.

The Ordnance Section finally abandoned OBD–1, moved to another location, and started over again. I've often worried about the terrible waste of money and materiel this represented. I learned my lesson about item identification by making all the mistakes myself, but I was never able to convince my bosses that the mess was a Transportation Corps problem more than a depot problem. The depot was the victim. Ever since, I've preached the need for item identification to both logisticians and transportation experts, but I have generally struck out.

Soon after Colonel Bratcher left and I took over the terminal operations at Pusan, we established a very innovative operation center on the recommendation of the Korean Base Section commander, Brig. Gen. Richard F. Whitcomb. General Whitcomb commanded a reserve transportation major port and had commanded ports of embarkation and debarkation in the United States and Europe during World War II. Called to active duty soon after the Korean War began, he devoted most of his days to managing the Korean Base Section, a very extensive operation.

At night, he would come to the port and travel its length to observe the various port operations. This was apparently his first love and he always came unannounced. He would never ask for anyone to accompany him on these nightly runs. After I learned he was doing this, I would meet him when he arrived. My assistant chief of staff for intelligence (G2) would tell me when General Whitcomb was on the way to my port.

I spent two or three hours almost every night observing port operations with Whitcomb. This was routine for me because I had made it a practice to tour the port myself every night before I turned in. I started by touring the port the first thing in the morning, before the night shift had departed, to see the results of their work. I would tour the piers again during the day and then again at night for the same reasons. Touring with General Whitcomb not only satisfied this evening task, but touring the port with a senior man of his experience was helpful. Early on, he pointed out much that needed some form of attention.

General Whitcomb told me he had made it a practice to establish an operation center with information boards on which were maintained the current status of each hatch aboard each ship. The same sort of system kept track of all warehouse open storage areas and all other work areas in the port. He equipped an agent at each work site with a small two-way radio which kept him in constant touch with the operation center. Normally every hour, the work area agent would report its status to the operation center. Any time a ship's gear broke down, trucks failed to show up or were not handled properly, the operation center knew about it. If it was serious, the agent notified whoever was in charge of the port. The port could then take corrective action immediately, instead of waiting until the end of the shift.

After learning about the operation center from General Whitcomb, I briefed Colonel Garretson, the port commander, and his director of operations. They went along with the idea and provided me with the equipment necessary to establish an operation center. Everyone soon knew of its importance. From then on, I used this procedure every time I had this kind of responsibility, including the port of Saigon during the Vietnam War.

Securing shipments for transport by rail was another of our problems in Pusan. Although we moved a lot of cargo short distances by truck and barge, lashing and securing was never a problem. But highways in Korea were practically nonexistent. For long distances we used the railroad, which required different preparation for shipment. Each long distance rail trip would be made over poorly maintained old track that crossed rough and mountainous terrain. Consequently, the rail cargo had to be properly blocked, braced, and lashed down; otherwise, it would fall off the cars enroute. When this happened, the Military Railway Service would have to stop the train to reload and secure the cargo before resuming the trip. The well-trained rail inspectors that supported the railroad operating battalion were very strict about releasing loaded rail cars for forward movement. They would reject a car if its load was at all questionable.

At that time, we were loading and forwarding hundreds of rail cars to the Eighth Army 24 hours a day. We generally loaded bulk cargo, such as vehicles and lumber, on flat cars. Vehicles were not difficult to secure on the flat cars, but lumber was a problem. Lumber had to be loaded and lashed down correctly so that it did not shift and fall off the cars. If the rugged terrain caused the lumber to slide off the train, it usually happened in areas that were difficult to access. If it happened near the port, the rail inspectors would ask the port to help reload, and we would generally oblige. If it happened in the mountains on the way north, we would pass the responsibility on to the MRS who had accepted the load. It became an MRS job to reload and clear the tracks. This made them very careful about accepting lumber loads.

Many times I was awakened in the middle of the night because an inspector had rejected a train of 100 or so rail cars loaded with lumber. Because all the rail cars would have to be reloaded, a standoff generally resulted between the rail inspectors and my stevedores. I would have to get out of bed to resolve the matter, usually in favor of the rail operations. They wouldn't move the cars unless they were loaded properly and we had to continue to unload the ships.

We had established major vehicle rebuild facilities at our depot in Japan at the end of World War II. We used them to rebuild vehicles for reissue to the American troops remaining in the theater, or to rebuild vehicles for military aid customers in the Far East and throughout the world. It was more economical to rebuild the old vehicles left behind by American forces in Japan than to return them to the States. (Our units returning to be demobilized after World War II had taken very little equipment with them.) It was more economical to ship rebuilt vehicles by water directly to overseas destinations from Japan rather than through ports in the United States. This policy also assisted the Japanese in rebuilding their economy. The overhaul capability in Japan created during the Korean War would later support our efforts during the Vietnamese conflict.

We back-loaded two or three ships with wrecked vehicles and equipment, 24 hours a day, for shipment to our rebuild depot in Japan. This equipment had been moved by rail from the Eighth Army area to the port. The only problem was pilferage of the equipment while enroute to the port. The wheels would be removed, the axles stolen, and the wheels replaced and lashed to the vehicle. Axles seemed to be high priority items. The thieves apparently used them for all sorts of things.

In addition to pilfering from rail cars, the Koreans pilfered the ships. Because they lived in extreme poverty, they would steal anything and everything. They had developed these skills during fifty years of Japanese occupation. They became very good at getting aboard ship, stealing something, and making off without being seen. They came by boat or swam out.

We stationed armed U.S. guards at both ends and on both sides of every ship with open hatches, whether or not the ship was being worked. It was difficult to keep the guards alert throughout their watches. Many Koreans would still come aboard, break into the cargo, and escape. If a guard detected a Korean aboard ship, he would order the Korean out and attempt to make an arrest; but, because of the language barrier, the thief usually would not respond to the guard. The Japanese had taught them that if they were caught, they would be shot on the spot, so they never surrendered. The thief generally ran for cover and the guard fired. Every night we would have several Korean casualties, usually fatal.

We also sustained many pilferage losses from our own troops and civilian port laborers. Marriage and temporary liaisons between U.S. men and local women were more common in Korea than anywhere else I have ever been stationed. The soldier or officer moved in with his Korean wife or girlfriend and because his Army salary would not support them, he had to find other ways to obtain money. In many cases, this would mean the soldier bought articles from the post exchange to sell on the black market. If this wasn't adequate, the soldier would begin pilfering and many times would become a drug dealer. Usually, the soldier was caught and his career was over. This sequence occurred more times in Korea than anywhere else I have ever been. To my real amazement, our provost marshall—a Regular Army lieutenant colonel in the Military Police Corps—decided to make some easy money. Until we discovered what he was doing, many things disappeared from the port. He ended up in the federal prison at Fort Leavenworth, Kansas.

At the same time we moved all of this military cargo to support the Allied and Korean forces, we also handled cargo to support the Korean civilian economy. We had previously sustained almost all of the Korean economy after taking over in 1945 and moving the Japanese out. During the next five years, the Koreans developed some capability for self support but, as the war between the North and the South developed, nearly all of this stopped. We found ourselves once again supporting South Korea almost entirely, including the offshore islands and the large POW camps.

Lifting very heavy cargo caused another major problem. Among the most difficult of the large, heavy items we moved into Korea were rail locomotives. We initially brought in steam locomotives because they were the standard engine used then. Later, we started improving their rail system with diesel locomotives, each weighing over 100 tons. In the port we had only one heavy-lift floating crane, an old Japanese 150-ton stiff-leg crane. Because the crane could not rotate on the barge, we had to rotate the entire barge to change directions. The ships that brought in the heavy loads could not discharge them by themselves. Consequently, we had to use our heavy-lift crane to unload the ship directly to our shore facilities. We lifted locomotives from the ship directly onto our port tracks. This process was very slow and difficult using the old stiff-leg Japanese crane.

A few years later, the Army provided us with standard 30- and 100-ton floating cranes that could rotate 360 degrees on their floating barge platforms. Far more efficient, they enabled us to discharge heavy loads much faster. Most of the heavy loads like locomotives and tanks would later be moved on ships with built-in heavy-lift cranes.

The Pusan fire occurred during the winter of 1953. This fire was the most serious and destructive disaster to happen during my tour. The port proper was located at the foot of the city of Pusan and the Korean peninsula. A mountain ridge divided Pusan into two valleys. The mountain came right down the middle of the valley and reached almost to the port. Large residential and business areas ran up each valley from the port. The buildings were made mostly of paper and cardboard with just enough lumber to hold them together. It gave the city the look of a shanty town. Early one evening, we heard that a fire had started far up on the western side of Pusan. We had no idea of its extent or what might happen.

As the evening progressed, we began to notice bright lights appearing from the valley. The lights became brighter and brighter.

Then we noticed that the fire was coming right down the valley, burning everything in its path from the foot of the mountain to the water. The wind was moving down the valley, pushing the fire ahead of it as it came. It became obvious that the fire would reach the port and, at the rate it was moving, the port would go. We alerted all the ships to button up hatches and move out to the anchorage. We moved our own floating equipment away from the docks and manned all the firefighting equipment we owned or had borrowed from the ships before they departed.

As the fire kept coming, moving faster and faster, the situation did not look good. The fire would reach Pier 1 first. This pier had working berths on one side, our main barracks barge on the other side, and all of our headquarters and administrative facilities on the pier itself. The barracks barge housed all our officer and enlisted headquarters personnel.

We did everything we could to prepare to fight the fire. Just as the fire actually began burning the entrance gate to the pier, the wind shifted. It changed from blowing north to south and blew from west to east. The fire followed the wind and moved east, sparing the port. It continued right down the street in front of the port all the way beyond it and then moved up the eastern valley of Pusan. Without the wind behind it, it did not move very far up the eastern valley and eventually burned itself out. The fire had destroyed the western valley half of Pusan. The sudden wind shift that saved the port seemed almost like a miracle.

The fire burned all night, and the next morning we could see the extent of the disaster. Destruction was everywhere, with thousands of Koreans left homeless. Needless to say, the remaining civilian community could not handle all the refugees. The U.S. military had to assume responsibility to provide shelter, food, and clothing for thousands of Korean families.

To house some of the displaced Koreans, we provided the well-covered and protected warehouse facilities on Pier 3. The largest in the port, Pier 3 had three deep-draft berths on each side and two at the end. Warehouses completely covered the center of this enormous area. We installed Herman Nelson heaters outside each warehouse door, with heat ducts leading into each warehouse, and built outside toilet facilities over the water on the side of the pier. Along the pier, we installed field kitchens with serving tables. We issued four 5x7-foot marine pallets to each family with enough straw matting to cover them. Very soon, we had filled the warehouses with some 10,000 Koreans, leaving only aisle room between the pallets. It was not like a hotel, but it was much better than lying on the ground during the very cold Korean winter. We housed and fed these homeless families for many weeks.

Lieutenant Fuson, Camp
Edwards, Massachusetts,
1942.

Combined amphibious and infantry unit training along eastern U.S. coastline, 1941; *below*, two LCIs and an LST during beach training exercises, Monterey Beach, California, 1943.

Captain Fuson with a
colleague, New Guinea,
1943.

Coast Guardmen trying to free an LCVP in New Guinea, 1942; *below*, amphibian truck, 2^1/2-ton 6x6, nicknamed "the Duck," standardized in 1942.

Supply operations on a beach near Hollandia; *below*, unloading at a beach on Leyte, 1944.

U.S. Army Transportation Center, Fort Eustis,
Virginia, circa 1948.

Open storage of supplies at Inchon port, 1948.

Stores of supplies in the open near the docks at Pusan; *right*, crane unloading a boxcar at Pusan port.

LST loaded with boxcars moving into Pusan Harbor, 1951; *below*, all hands join to fight a raging fire, Pusan, 1953.

Lieutenant Colonel Fuson meets with Brigadier General Lastago at Outpost #2, Ulsan, Korea, 1952.

CHAPTER 6

The Transportation Corps

My family remained in Alexandria, Virginia, during my eighteen-month tour in Korea from late 1952 to early 1954. It had been a very difficult period for my wife and our three children, ages 3, 5, and 7. The youngest, our three-year-old son, contracted nephritis and became very ill. He stayed in Walter Reed Army Medical Center for many weeks and at first had not been expected to live. My wife spent long hours at the hospital with him while friends and neighbors cared for our two other children. Fortunately, our exceptionally good friends provided all kinds of support for my wife. I did not learn about our son's problem until I had finished my tour and returned to the United States.

Before I finished my Korean tour, I was delighted to receive orders to attend the Army Command and General Staff College. I returned to Alexandria, put our house on the market, and packed up our household goods for the move to Fort Leavenworth, Kansas. We sold our house very quickly, fortunately, stored our household goods, and returned to my family's home in St. Joseph, Missouri, very close to Leavenworth. The family remained with my parents while I reported to Fort Leavenworth in the early spring of 1954. Since our class would not begin until August, I was given an interim assignment on the academic staff in the assistant chief of staff, logistics (G4) section.

During the summer, I was able to orient myself and my family around the school and post. Because the current class was still in session, regular student quarters were not yet available. We were assigned very satisfactory interim quarters, and we left our household goods in storage until the permanent quarters became available. My wife and children spent a lot of time back in St. Joseph with my family. At the end of the class, school quarters became available and we settled down into a very nice, small house. The fact that Fort Leavenworth and the school make a great effort to take care of the student's dependents meant a great deal to my family, who had just been through a very difficult ordeal while I was in Korea.

I knew that my staff school assignment was important for my Army career. My four years in the Transportation School had convinced me of the importance of the Army's career school system. The experience had also given me a much better preparation for staff college than the average student. In addition to the academic training, the staff college provided many other features of value to my career. I had a chance to meet and make friends with the fellow officers with whom I would work for the rest of my Army career.

The experience improved my morale and increased my appreciation for the Army. There wasn't a deadbeat in the entire class or on the faculty. The student officers and their families were all top-notch people. Often in logistics, out at the end of the supply line, you can become discouraged by working with officers who really don't measure up. All of my classmates worked hard and were very competitive, but in a most positive way. I found this to be true of students in all the career schools in the system during my later years.

Before graduation, I received orders that sent me back to Fort Eustis to be the command's deputy chief of staff. My family and I were happy to return to Eustis because we liked it and the surrounding community. We were delighted to know that we would rate quarters on post. As deputy chief of staff, I would work directly for the commanding general, Maj. Gen. Rush B. Lincoln, and I was certainly pleased about this. General Lincoln had been the Transportation School commandant in 1947 when I was first assigned there. I had learned a lot about movement planning and control in the Army from this brilliant man and had come to respect him very much. As much as any one person, he had been responsible for the success of my career.

During this three-year tour as the deputy chief of staff for operations, I worked for three different top-notch chiefs: Col. (later Maj. Gen.) Edward W. Sawyer, Col. Robert A. Cliffe, and Col. (later Brig. Gen.) William L. Calhoun.

During this tour, I was exposed for the first time to the manifold functions of a large military post: the operation of the school, training of all types of units, the many post administrative functions, and the large staff of civilian personnel required to support these units and their families. It was an extremely educational eye-opener for me and helped me prepare for future assignments on military posts, including Fort Eustis.

During my previous assignment at the Transportation School, I had encouraged amphibious training for our transportation units with exercises on the James River beaches and at our satellite installation at Fort Story, Virginia. These had continued during my absence, especially during the tour of General Frank S. Besson, Jr., General Lincoln's predecessor.

While commander of Fort Eustis, General Besson had initiated several innovative approaches to amphibious operations. Besson had gotten the idea for an innovative overhead aerial tramway from Mr.

Dick Kerr, who helped in the development of the DUKW. In his capacity with the Arab-American Oil Company, Kerr had developed an aerial tramway to move oil rigs and other equipment ashore for the construction of oil wells in Saudi Arabia. The tramway could be used for ship-to-shore loading and unloading of cargo and equipment in an amphibious operation if adequate beaches were not available.

The system consisted of an offshore pier with an overhead structure onto which was mounted one end of a cable. The cable was attached to a similar pier ashore. Cargo and equipment would be pulled ashore from supply ships using slings and pulleys that rode on this cable. This made over-the-beach operations unnecessary, regardless of the condition of the shoreline. General Besson had developed the idea and procured one system at Fort Eustis.

The offshore pier itself was a new idea developed by retired Col. L. B. ("Slim") DeLong. DeLong based his theory for the pier on first modifying a barge large enough to berth a deep-draft cargo vessel alongside. Several long circular steel studs that would reach the bottom were dropped through openings built into the barge. The openings for the steel shafts were fitted with lifting pumps that could lift the barge onto the studs.

To create the offshore pier, tugs would float the barge into position. The studs were stacked on the deck of the barge which was fitted with a crane. When the barge had been moved to its anchorage spot, the studs would be lowered through the openings to firmly penetrate the bottom of the ocean. Pumps would then raise the barge onto the studs; at the same time its weight would drive the ends of the studs into the bottom. After the barge had been pushed up to its proper height and secured to the studs, the overhead cranes and the cable would be installed on the DeLong barge and on the shore. After the cables had been secured, the cable cars for moving the cargo would be installed. The rig was then ready for a ship to berth alongside and be worked.

Besson was one of the very few in the Army who liked DeLong's idea. The Army first used the DeLong pier as part of Besson's overhead tramway. The entire tramway had been installed on our James River training area site and we began testing it.

During this same period, the Army and Navy had been conducting annual over-the-beach amphibious exercises in France. General Besson was next assigned to the Combined Command of the North Atlantic Treaty Organization (NATO) and the Supreme Headquarters, Allied Powers Europe (SHAPE). Still very much interested in innovative transportation ideas, he was instrumental in adding testing of the overhead tramway to the 1957 amphibious over-the-beach exercise off the southern coast of France. The Army procured another tramway and shipped it to Europe with the other equipment to be used in the exercise.

General Lincoln, our major troop unit commander at Fort Eustis, Col. Phillip E. Pons, and I went to Europe to observe the exercise. On the way, we visited and were briefed by the European Command (EUCOM) in Paris and U.S. Army, Europe, in Heidelberg. In Paris, General Besson briefed us and gave a cocktail party in our honor.

At the beginning of the exercise, we observed the installation of the DeLong pier from the shore. The water was very rough, with a large surf developing. At dusk, the operation was called off until the next day. By this time, the barge had been jacked up on only two studs, and it was still floating on the surface of the water. They secured it for the night in this condition. Unfortunately, during the night a storm came up. Because the barge pumps had not been able to jack the barge up and out of the water, the pounding surf knocked it off the two studs and washed it ashore. The barge and all of its equipment were wrecked. This ended the test of the aerial tramway during the 1957 exercise. It also ended the idea of the aerial tramway. Besson remained the only optimistic supporter of the concept in the Army, but he did not push the idea any further. The tramway was one of the few ideas of his which did not work out.[1]

It was about this time that General Besson started thinking about containerization. He realized that to use the tramway effectively, we would have to move break bulk cargo in containers of some sort. This concept would not be fully realized until the Vietnam War, but I am convinced that following the aerial tramway failure, Besson worked on this idea with some of his research and development people. Mr. Malcolm McLean, who later created the Sea-Land Services, was one of these researchers.

After witnessing the failure in France, we returned to Fort Eustis. Although we used the tramway in later exercises, we really did not carry development of the idea or the equipment any further. We did, however, think a lot about the DeLong pier and how we could use it in the future.

During my tour at Fort Eustis from 1955 to 1958, our fourth child, a son, was born at the Fort Eustis Hospital. We named him for Georgia's father, Peter Bahnsen. Also during this tour, I realized that I should take advantage of the convenient night school to finish my college degree. Although I attended evening classes for the entire three years, I did not receive my college degree until several years later.

The tour at Fort Eustis also made me realize that the officers' wives, especially the senior officers' wives, made significant contri-

---

[1] British engineers had attempted a similar but more primitive system off the Normandy beaches in 1944 with nearly identical results. (*See World War II green book.*)

butions to the post community. The variety of daily activities on the post require the help of volunteers. Volunteers play important roles in activities such as the Red Cross, the post medical facilities, the special service center, and child-care and youth centers.

The post information center is one of the most important operations that requires such individuals. Volunteers help and teach young soldiers and their wives about relocating to a new post and a new life. Many of these young couples have never made a budget, never comparison-shopped, and never taken advantage of post services. Because unit commanders no longer had time for this type work, volunteer training programs became vital. In the old days, young soldiers, mostly single men, required no introduction to family services. Today, it is not uncommon to have 18- or 19-year-old soldiers with even younger wives and one or two children. Many times young families arrived accompanied by letters of indebtedness. Helping these young soldiers and their families made the three years from 1955 to 1958 at Fort Eustis interesting, educational, and rewarding for both my wife and myself.

I received orders to attend the Armed Forces Staff College in Norfolk, Virginia, just across the James River from Fort Eustis. During this relatively easy permanent change of station, the only difficult part was moving from very ample quarters at Fort Eustis to the much less than adequate quarters at the staff college. Although the staff college tour lasts only five months, it is one of the few assignments for less than six months that is considered a permanent change of station. Including families in the program was very important. Having become a real advocate for the career school system, I was delighted with this opportunity. In those days, it was not necessary to attend both the Command and General Staff College and the Armed Forces Staff College, but I thought it would be helpful.

Soon after entering the staff college, I realized its many advantages. For the first time I had close contact with officers from the Navy, Marine Corps, and Air Force. All were dedicated career officers with interests and experiences very different from mine. Exposure to officers from the other services and regular classroom dialogues proved to be a valuable educational milestone. The college offered me the chance to meet many officers from Allied countries and their families as well. All of us had been encouraged to bring our families to the school to foster this sort of interaction. Just as we did at Leavenworth, we made many friends in the U.S. services and our Allies, whom I continued to see and work with for the rest of my active duty career.

The first three weeks of the curriculum were known as service orientation weeks. Students from each of the services were given a week to orient the students from the other services about their organization, functions, and missions. These briefings broadened our knowledge of the other services and allowed us to get to know our college associates quickly.

The differences between the theories of career education in each service became immediately apparent. The Army system stressed Army career schools and required each officer to attend the basic and advanced courses for his branch. The officer was then ordered to the Command and General Staff College and others if his career potential warranted. The Air Force stressed some of this, but did not require the career officer to complete all of his branch courses except for the Air Force Command and General Staff College. The Navy stressed on-the-job training and a master's degree program in an area allied to the officer's military specialty. The Navy did not have career courses like the Army.

Having been through preparation and presentation of this information before, we in the Army were much better prepared to present the first week service orientation program than those in the other two services. Most of us had already had tours at other service schools. The Army always led off with the first week, followed by the Air Force, then the Navy/Marine Corps. We students got together, decided what we should present, and divided up the work. We did not have a difficult job presenting our organization to the other services for that first week, but we received considerable help from our faculty advisers.

During our week, the other services struggled to prepare their presentations. They told us as much during the "happy hour," an informal social gathering at the post officers' club. We finished easily and then sat back to watch the other students. It became apparent that they were having problems. Many of them had never thought about their total service organization, missions, and functions. They also had a hard time finding reference material that provided this information. The staff and faculty assisted them because they had seen this before.

The Armed Forces Staff College was very informative and very enjoyable. The importance of joint and combined operations became more clear to me than before and better prepared me for future joint operations assignments. It also prepared me for several future assignments in Europe and the Pacific, where I worked closely with Allied forces. The Allied officers who attended our class had been selected with the same great care exercised to select officers from the U.S. services and they participated in all activities with great enthusiasm, contributing much to the success of the class.

CHAPTER 7

Duty in the United States Army, Europe

About halfway through the staff college course, the Office of the Chief of Transportation notified me that I was scheduled for an assignment in France following graduation. I would be assigned to COMZ, headquarters for about two years, then given the command of the 53d Truck Battalion in Germany. This was absolutely the best news I could have received. My only experience in Europe up to that time had been the trip with General Lincoln to observe the over-the-beach mobilization exercise in 1957. All of my previous overseas experience had been in the Pacific, but at that time the Army's main mission was supporting NATO. Except for the classroom, most of my experience had been in transportation. I was glad to be assigned to Headquarters, COMZ Europe, which would broaden my experience. My family and I would travel to Europe by surface transportation on the *United States*—then the newest and most modern ocean liner in the world.

After graduation in the spring of 1959, we packed up the household goods that we had moved to Leavenworth and prepared for our move to France. We were told to leave most of our belongings in storage. In order to reduce transportation costs, most of the main household goods would be issued to us in Europe. In those days, families could take overseas only those personal things thought to be absolutely necessary. Our trip on the *United States* was enjoyable even though we sailed through the rough water of the North Atlantic during winter.

Old friends met us in Orleans, France, the headquarters for COMZ. As always, we were looked after until we could find a place to live and become established. Once again, we witnessed the Army taking care of its own. Because of limited government quarters, we moved into an adequate privately owned house. We enrolled our children in school and I reported to work.

In 1959, the COMZ still functioned much as it had immediately following World War II. Its headquarters was in Orleans, with a base section in the western part of France, an intermediate section in the Orleans area, and an advanced section in eastern France. I was assigned as executive officer in the Office of the Director of Supply and Services, the G4 of COMZ. This opportunity permitted me, for the first time in my career, to work in aspects of logistics other than transportation. I had studied and taught "Movement Planning and Control in COMZ Europe." On a theoretical basis, I was familiar with the organization, the COMZ mission, and its command functions. I served as the G4 member of the command briefing team and participated in all of the command briefings. This work allowed all of us to visit and learn about all parts of the command in great detail.

The Technical Services still operated the Army's logistics system.[1] Headquarters COMZ consisted of a general staff and Technical Services staffs. The general staff provided overall command and control while a technical service staff operated each separate system. Each Technical Service had its own supply and maintenance facility in each COMZ section, as well as in the Army rear area. They maintained war reserve stocks at the COMZ facilities, while active supply and equipment moved directly forward to Seventh Army units or to Seventh Army supply and maintenance facilities.

At the time, approximately 120 days of war reserve stocks were maintained in theater, mainly in France. Bulk POL were provided by a petroleum distribution system under the chief of the quartermaster general. This POL supply line ran from the Biscay Bay on the west coast of France to Metz on the east. The COMZ chief of transportation provided POL transportation, which consisted mainly of commercial rail and Army trucks.

Both the French and German railroads had been reestablished, having been rebuilt by the U.S. Military Railway Service after World War II. By that time, the trains were running as well as they had before the war. Some commercial trucking was available, but the U.S. Army's 37th Transportation Command provided most of the highway transport.

The 37th had a truck battalion in the French port area on the Bay of Biscay, one in Orleans, one in eastern France, and a fourth in Kaiserslautern, Germany. For the most part, the fleet comprised five-ton tractors, flatbed trailers, and vans. The 37th's trucks moved most of the freight from the Biscay Bay ports to supply and maintenance facilities in the COMZ and to the Seventh Army. Each battalion had truck parks along the line of communications (LOC) and was responsible for the forward movement of trucks and trailers from park to park and the retrograde movement of cargo and trucks to the rear.

The LOC was well-established and adequate to support peacetime operations, but could also be expanded rapidly in case of war. Although the LOC required some contractor help, U.S. military or direct hire civilians performed most of the work.

---

[1] The seven Technical Services were: Medical, Quartermaster, Engineer, Ordnance, Signal, Transportation, and Chemical.

All of my previous experience in movement planning and movement control had been academic, and I could now observe and participate in operating the actual systems. The real world varied from the text book concept and doctrine from time to time, but not significantly. I found it most interesting to observe that the command required that all customers forecast their transportation requirements in advance. Then the Movement Branch of the Office of the COMZ Chief of Transportation programmed transportation movements to meet this forecast. They published program requirements monthly, which became the basis for most movements.

Standard procedures were not always followed precisely. Many transportation requirements developed that had not been forecast. However, because there were plenty of transportation resources available, as is the case in peacetime, unscheduled transportation could always be furnished. Very little attempt was made to discipline the system. Such lack of discipline is poor training for wartime movements, when transportation shortages always develop and must be planned for and controlled.

From my vantage point, I could observe the entire operation of this theater logistics system in great detail. Although I quickly became familiar with general supply and maintenance functions, I soon realized that this knowledge was not enough. An effective supervisor of supply and maintenance must first understand, in great detail, the commodities being supplied. There is a large difference between knowing about and managing field radios, bridge timbers, or truck repair parts.[2] In just a few years the Army reorganization of supply would render the commodity expert very difficult to find.

I also realized that the need for expertise applied to transportation as well. An effective transportation planner and operator must become a specialist in one mode of transportation such as highway, rail, or terminal and water transportation. My field remained ports and shipping.

When I was made deputy commander of a reserve logistics command under the chief of our Supply and Maintenance Division of COMZ, Colonel Scott, my experience again broadened. President Eisenhower had sent U.S. troops into Lebanon to stabilize that area. After their departure, plans were prepared for similar operations in the Middle East if conditions warranted. The combat troops to be deployed there would be taken from U.S. forces in Europe as before. However, no support unit was available that could be easily deployed.

A plan was prepared to use logistics troops already in the theater for deployment. A reserve logistics command drawn from our personnel in

---

[2] This subject is described very well in Joseph M. Heiser, Jr., *A Soldier Supporting Soldiers* (Washington D.C.: U.S. Army Center of Military History, 1991).

COMZ headquarters would manage this support operation. This reserve unit was formed on paper and met occasionally to prepare plans and to participate in exercises to be ready to move out if needed. Some 10,000 tons of reserve stocks were prestocked in the Middle East for immediate availability in case of deployment. These supplies were positioned at the U.S. air base at Adana, Turkey, which the commander and I took turns inspecting.

While we were stationed in Orleans, our fifth child was born at the St. Chapel's Hospital, an old French hospital building which the U.S. Army took over. We named our new daughter Jennie Chestnut after my grandmother, a memorable woman.

While assigned to COMZ in Orleans, I also participated in a study to decide whether the Technical Services and their staffs should be moved from COMZ to USAREUR headquarters to be consolidated with the Technical Service staffs there. Because the chief of staff of USAREUR supported such a move, the study recommended consolidation and the move took place.

My original orders had assigned me to COMZ for two years, to be followed by command of the 53d Truck Battalion of the 37th Group in Kaiserslautern. These plans changed after I had been in the COMZ only nine months. The officer who was to precede me as battalion commander, Lt. Col. Arthur Hurow, had just taken command when his wife became seriously ill and had to be evacuated back to the States. On 1 December 1959, I was told to take over the battalion at once. I hated to leave France and my job at COMZ, but was anxious to assume a command.

The 53d Truck Battalion, the 37th's largest, consisted of six truck companies: two light 2½-ton truck companies and four medium truck companies with 5-ton tractors. We also had operational control of a German labor service battalion which had three companies of 5-ton diesel tractors. This service battalion had been operating in the area for many years with an excellent reputation. Its commander and I became very good friends. On later trips to Europe I was able to visit his unit many times to maintain our very friendly relationship.

The 53d and the German labor service battalion received and distributed supplies and equipment by trailer and van from the LOC, through France, into Germany. The group covered a very large area and had some 3,000 trailers to perform its mission. Our sister battalion, located in eastern France, had truck terminals in Nancy and Metz, France. We would pick up most of the trailers and vans from these terminals, move them to our terminal in Kaiserslautern, and from there to their final destinations at the various COMZ supply and maintenance facilities and Seventh Army facilities in Germany.

Because we were having scheduling difficulties in marrying up our tractors with the trailers coming up the French LOC to Kaiserslautern, I obtained permission to establish our own terminal downstream in France. After that, I coordinated my tractors and the trailers more efficiently.

We moved the trailers and vans to their destinations along with the documentation of their contents. After unloading the trailers, the receiving personnel were supposed to notify us of their status. Often they would not unload them, or would back load them or move them to other terminal facilities or installations. We, of course, were required to pick up the empty trailers wherever they were and return them to the LOC for subsequent return to the coastal area. To keep track of these trailers, we established a system of daily checks of the trailer locations. My operational staff and I spent many hours every week riding the German autobahns to visit the military transfer depots, to check on our tractors and locate our trailers. This proved to be a very effective system to maintain control.

We were called upon to perform an interesting political operation. After the Berlin blockade and the U.S. airlift, the Allied nations and the Soviets had agreed that we would use the main highway into Berlin that passed through the Soviet sector of Germany. In order to prove that the Allies actually needed to use this highway, we had to run frequent convoys of our trucks in and out of Berlin. I had to dedicate most of the 501st Light Truck Company to this mission. More often than not, these trucks moved in and out of Berlin with their empty beds covered by tarps.

My wife and I set about to establish good relationships with the officers and wives in the battalion. My wife was particularly adept at organizing the wives for all sorts of battalion activities and activities with the community outside. These interpersonal affairs are critical to unit cohesion, especially when dependents accompany units overseas. We spent a most enjoyable year with the 53d Truck Battalion and were reluctant to turn over command after only one year.

When our first year ended on 1 December 1960, we still had more than a year before our return to the States. We then went to USAREUR in Heidelberg, where I was assigned to the Planning Division of the Office of the Deputy Chief of Staff for Logistics. The next organizational step up from COMZ, this further enlarged my view. It was my first experience planning and coordinating logistics for a field Army, its many organizations, and the communications zone.

When I arrived at USAREUR, the United States faced a serious "gold flow" problem. Our overseas expenditures greatly exceeded European purchases of our products, leaving the country with a negative balance of payments. The military was under pressure to reduce the expenditure of many millions of dollars to support our military forces in Europe. While I was assigned to the USAREUR staff, this economic constraint influenced nearly all our work.

During my tour at COMZ, before I took over the 53d Battalion, I had participated in a Headquarters COMZ and Headquarters USAREUR joint study designed to prove that the Technical Service staffs should be consolidated at Headquarters USAREUR to save money. Because the results of this directed study proved this point, the plan was set in motion.

When I joined USAREUR, a second joint COMZ-USAREUR study was initiated. We were told that we could save even more money and help stem the gold flow if we moved the Technical Service staffs back to Orleans. Our second staff study precisely proved this conclusion. The second time, the new commanding general of COMZ had more influence on the commander in chief than had the previous commander. I witnessed an excellent example of the influence personality can play on actions in the field. As a result of this second study, the Technical Service chiefs and their staffs moved back to COMZ in Orleans.

While on the planning staff at USAREUR, I had an interesting job taking part in the annual updating of USAREUR's major contingency plan. This plan would be followed if NATO went to war with the Russians. One of its key annexes was the wartime movement plan and program. To prepare this annex, we requested the transportation customers, Seventh Army and COMZ, to submit what they believed would be their wartime movement requirements. During my entire term on the planning staff, I could never obtain these estimates from the various customers. In the end, I would repeat the movement requirements presented in previous plans. The transportation staff, in turn, would prepare the wartime movement program.

Years later, when I had a similar job at the DA level, I once again tried to obtain estimates from transportation customers. I was never successful nor was I ever able to arouse enough interest at the command level, in either USAREUR or DA, to force the customers to respond. I do not want to minimize the difficulty of making these estimates: many uncertainties exist. But I have always attempted to prove, as I've been taught, that a poor estimate is better than none at all. My assignments at COMZ and USAREUR were very interesting and eye-opening. I have always been glad that I had this kind of opportunity.

My chance to command the 53d Truck Battalion, an invaluable leadership opportunity, broadened my understanding of highway transportation operations. It gave me on-the-job experience with highway transportation in addition to landing craft, harbor craft, intercoastal water transportation, harbor terminal operations, and rail operations. My experiences greatly broadened my knowledge of overall transportation and logistics management.

CHAPTER 8

The Army Reorganizes

Soon after arriving at USAREUR headquarters and the Office of the Deputy Chief of Staff for Logistics, I found my name on the list to attend the Industrial College of the Armed Forces. Being a logistician, I had asked for the Industrial College rather than the Army War College. This meant we packed up again to leave Europe in the early spring of 1961 to return to Washington. Our family, now grown to five children, was lucky to move by ship again. This time it was a regular military transport and not a luxury liner.

As soon as we were settled with our children in school, the class of 1961–1962 commenced. Once again, the caliber of the faculty and of my fellow students impressed me. The Industrial College, a joint service school, had Army, Air Force, Navy, and Marine Corps officer students. Senior executives from other government agencies, such as the State Department, Treasury Department, Interior Department, Central Intelligence Agency, and General Accounting Office (GAO), also attended. The college gave me my first opportunity to know and work with top-level civilian professionals. As the college moved us from office to office to work with people in different fields, I appreciated my opportunity even more.

The college curriculum gave us a very valuable understanding of this country's industrial base, a whole new field for me. For the required master's thesis, I chose control of commercial transportation in the United States at the national level. This subject had fascinated me since General Lincoln introduced me to it during my first years at the Transportation School. I had never before had an opportunity to study it in detail to learn how it was managed and how management differed during peacetime and wartime.

During peacetime, transportation is plentiful and the dollar drives transportation decisions. The profit motive creates a cooperative and cordial customer/carrier relationship. During wartime, the carrier is always privately concerned with staying "full and down," that is, the carrier wants to move the most cargo he can handle regardless of the type of cargo or the needs of the customer. On the other hand, the customer wants his cargo moved immediately whether or not the carrier's truck or train is full.

When an emergency occurs, transportation always becomes scarce. Top-level authority must make allocation decisions. Command decisions on allocations of resources can only be made at the top, whether for a combat unit in the field competing with other units, or whether one must decide to allocate transportation space to the military or allow it to remain available for the civilian economy. The only time these problems ever really occurred was during World War II. The War Shipping Administration, which President Roosevelt created, decided on transportation priorities while the War Production Board controlled other critical items. The civilian/government joint cooperation was most interesting to review.

Dr. James A. Huston, an eminent historian of logistics, described in great detail how the Army Service Forces handled the allocation of transportation resources during World War II.[1] (The Army Service Forces were the combat service support units.) History indicated that almost daily Maj. Gen. LeRoy Lutes, the operations officer (G3) of the Army Service Forces, demanded that Maj. Gen. Charles P. Gross, chief of transportation, move goods regardless of efficient utilization of transportation. General Gross would insist that transportation be used carefully because it was so critical. Lt. Gen. Brehon B. Somervell, Army Service Forces commander, would then have to decide, exemplifying the need for decisions to be made at the top.

During World War II in Europe, transportation decisions were frequently pushed up to the COMZ commander, General Lee. As noted earlier, Lee believed in the British Q-movement system and demanded that this system be followed to the letter. General Lee was apparently a real martinet who believed in doing everything in accordance with proper orders and regulations. Through the force of his personality, he had been instrumental in making sure that the British system for movement planning and control was followed. By the end of the war, this system had become, and still is, the basis of our movement system.

Two field trips made the course even more interesting. We made one trip to industries in the United States and another to visit industries and government agencies in three European countries. We were allowed to choose the itinerary for our trips. For my U.S. trip, I chose to visit the Gulf Coast to be briefed by oil companies, especially those engaged in offshore oil drilling. During this most valuable experience, I learned about a completely new type of offshore operation.

For my trip to Europe, I selected Great Britain and NATO. A member of Parliament entertained and escorted us through the House of Commons during our visit to England. After briefings on the economy and its industrial base, we left London to tour industries in

---

[1] James A. Huston, *Sinews of War, Army Logistics 1775-1953* (Washington D.C.: U.S. Army Center of Military History, 1988).

the Liverpool and Birmingham areas. After a week in England, we visited Brussels and NATO headquarters and then traveled to Paris for briefings at SHAPE and the U.S. European Command. The entire trip was well organized and informative.

While at NATO in Brussels, I was reminded that NATO's logistical problems are very different. Where actual operations are concerned, commanders have no problem agreeing on combined and joint doctrines. Logistics support is a different matter, because each country considers logistics to be its national responsibility, even though this could not work during a war.[2] It also contradicts NATO policy.[3]

My Industrial College year was enjoyable as well as educational. My family associated with my fellow students and their families, an added benefit we experienced at each career school. My promotion to colonel while at the Industrial College increased my satisfaction.

Following graduation, I moved over to the Army staff. I had earlier been assigned to the Office of the Chief of Transportation, but this was my first tour with the general staff. As a colonel in logistics, I was assigned to the Office of the Deputy Chief of Staff for Logistics (DCSLOG) in the European Branch of the Plans Division. I was chosen for this slot because most of my previous staff experience had been in logistics planning and my last assignment had been in Europe. I thought I knew everything about logistics in Europe but I found out soon enough this was not the case. Our principal staff action continued to be the fight against "gold flow" out of the country. This was more of the work I had done on the USAREUR staff.

Before I had a chance to become familiar with the job, I was ordered to join an orientation tour of Vietnam. The Vietnam conflict was heating up in 1962, and President Kennedy had initiated a Senior Officers' Orientation Program for a group of colonels or Navy captains to travel to Vietnam for several weeks to learn about conditions in the country. On this first trip, twenty-five colonels or Navy captains participated, along with two brigadier generals. First the Defense Department and the joint staff in Washington briefed us, followed by the commander in chief, Pacific, and the three service commanders in Hawaii. After these meetings, we flew on to Vietnam in a special mission plane.

In Saigon, we spent the first week in briefings with the American ambassador, the Military Assistance Command, Vietnam (MACV), staff, and the three services. We then divided into four groups for travel out of Saigon to spend a week thoroughly investigating each of the four

[2] Heiser, *A Soldier Supporting Soldiers.*

[3] *NATO Long Term Defense Program*, NATO Military Committee Document 32/2 (NATO Headquarters: Approved by the Heads of State on 30–31 May 1978).

areas of the country. Each weekend we returned to Saigon to discuss what we had seen. The four groups visited a different area each week.

My group first visited the northern area, where both political and military personnel briefed us. Next, we went to the Qui Nhon area, then Saigon, and finally the Delta. The ambassador and his staff spent an entire day with us, discussing the political problems as they saw them. General Paul D. Harkins, the MACV commander, also devoted a day to reviewing the military situation as he and his staff understood it. Although I would have two wartime tours in Vietnam and would make many trips there, I saw and learned more about Vietnam and its people during this orientation tour than during any longer stays in the country.

For the next ten years, as the U.S. position in Vietnam deteriorated, I kept wondering why we did so badly, both politically and militarily. When I left Vietnam in 1962, I believed that the United States was going to help the Vietnamese people help themselves, rather than treat them as inferior colonial people as the French had.

We seemed to start out being helpful. We sent our best people there to advise the Vietnamese both politically and militarily, but as the years went by we changed. Instead of helping them to learn and to do the job on their own, we started to bring in our forces and to take over the job of fighting the Viet Cong and the North Vietnamese. The South Vietnamese observed this shift and adopted the attitude that if the Americans want to fight our war, we will let them. The finger can't be pointed to any one person or group: everyone made mistakes, starting with the White House and President Johnson.

Almost ten years later, during 1970 and 1971, when I was assigned as the DCSLOG of U.S. Army, Pacific (USARPAC), I worked directly with Lt. Gen. William P. Yarborough, the deputy commander. As one of the original members of the Special Forces, he had spent years in and around Vietnam. Yarborough felt strongly that when we shifted our strategy from helping to taking over, we made a serious mistake. Apparently, his strong views on this subject became so well-known that he was not reassigned to Vietnam in a senior position even though he was extremely well qualified. At the time I served with him, I did not realize how correct General Yarborough was, but I certainly learned it before the war was over.

In 1961, great organizational perturbations began to affect the Army staff under the new secretary of defense, Robert S. McNamara. First, a newly created Defense Supply Agency (DSA) assumed control of all wholesale supply for common use items for the Defense Department. Then, by direction of McNamara, the Army began a study of its administration to meet the goals of the new Project 80.

Project 80's most drastic requirement was the elimination of the Technical Services and the creation of the Army Materiel Command

(AMC) to assume all the wholesale logistics functions previously performed by the Technical Services. Mr. Leonard W. Hoelscher, deputy comptroller of the Army, had many years of experience in the Defense Department. His committee, charged with implementing Project 80, concluded that effective management of the Army's logistic system required that the Army staff confine itself to planning and policy making and divorce itself from the details of administration and operations.

The Office of the DCSLOG had become so involved in overseeing the administrative operations of the Technical Services that it had neglected its planning functions. It could not function effectively as commander of the Technical Services because of the concurrent jurisdiction exercised by other staff agencies over those services. As a result, AMC was established to take over the wholesale logistics system. Personnel management was transferred from the Technical Services to the Office of Personnel Operations.

The study also created other major commands: a Combat Developments Command (CDC) and Continental Army Command (CONARC). Each would exercise similar consolidated functions in their respective areas. CONARC would have no responsibility for combat development, but would command the Army school system, including the Technical Services school systems.

Project 80 did not completely abolish the Technical Services. Most were initially left at the departmental level, to be administered by special staff officers. The surgeon general, who had already lost his procurement function to DSA, continued to exercise his former functions as the head of the Medical Corps. The chief of engineers retained responsibility for mapping, civil works, military construction, and real estate. The chief signal officer retained responsibility for Army-wide communications and photographic services. The transportation officer retained responsibility for coordinating and planning all transportation required by the Army. Those responsibilities of the quartermaster general not turned over to DSA were reassigned to a chief of support services. The positions of chief of ordnance and the chief chemical officer were abolished. Their staff functions were transferred to DCSLOG.

Certainly the central feature of the Project 80 reorganization was the loss of the Technical Services' traditional birth-to-death responsibility for the commodities under their control. This led to the loss of technical supervision and commodity-related personnel training, commodity-related military occupational specialty, and unit responsibilities for commodities.

A year after the Project 80 reorganization, one management expert, a leading participant in the reorganization process, expressed that the old Technical Services were sorely missed. Efforts to decentralize control of them and homogenize their efforts had failed, and had also failed to achieve wholehearted cooperation with respect to complex weapons systems such as missiles and tanks. The Technical Services had provided manpower and experts to the general staff for surveys, studies, and normal staff actions. The general staff had become quite dependent on this support and it no longer existed. The chiefs of the Technical Services had been responsible for doctrine and for research and development. They also provided service units to the field and supervised their operation throughout the Army. This function was now lost.

Project 80's major intent was to consolidate the seven Technical Services into a single coherent system. This was pretty well accomplished at the national wholesale level, but it had the exact opposite effect at the operating level.

To make logistics operations feasible and to continue their operations until CDC could develop doctrine for a retail logistics system, each major command, and in some cases their subordinate commands, integrated the available literature, regulations, and organizations, and prescribed their own systems. As a result, we had a different system in each major command. Europe had one system and the Pacific a different one. This made it extremely difficult to train personnel and units to deploy to the field and be prepared for the logistics system they would find there.

As a result of Project 80, the wholesale logistics function perhaps benefited, but at the expense of training, combat development, and other similar activities. Without technical service support, the Technical Service schools suffered. CONARC had already begun to emphasize its tactical mission at the expense of its school operations. This problem may have been compounded when CONARC was given more schools to operate. This trend was further emphasized when the CONARC commanding general received a second role as the Army component commander of the U.S. Strike Command.

Although the Technical Services had created many problems because of the seven separate systems, at least each system was standard from top to bottom. The chief of each Technical Service developed his own doctrine, created his own organization, and trained his own personnel. He received new personnel and trained them, organized them into units, and then deployed them as requested by the theater commander. The service units were under the command of the theater, but they continued to follow the standard technical system when supporting the theater. If they were not doing their job, the commander did not attempt to correct them but merely told the chief of the Technical Service, who would replace the commander or do whatever was required to satisfy the combat commander and do the job that was needed.

After AMC was created, the wholesale and the retail systems began to separate from each other. AMC had no authority over logistics support in the field. Logistics doctrine was to be developed by CDC, which would require lead time before the doctrine could reach the theater and the CONUS commands. As a result, during this void, each theater developed its own doctrine and managed its own unique system.

We entered the Vietnam War that way. People trained in CONUS really couldn't be readied for what they would find when they arrived in the theater. The systems in each theater were different.

Following my 1962 orientation tour in Vietnam, I returned to the Pentagon and resumed my assignment as chief of European Plans of the Office of Plans and Operations Division, Department of the Army/DCSLOG. For the next two years, followed by another two years on the joint staff, my eyes were trained toward Europe and the problems there.

By then, McNamara had served as secretary of defense for two years and many of his changes were beginning to appear. The gold flow was certainly high on his priority list. He wanted to get the United States out of France in order to reduce the great expenditures for maintaining our line of communications across France. He sensed that this would not be politically acceptable either in our country or in NATO, but he started to reduce the LOC a little at a time. These policies are covered very well in a report issued by USAREUR.[4]

The report pointed out that in fiscal year 1961, the annual foreign exchange cost for maintaining the U.S. military forces in Europe was approximately two billion dollars, of which some $275 million was spent in France. The government had conducted several studies to determine what could be done to reduce this money flow. The Headquarters, European Command (EUCOM), was also directed to study the problem and recommend how to reduce costs without seriously reducing combat capability. Because most of the money spent in France went to support the Army, Secretary McNamara directed that the Army prepare a plan to reduce its costs.

The Department of the Army formed the U.S. Army Logistics Evaluation Group (USALEG) under Brig. Gen. Ferdinand J. Chesarek, the director of supply and maintenance in DCSLOG at the time. This USALEG was tasked to reduce expenditures in Europe by $32 million while the Army's peacetime support of its combat forces would have to

---

[4] *U.S. Army Lines of Communication in Europe, 1945-1967* (Headquarters, U.S. Army, Europe, and 7th Army, Office of the Deputy Chief of Staff for Logistics [Operations], 1968).

remain intact. The reduced organization would have to be capable of being expanded rapidly in time of emergency. General Chesarek selected four or five of us from the DCSLOG staff to assist him; I became his deputy. We were all familiar with Europe, having had tours there recently. Chesarek himself had commanded the 4th Logistical Command, part of the COMZ, before being assigned to the DCSLOG.

At the time, our LOC across France was a mammoth operation. We visited every facility and reviewed all their functions and activities. We spent our final two weeks at Headquarters, USAREUR, finalizing the plan which General Chesarek would brief to CINCUSAREUR and through the chain of command back to the Defense Department. Through Chesarek's superior briefing skills this plan was briefed all the way up to the secretary of the Army and then to the secretary of defense, who approved it. Insignificant changes were suggested as the plan went up the line.

This was not what the CINCUSAREUR wanted. He objected to it violently, but he realized he had no other course of action. The Army staff principals didn't particularly like it either, but they realized they were under pressure to do what General Chesarek had recommended. No one else could think of a better way to save $32 million.

His major recommendations included reducing theater supply levels from 120 to 90 days; closing depots in western France; deactivating the Petroleum Distribution Command or putting it on standby status; moving stocks to be issued from rear depots to forward depots as space became available in the forward area; returning the 4th Logistical Command along with the 32d Engineer Group to the States; reducing port activities to the single port of Saint Nazaire and imposing a ceiling of 10,000 tons per month; providing for joint United States/Federal Republic of Germany (FRG) use of depots in eastern France under cooperative logistic agreements; and reducing other activities.

After Secretary of Defense McNamara had approved the plan, the secretary of the Army directed its implementation. The secretary of the Army commented that this line of communication retrenchment would neither achieve a better organization nor improve management. He saw it as solely a gold flow measure with the clear understanding that these reductions would require the acceptance of a higher degree of risk than before. Much to my later regret, this was the last time this caveat was heard. It soon became U.S. policy and everyone assumed that we just didn't need these extra resources to support our forces in case of war. In fact, this was just the beginning of further reduction of the LOC, until ultimately it was eliminated entirely.

Our plan also contained a proviso that the units returned to the States would be stationed on the East Coast with the primary mission to continue to train for Europe. In case of an emergency, they would return to Europe and to the line of communications. This proviso was honored for less than a year. After that the mission was forgotten and most of the units disappeared from inventory. This was only the first of many such reductions to the logistics support structure in Europe.

In the 1960s, after a great deal of discussion between the United States and France, President Charles DeGaulle announced that he was determined to reestablish normal French sovereignty. All French soil, air, and sea would be under the control of the French government. The French claim was really not much different than the agreements we had with other countries such as Turkey, Spain, and Great Britain. In these countries, we operated and controlled our bases. Each country had its own commander on base, who flew the host country's flag. American commanders in France, however, had retained complete control inside the base. We assumed that, because President DeGaulle wanted this changed, Secretary McNamara used his demand as an excuse to reduce the gold flow to France to zero. In 1966, all U.S. troops, their dependents, equipment, and supplies were moved out of France to other locations.

EUCOM then began to draw up a plan, called the Fast Relocation (FRELOC). When the joint staff approved this plan on 2 July 1966, EUCOM immediately began its implementation. A tremendous task at the time, this involved some 70,000 U.S. personnel (including dependents) in France and many thousand tons of supplies, of which USAREUR owned over 90 percent.

The major effort for implementation fell to USAREUR. The major objective of the FRELOC Phase I plan was to move sixty days of combat support supplies to add to the thirty-day supply in the United Kingdom, Belgium, Luxembourg, and Germany. All the supplies remaining in France beyond these requirements would be disposed of, and all U.S. personnel in France would relocate. Most of the COMZ depots and supply installations in Germany were in Kaiserslautern, Pirmansens, and Nabollenbach. Consequently, that is where most of the equipment and supplies were sent. Although unprepared to receive this tremendous load, they did their best. Even some ten years later, as I revisited these areas as DCSLOG, I could still see some of the unfortunate effects of this move.

Since the French agency Trapil already controlled the petroleum distribution system from Donges to Metz, it was not necessary to make any change. France, however, would only guarantee its use in peacetime; its availability to U.S. forces in wartime would be up to the French. We could either take our chances on having French petroleum support in wartime or build another very expensive pipeline system. A second pipeline had been laid out of the Benelux countries for peacetime use, but its availability in wartime was questionable. For a time, we really had no alternative but to depend on the French.

The final step of the FRELOC plan was to relocate the COMZ headquarters and its supply and maintenance agency to Germany. On the surface, FRELOC had been a success; it had met its deadline of 31 March 1967. The military liquidation section, attached to the U.S. Embassy in Paris, was charged with disposing of residual matters after the relocation had been completed. Germany and England required extensive new construction, and it took years to recover from the confusion the move caused.

Secretary McNamara expressed his satisfaction that, although FRELOC had been estimated to cost more than a billion dollars, the actual cost totaled less than $150 million of which less than a third was gold flow or exported U.S. funds. He conceded that the new LOC would be more vulnerable than the LOC across France, but considered the increased risk insignificant. He believed that the use of long range aircraft to transport military equipment would compensate for the conditions imposed by the relocation from France. In fact, he felt this represented a definite logistics advantage. Few logisticians agreed, then or now.

The withdrawal from France strained USAREUR's capability to perform its mission. Twenty-four major installations in an area extending 750 miles, from the French Atlantic coast into the Federal Republic of Germany, had been reduced to one storage depot in England and seven active depots in Germany. Such a dramatic reduction severely diminished our capability to provide effective logistics support. More than ninety percent of COMZ supplies were stored within a thirty-mile radius of Kaiserslautern. In the same area were also concentrated such important assets as the Supply and Maintenance Agency, several truck battalions, and many active Seventh Army units. I knew this area well, having covered it extensively while commanding the 53d Truck Battalion out of Kaiserslautern.

By the end of 1967, USAREUR's capability to extend its logistics resources to provide an effective and efficient wartime support posture was questionable. COMZ no longer had a technical signal or engineer capability. It had limited potential to provide logistics support across the English Channel to deployed combat units and it could not expand its depot system to the west. For several years, all U.S. European commands continued studying and planning to use the LOC from England through the Benelux countries into Germany. We also secretly planned to reestablish some kind of LOC across France. These schemes were always highly classified.

It soon became evident to the planners that this same LOC through channel ports and into the Benelux countries would be used by all our NATO Allies to support their own forces. All the NATO Allies depended on the same railroads, waterways, and highways. The logical solution was the development of some kind of cooperative effort. Our principal LOC to support the Seventh Army was a line starting from the Benelux and Bremerhaven ports to the LOC facilities in western Germany. This line paralleled the USSR's western positions only a few miles to the northeast.

From the late sixties into the early seventies, the logistics support structure continued to reduce under the popular motto, reduction of the "tooth to tail." During this period, I kept pointing out that the LOC was not capable of supporting an all out war. I maintained that we should stop rationalizing and admit that this was a risk we were willing to take. As was frequently the case in long-range planning, when the problem couldn't be solved, it was assumed that the problem didn't exist.

We began consulting with our representatives from SHAPE and through them to our Allied logisticians. We worked particularly closely with the Germans. Next to the U.S. Army, the FRG was our largest customer. At that time most of their equipment and supplies still came from U.S. sources. The Allies initially secured a great deal of this equipment from the United States through grant aid, but they later obtained their supplies through our military sales program. The Germans found no problem with procuring this support in peacetime, but they were apprehensive about maintaining a supply line during wartime when shortages were bound to occur.

The U.S. Army DCSLOG had the main responsibility to solve this problem. To better cope with the problem, the DCSLOG created a new Directorate for International Logistics which included the divisions for military grant aid and military sales and added a new division for cooperative logistics. My European Plans Branch was transferred intact to constitute the new Cooperative Logistics Division.

As chief of the Cooperative Logistics Division, I began working full time with NATO Allies including the FRG. I concentrated mainly on creating a U.S./FRG combat logistics support plan. The FRG was concerned as to whether the United States would continue to support them when equipment and supplies became critical for U.S. troops. The FRG was especially worried about the continued support with repair parts for the trucks and tanks they had purchased from the U.S. There was no other source for these parts.

Our office began a combined effort with the FRG to solve this problem. We held many planning meetings to work out the details: totaling the end items they possessed; estimating additional end items they might need; estimating wartime consumption rate of repair parts and components; deciding where to store these items; and determining how they would pay for this logistics support. A major problem was to integrate FRG needs into the various U.S. storage levels in theater and in CONUS. How much of the peacetime stocks should FRG fund? What part of wartime reserve stocks? How would their supply system fit into our system so they could submit requisitions and receive supplies in peace and war the same as our forces? This became far more complicated than it first appeared.

The politics got very complicated. By this time, each country was sensitive about the other country taking advantage of it. For example, because of all the emphasis on stemming the gold flow, the United States had required the FRG to assume a large percentage of the cost of maintaining our forces in Germany. Every time we assessed the Germans with another cost, their politicians became involved. During my last year in DCSLOG and for the next two years in joint staff logistics, I devoted nearly all of my time to this joint planning.

One historic event is forever associated with our first complete U.S./FRG Cooperative Logistics Plan. After our entire staff had reviewed the plan, we turned it over to the FRG for their staff to review. A special assistant to the secretary of the Army translated the plan from English into German. He was a German national who had been employed by the American forces and then worked his way up to this high level position on the secretary's staff. As soon as he finished the final translation, he and I made an appointment with the senior German representative in the United States for FRG planning at the German Embassy in Washington. We knew that he would have to take it back to Germany for staff review, but we first wanted to answer any questions that he might have.

As soon as we arrived and entered the embassy, our friend met us and ushered us into his office. We immediately began talking about our plan, but very soon our German friend, who had looked rather surprised as we arrived, asked us what we thought about the latest news. We asked what he was talking about. He told us that President John F. Kennedy had just been assassinated. We had not heard the awful news. We were dumbfounded. It had been announced while we were enroute from the Pentagon. We thanked him, gathered up our papers and left, telling him we would talk later.

Shortly after the President's death, we resumed our joint planning. Combined staff reviews were extremely time consuming and difficult. The plan was not fully agreed upon until many years after my tour of duty. Politics played a tremendous part.

We embarked on similar planning with the other Allies using the same LOC through the Benelux countries into Germany. Many of these Allies also had U.S. equipment and required our continued support for repair parts, maintenance, and other supplies.

After two years on the Army staff, I transferred to the Logistics Directorate (J4) of the joint staff, where I continued in cooperative logistics. NATO logistics had developed from just an Army problem into a joint staff problem. Our combined joint planning group met at least monthly to discuss progress and to lay out our next actions. Military solutions were simple compared to the political considerations. One month we would meet in the United States, the next in Europe. I spent a lot of time on airplanes.

By 1964–1965, Vietnam had become a full-scale Department of Defense preoccupation. We were in the process of building up our forces in Vietnam to over 500,000 troops. McNamara operated differently from any of his predecessors, or his successors as far as that is concerned.

McNamara soon learned that the bureaucratic process of moving actions through the services and joint staff for review was slow and tedious. It certainly did not satisfy his needs. Once he decided to do something, he wanted to take action immediately. He not only wanted to change the staff procedures, but he also had the administrative and the legislative authority and support to do it. Many of his actions initially helped to move troops, their equipment, supplies, and construction material to Vietnam or offshore and to reposition additional equipment and supplies. He insisted on personally approving each and every one of these actions regardless of size. I remember one case of a troop list of five men for a well-drilling detachment that had to go up as a separate action for approval by Secretary McNamara.

He established a procedure of directly telling the joint staff logistics director, Lt. Gen. Richard D. Meyer, to take an action rather than following normal channels. General Meyer, after graduating from West Point, had entered the Corps of Engineers. General Gross had selected him to move over to the Transportation Corps upon its establishment during World War II. He was equally as brilliant as the ten other original engineer officers who had joined General Gross.

I had known Meyer at both Fort Eustis and at the chief's office. He was, of course, a good friend of both Generals Besson and Lincoln. He had been responsible for my transferring from DCSLOG to his directorate to continue this cooperative logistics effort. Although he initially set me to work in cooperative logistics, more and more he shifted me into Vietnamese actions and Mr. McNamara's plans. The secretary would task General Meyer and apparently tell him not to wait for the normal staffing procedure. General Meyer, working with the services, would direct implementation of McNamara's requirements. This was unheard of at the time and the services objected violently. McNamara ignored them. He apparently also told the service secretaries what he wanted done, and they cooperated.

The service chiefs and their staffs could not do anything about this. General Meyer was very effective at accomplishing his tasks. He understood the system very well and knew how to work around it if necessary. He also understood the system so well that the services could not inadvertently interfere with his tasks.

Secretary McNamara, his assistant secretary for installations and logistics, Thomas D. Morris, and General Meyer brought the assistant secretaries for logistics in each of the services and their DCSLOGs into the net. They developed a new chain of command so that orders passed down through these logistics channels and the results flowed back up to General Meyer, Tom Morris, and Secretary McNamara. These gentlemen established a steering committee that met weekly to discuss issues and to assign future actions. This was an extremely efficient and unique organization for logistics actions. It had been set up in 1961 and was ready when the war in Vietnam escalated.

McNamara developed another controversial idea. After having established DSA to handle common supplies for all the services, Mr. McNamara wanted to do the same thing for the retail logistics systems. He again asked General Meyer to develop his idea. To head up the planning group, Meyer chose Maj. Gen. Frank A. Osmanski, the first logistics director on the MACV staff in Vietnam, who understood Vietnam and its problems. He had been a field artillery officer with a strong supply and maintenance background. He organized a small planning group consisting of three members from each of the services. I was the Joint Logistics Directorate member along with General Osmanski, who assigned me as his deputy.

We spent about a year on this combined operations support project that included several trips to the Pacific and Vietnam. Each of the services provided excellent specialists to the group. Although loyal to their respective services, they all tackled this project with knowledge and enthusiasm. As a matter of fact, we developed a system that when connected with DSA could probably have done a better job than the systems each service followed to provide supplies to the forces in the field—certainly better than the Army's system.

Secretary McNamara's steering committee met periodically to evaluate our plan. As we presented each phase to the committee, they either approved it or suggested changes. Although committed to producing the plan, we really didn't believe it was something Secretary McNamara could force down the throats of the services. As it turned out, we were right. This was one time he met with failure.

I certainly learned an awful lot about supply and maintenance working on this project. I did most of the transportation planning, but I also became much more familiar with supply and maintenance. This work also proved very useful for future assignments. General Meyer

asked me to extend my tour for another year after the normal two
years on the joint staff, and I accepted.

CHAPTER 9

War in Vietnam

During the buildup of troops in Vietnam and the ensuing surge of weapons and supplies, the port of Saigon became a bottleneck. Most of the troops, equipment, and supplies came through the port facilities of Saigon, which also served as the major port of entry for all commercial cargo. (*See Map 3.*) The Saigon port is located on the southern coast, fifty miles up the Saigon River from Vung Tau and Cape St. Jacques. Although Saigon was a river port, it had adequate depth for deep-draft shipping. The port had several deep-draft berths and quays along the Saigon side of the river. The muddy opposite bank was almost impassible.

I had visited the commercial port of Saigon a few times on earlier trips to Vietnam, not on official business, but only to satisfy my own curiosity. During these earlier visits, when U.S. personnel were there only as advisers, the port operation appeared relatively small. We had few troops in the country, and the flow of U.S. Agency for International Development (AID) cargo had not yet begun.

Each time I visited the port, one thing impressed me: crews unloaded military cargo from the few ships being worked at a speed that permitted the crews to identify and document the cargo for movement to its destination. If the first destination backed up, ship discharge would stop until they relieved the backup. I couldn't help but recall the old days in Pusan, Korea, when we had to stuff the cargo down the customer's throat whether he could handle it or not. The process in Saigon, geared to the whole team's capabilities, impressed me very much. This was certainly an improvement over my previous experiences with overseas port operations during wartime. The key to the smooth operation was matched capabilities—both the port and the customer.

During late 1964 and into 1965, as the buildup of U.S. and other military assistance forces in South Vietnam went forward, large increases in both initial unit tonnage and resupply tonnage flowed through Vietnam's ports, especially Saigon. By December 1965, the backlog of ships waiting in South Vietnam waters, or in holding areas elsewhere, was so large that it created a buildup of cargo in U.S. ports that could not be shipped to Vietnam.

Although several factors contributed to this shipping backlog, the lack of adequate deep water port facilities in Vietnam was the major cause. In addition, the number of transportation units at Vietnam ports had not kept pace with the shipping increase. The construction of port facilities, roads, and hard stands for storage had also lagged behind requirements. MACV's 1st Logistical Command, under Col. Robert W. Duke and then Maj. Gen. Charles W. Eifler, had studied the problems and developed a plan to solve them. The steps required to correct the problems would take time. Major engineering projects included expanding Saigon's harbor facilities and building a new port at Cam Ranh Bay, half-way between Saigon and Da Nang.

Commercial, mostly AID cargo was being shipped through the same port facilities as military goods, which further congested the ports of Vietnam. Initially four deep-draft berths had been assigned to the U.S. Army for handling military cargo ships, which had reduced the capability of the commercial port. Commercial port personnel, even with some help from AID representatives, did not have the necessary know-how nor the capacity to do the job. AID cargo was generally of two types: AID-sponsored Center Procurement Agency (CPA) cargo, consisting of bulk products such as rice and fertilizer, and other materials being shipped to stimulate the Vietnamese economy under the commercial import program (CIP).

CIP cargo included items like bicycles, motorcycles, refrigerators, radios, and other consumer goods sent in at the request of the few importers. The importers were supposed to bring them into Vietnam on U.S. credit, enter them into their normal commercial supply and distribution system, and sell them to their customers for profit to generate capital for their economy. This long-range idea was noble, if it would work.

The major flaw in the plan was that little or no supply or distribution system existed in Vietnam to handle these goods. Before the CIP program, Vietnamese importers would import such items and store them at the port until they could sell them. The customer came to the port, paid for an item and its custom duties, and took it away with him. The importers lacked the capital to carry on business the way the CIP people envisioned. The port soon began to bog down with military, CPA, and CIP imports.

The Army, directed to move in an Army terminal command to control the military cargo, chose to send the 4th Transportation Command from Fort Eustis. It was a type A command, the smallest. Even with support by several terminal service companies and harbor craft units, it soon bogged down as well. The port command was soon converted to type C, which meant increased size and capability.

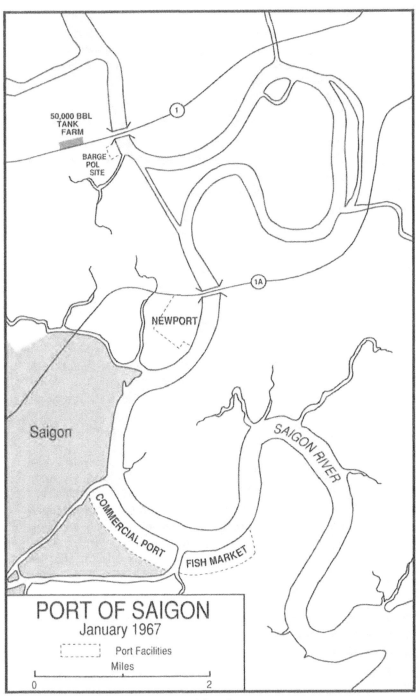

PORT OF SAIGON
January 1967

Port Facilities
Miles
0   2

Map 3

Lt. Gen. Jean Engler, U.S. Army, Vietnam, commander, along with General Eifler, heading the 1st Logistical Command, asked that General Besson, AMC commander, provide a Transportation Corps colonel to assume command of the port. Besson responded by asking that the Department of the Army send me over to assume command. Although General Meyer had recently extended my tour with the joint staff, he permitted me to leave. I was very pleased and could not have asked for a better job. (Nearly every time I had been assigned a new job, General Besson had been in the background. He had been responsible for both the Pusan port job and my command of the 53d Truck Battalion in Europe.)

By the time I arrived in Saigon in July 1966, the buildup in Vietnam was really underway. We were moving U.S. troops in to take over the war and to show the Vietnamese how to do it. Unfortunately, the major port to receive incoming shipments was still Saigon. At that time the port areas at Cam Ranh Bay, Qui Nhon, and Da Nang were just beginning to be expanded and could not handle the loads they would be able to later.

When I arrived to take command of the 4th Transportation Command, I found a very demoralized unit. The 4th had been there less than a year but it was already being blamed for all the logistical problems that had occurred while supporting the military and the entire civilian community. The situation was appalling. I found many ships with commercial AID cargo at anchor off Vung Tau, at the mouth of the river coming up to Saigon, that had been waiting to be unloaded for months.

The warehouses at the Saigon port were absolutely full of cargo and accountability was completely out of control—asset visibility was almost nonexistent. With all of the pier space full, nothing could move. We quickly found out that the materiel handling equipment available to our dock and warehouse crews was inadequate. The port command had some 1,500 to 2,000 civilian Vietnamese barges under contract and fully loaded. The barges, with families aboard, were just floating around while their cargo was pilfered or rotting. Documentation for the cargo on these barges was missing, but we thought most of the cargo was AID material, such as rice, fertilizer, and some general cargo.

AID had first attempted to solve the problem by inviting Mr. Teddy Gleason, president of the longshoremen's union on the East Coast of the U.S., to straighten it out. Before I arrived, he had visited the port with twelve of his longshoremen to try to improve the port warehousing. All but one man did work in the warehouses, attempting to improve the situation, but this alone was not the solution. After a short period of time, they returned to the States. One man, Mr.

Schultz, stayed on and proved invaluable in assisting us to improve the port situation.

Upon my arrival, I first attempted to sort out the problems. I found they fell into two areas: military and civilian. Sometimes they overlapped. One potentially dangerous problem existed because the port crews were working general cargo ships in the Saigon commercial port and military POL and ammunition ships at Nha Be just to the south. No one central authority was in charge.

The military and commercial cargo had been mixed throughout the port area. To make matters worse, the military and commercial customers waiting for this cargo could not receive, identify, or place their cargo in proper storage. Facilities were inadequate and trained personnel were not available. Although the military port troops were being blamed, they could do nothing about it.

Up to this period in Vietnam, the Transportation Corps' principles of movement planning and movement control did not govern shipments to or within the country. Each service requested and shipped its own equipment and supplies into Vietnam, as did the AID and other agencies. The MACV had established the Traffic Management Agency (TMA) to control movement, but it did not become effective until early 1967.

The existing procedures and organizations had four deficiencies at the outset.[1] First, a coordinated movement organization did not exist within the combat zone. Second, no agency had responsibility for providing CINCPAC with logistics information, for advising CONUS of the immediate requirements of CINCPAC and COMUSMACV and the component commanders, or projecting the cargo input to Vietnam, to CINCPAC and MACV headquarters. Third, procedures had not been established to coordinate inter- and/or intra-theater shipping with its ability to be received in Vietnam. Lastly, considerable cargo was moving to Vietnam outside of the Defense Transportation System and without the knowledge of any DOD movement control agency.

Because of the lack of port facilities, materiel handling equipment, and receiving capability, during the early days COMUS-MACV's General William C. Westmoreland made it a practice to open and close hatches and unload ships as the cargo was needed. Selective off-loading and using ship's holds as warehouses was necessary because of the shortage of adequate shore facilities.

This procedure, which tied up ships indefinitely, caused the ship owners and operators to bring strong political pressure to bear on the President of the United States. The solution to the problem then became political. Before I arrived in Saigon, the civilian port operated

---

[1] General Frank S. Besson, Jr., Chairman, A Report by the Joint Logistics Review Board, Transportation and Movement Control.

completely separately from the military port. Although in many cases both jurisdictions used some of the same facilities, cooperation and coordination were nonexistent. The problem had been under discussion at all levels for some time and a decision had finally been reached that the 4th Transportation Command would have operational control of CPA/AID cargo. Both the United States and Vietnamese governments concurred in this decision. The decision on control of CIP cargo and the entire commercial port would be made later. We were told that President Johnson sent a message through channels to Westmoreland, ordering that all ships be unloaded within thirty days.

When I took charge of the 4th Transportation Command, it appeared to me that with few exceptions, the facilities were adequate to handle the cargo being unloaded from the ships waiting in the river. Trained civilian contract stevedores handled both military and commercial cargo. Army terminal service companies supervised the crews moving military cargo. However, although both military and civilian cargo checkers were available, their performance was marginal. Materiel handling equipment remained inadequate.

Port clearance was problematic. We had both military and civilian contract trucks to clear the port but, as generally happens when operating overseas during wartime, the recipients of the cargo were not equipped to handle the volume of cargo being directed to them. It was a replay of the port at Pusan during the Korean War.

I reviewed the situation, realizing I had three generals looking over my shoulder: General Westmoreland, the MACV commander; General Engler, his deputy; and General Eifler, the 1st Logistical Command chief. After explaining the problems to them, I told them what I thought should be done and our chances of solving the problems. They told me to start and to let them know when I needed help. The only help I requested was additional port personnel to help supervise the AID commercial stevedores under my command.

From then on, I had a completely cooperative working relationship with my three bosses. I kept them informed with periodic oral and written status reports. Any time I needed support from areas over which I had no control, I requested help through channels, and it arrived without a problem. Generals Engler and Eifler frequently visited and I always kept them aware of what was going on. General Westmoreland had too many other problems to be able to keep well informed about the port. Most of our problems could be solved without his intervention.

The one major problem continued to be handling of the AID commercial cargo. AID personnel had been quick to tell top administrative officials that all the problems lay with the military port administration. I soon realized that the principal culprit was AID itself.

Mr. Robert W. Komer, President Johnson's chief adviser from the White House, visited Vietnam every month and always told the Army, the American ambassador, and General Westmoreland that something should be done about the port problem. On one such occasion, while I was meeting with Mr. Komer at AID headquarters, I asked him to come to the port and let me show him what the problems were and what we were doing about them. Komer told me to stop trying to confuse him with facts, but just get the port mess cleaned up. I gave up trying to be reasonable with Bob Komer, who later acquired a nickname, "the blow torch."

On the military cargo side, I immediately began looking for a new location for the ammunition ship working area. I asked one of my terminal battalion commanders, Lt. Col. Thomas H. Hoy, to find a new location for the ammunition discharge facilities. He recommended an area known as Cat Lai, a point of land that extended out into an adjacent river canal, within working distance of the port proper.

The water at Cat Lai was deep enough to handle the ammo ships. The small landing area would allow construction of a large barge-discharge facility so we could unload the ammo ships in the stream. The major setback was that the land ashore was a tidal swamp. We decided to go with Cat Lai anyway, intending to move in masses of fill material and build the barge facilities.

As soon as I explained the situation to Generals Eifler and Engler, they took the necessary actions to meet our needs. Dump trucks began to haul in fill and continued to haul it for months afterwards. It was a big job, but the swamp was finally reclaimed, the engineers built our discharge facility, and Colonel Hoy erected a tent city for his battalion. We immediately moved our entire ammunition discharge operation to Cat Lai and began unloading all the ammo for the Army, Air Force, and Vietnamese armed forces. Cat Lai became the transfer point for most of the ammunition going to the Delta.

To alleviate port congestion, we had to move general military cargo out to its destination regardless of the customer's ability to receive it. One of the principal recipients of this treatment was Col. (later Maj. Gen.) Joseph E. Pieklik, the commander of the "Fish Market" supply depot. ("Fish Market" was the Vietnamese name for this area, which in earlier days had actually been a fish market.) This depot was just south of the port proper, a very short haul by truck. (*See Map 3.*) But Pieklik had inadequate space, personnel, facilities, and materiel handling equipment to cope with the incoming cargo.

The recent change from a technical service to a functional supply system made the situation worse. Supply organizations had not had time to reorganize, to retrain, to change concepts or doctrines, or take the steps necessary to competently operate an overseas depot. Even though we had had supply problems in Korea and during World War II, at least we knew to move boxes with red corners to the ordnance depots. Ordnance personnel, although understaffed, were trained to recognize, receive, and identify ordnance cargo. The same was true for the other Technical Services.

We now moved most of the general U.S. military cargo to the fish market depot, manned by personnel beset with myriad problems. We were about to deliver them much larger quantities than they could possibly handle. With General Eifler's approval, I sent crews and equipment to the depot to assist in unloading our trucks so we could turn them around to bring in even more cargo. Not surprisingly, cargo stacked up without proper receipt or identification. But we *were* moving cargo out of the port. The fish market depot, although not our only customer, was by far the largest. Because of the inadequate depot facilities at the fish market, the 1st Log Command established a much larger depot facility at Long Binh, approximately thirty miles north of Saigon, close to the Bien Hoa air base.

We relentlessly moved all cargo to our customers. We had to do this to meet President Johnson's demand that we unload the ships. To make matters worse, much of the cargo documentation was missing or inadequate to properly identify the items and their final destinations. This led to the creation of "gray boxes," a term coined to describe boxes with unknown contents or unknown destinations. After these unusable gray boxes sat around a depot for a certain period of time, we moved them back to Okinawa. Workers there opened the boxes, identified their contents, and put them back in operating condition or disposed of them. If possible, they returned them to Vietnam. I'm sure some boxes made more than one round trip between Vietnam and Okinawa.

To cope with the boxes in Okinawa, AMC established assembly-line type operations to process the gray boxes. It required well-trained experts, able to open a box and identify a part as well as its purpose. To recognize an item as a repair part for a $2\frac{1}{2}$-ton truck instead of a 5-ton truck or another vehicle is no easy job. It required that AMC send many of its CONUS depot experts to Okinawa to do this and train Okinawan labor to help. This was a very costly remedy considering that the Army had not been permitted to adequately man and equip the depots in Vietnam to do this same job. We always seem to repeat this mistake, as we did in the latest operation in Saudi Arabia.

A great deal of cargo was destined for the Vietnamese armed forces: their port clearance trucks moved it from the port under the watchful eye of the U.S. advisers, or we moved it to their depot facilities on U.S. military trucks or contractor-provided trucks. The Vietnamese seemed to have an adequate capacity to handle the cargo, but proper identification was another matter. Years later, as joint staff logistician (J4), MACV, I would learn that identification had been a real problem for them as well.

Much Air Force cargo was moved out of our port to Air Force facilities. The Air Force could handle the increased load better than the Army. Most of the Air Force cargo moved into the country by aircraft except for bulk cargo, such as rations and POL, which moved on land. The Navy received very little cargo.

About this same time, General Besson paid me a visit to see the port situation for himself. He wanted to learn what I had found and how I planned to solve the problem. I walked Besson over the entire port area and over to the fish market. As soon as General Besson saw the mess, he turned to me and said that he was going to change the method of sending supplies to Vietnam. From then on I would receive Army cargo in containers, not break bulk. The stevedores would unload containers, not individual boxes of parts. At the time, we had been receiving very limited quantities of cargo in CONEX containers. Once we moved the CONEX container to its destination, we never saw it again. The customer used it for storage or some other purpose. When General Besson heard this, he said, "Fine. It is well worth the cost, and we will continue to buy more CONEX containers."

He was not sure how he would containerize all general cargo, but he knew he would find a way. He admitted he should have done more on development of a standard container at the time of our test of the offshore aerial tramway in France in 1957. He also said something about working with a Mr. Malcolm McLean on the container project. By the next year, sea-land containerized services became available to Vietnam.

Very soon after General Besson left the country, we began receiving containerized cargo rather than break bulk cargo. It was not in actual overseas containers, but the cargo was lashed to standard warehouse or Marine pallets with wire bands or moved by CONEX containers.

I failed to mention our forklift problem while General Besson was there. Our materiel handling equipment was not adequate to handle our break bulk cargo and could not move the containerized cargo that we anticipated. As soon as I realized the scope of this problem, we submitted high priority requests for adequate forklifts and other materiel handling equipment. For the next six months, crews broke down the pallets in order to handle the boxes by hand or the pallets were discharged by ships' tackle directly into waiting vehicles.

Very soon we had the military cargo portion of our port operation under control. Our only continuing error was failure to document the cargo adequately. Our customers failed to notice this oversight because the cargo was being fed to them so fast they did not have time to spot the omission. Transportation Corps doctrine has always required that each piece of cargo be identified as it enters the system, from its point of origin until it is unloaded at dockside and shipped to the user.

The port must know in advance the amounts, weights, descriptions, sizes, classifications, stock and/or part numbers, stowage locations, and all pertinent details of all the cargo on ships bound for Vietnam. This information was supposed to be mailed to the port in advance, but this did not always happen. The ship also carried a copy of its manifest that detailed the necessary information, which they submitted to the port upon arrival. The port Accounting Division then translated the mass of information on the manifest into usable data to enable the ship to be unloaded, the supplies stored or shipped to the correct consignee quickly, and the vessel released for its next trip.

The port was required to transpose the information on the manifest manually into transportation control movement documents (TCMD) that would control movement of cargo to customers in Vietnam. If these TCMDs did not accompany the cargo, the customer would not be able to identify the items or their final destination. Incoming supplies generally replenished depot stock or filled a supply requisition from a combat unit. This total accountability of shipments, called "intransit asset visibility," is absolutely essential for the supply system to operate effectively.

Visibility has always been a problem during the buildup phase of every combat support operation, from World War II, Korea, Vietnam, up to Operation DESERT SHIELD. Cargo arrives much faster and in larger quantities than can ever be imagined; the number of support personnel available to handle this avalanche is never enough. Both of these conditions existed during the buildup for DESERT SHIELD. Even though the supply operation is now completely automated, it still requires individual human intervention to make the automation work.

At Saigon, in the 4th Transportation Command, we could not maintain 100 percent asset visibility of the cargo moving through the port. Because of this inability, the customers receiving the cargo were plagued with problems. However, even if we had been able to do our job in the port, most U.S. military customers would still not have been able to maintain asset visibility. They simply lacked sufficient personnel and depot facilities to handle the large quantities of cargo being moved to them. I discussed this problem with General Eifler many times, but he knew we had no recourse other than to unload the ships.

We had many other operating problems, but most of them were solved as they occurred. One recurring problem was the fact that operational difficulties were not brought to the attention of the operational supervision as they occurred. They were reported at the end of the shift, if then. This same problem had occurred in the Pusan port during the Korean War before we established our radio-monitored operations.

We established a similar operational center in Saigon with control boards showing the status of each work site, whether it was a ship discharging, a truck transfer point, or a warehouse operation. We linked each of the work sites with the operations center via a radio net so that each work site could report its status each hour. We used this data to update our control boards. If, for example, a crane were to break down, the problem would be reported immediately to the operations center, where it would receive corrective action. This network also gave me and my operations people a much better, more timely overview of the entire port operation.

In addition, I walked through the entire port working area at least three times a day. I would make my first trip early in the morning, before the night shift left, to see how they had done, again sometime during the day shift, and the third trip during the night shift. Operations staff members always accompanied me. We were thus constantly aware of the status of port operations. During these tours we boarded each working ship, including those AID cargo ships being worked on the river.

It seemed like every VIP from Washington had the port on his itinerary. Visitors would usually make the port operation center their first stop. We would brief them on our capabilities and the status of our ongoing operations. When we showed them around the port, they gained a much better understanding of our organization, operation, and problems. We received many compliments for our tours and briefings.

Before I arrived in Saigon, MACV had approved construction of additional port facilities for Saigon and construction began on the port addition, named Newport. (*See Map 3.*) It was located up the river from the existing port, just south of the main bridge that crossed the Saigon River, going north from Saigon toward Bien Hoa air base. This was the route from the port to our main ammunition depot and the Long Binh depot.

Newport was planned to have four deep-draft berths, one of which could handle roll-on and roll-off ships. Other facilities would include two ramps for landing LSTs, a wharf capable of handling seven barges, and a landing craft ramp. The Newport complex would also have both warehouses and open storage spaces behind each pier, plus a large parking space for the sea-land containerized shipping operation. Most facilities were operational in October 1966, but the four deep-draft piers were not available until July of the next year.

In 1967, when I departed Vietnam, Newport became entirely operational, which considerably increased our throughput capability. Newport also allowed us to direct most of the U.S. military cargo trucks directly onto the Saigon/Bien Hoa/Long Binh highway, bypassing the congested city of Saigon with our heavy equipment. Newport was completely manned by U.S. military personnel, the 71st Transportation Terminal Service Battalion, which also reduced pilferage. With Newport available and more convenient for military cargo, most of the main port of Saigon was used to handle the primarily AID commercial cargo. Newport also allowed improvement of the military cargo documentation procedures.

Newport did not receive its first container ship until October 1967. Small C2 container ships, with their own cranes aboard, shuttled containers between Cam Ranh, Da Nang, and Saigon about every two weeks. The C2 ship picked up containers from a container berth or from a large container ship being discharged at Cam Ranh Bay, then shuttled the cargo to either Newport or Da Nang. A DeLong pier, equipped with container cranes, had been installed at Cam Ranh Bay. General Besson, Slim DeLong, and Mr. McLean had worked out this arrangement. I later learned that this sophisticated installation had not been easy to sell and the deal nearly collapsed several times, surviving only because of Besson's persistence.

Although containerization had been used in ocean shipping before, this was the first major container operation anywhere in the world. McLean and Besson were testing an entirely new concept that had always been laughed at by most ocean transport companies and most large ports worldwide. The innovative Besson stuck his neck out for something he believed in, and was proved right in the long run. Almost immediately, all U.S. shipping companies were forced to follow his lead and worldwide shipping companies were not too far behind.

In Vietnam we experienced a tremendous, instant increase in our surface transportation capabilities, but containerization completely revolutionized the method of handling and moving cargo in surface shipping. Most people today don't realize that this major shipping innovation occurred little more than twenty-five years ago. Although it finally happened in 1967, Besson and McLean had been toying with the idea for many years. DeLong had for years been promoting his novel ideas for rapid construction of offshore facilities such as deep-draft piers and oil drilling platforms. DeLong went on to oversee construction and installation of his DeLong piers up and down the coast of Vietnam and the southern part of Thailand.

Although Newport relieved the military cargo pressures on Saigon port, the handling of AID cargo remained difficult. The warehouses were full of commercial AID cargo. When local Vietnamese importers learned that items which AID had imported on their behalf had arrived, they customarily left them in the port warehouse until they could be sold. At the time of sale, the customer and the importer would come to the port together to pay the customer's duty to the government and to remove the imports.

When I became aware of the procedures in Saigon, I realized that the AID cargo was being handled in a manner contrary to all standard port procedures. A document called the "port tariff" set forth all of the rules and regulations governing warehouses, along with the port rules and regulations and the schedule of fees to be charged for such services as towing, berthing, and line handling. The port tariff is a critical commercial document that specifies fees for each operation and controls all that goes on in the facility. Like all such transportation operations, no port can operate without a tariff; at least I had never heard of one that did until I arrived in Saigon.

When I asked to see the Port Tariff for Saigon, my transportation people didn't know what I was talking about. Neither did the Vietnamese commercial port commander when I confronted him. A Vietnamese army brigadier general with little or no port experience, he had apparently just been shuffled off to that job.

In Saigon the only bonded warehouses were at the port, a condition I had never experienced before. The port has the most expensive and the least available warehouse space anywhere. Because of this, the customer usually takes his cargo out of the port warehouse within three to five days. If he does not, the government moves the cargo out of the port warehouse to a government-operated, bonded warehouse for storage. The longer the importer leaves his items in bonded storage, the more the warehouse and custom fees mount up. Therefore, importers everywhere but Saigon move very fast to avoid these fees. After a period of time, if an item hasn't been claimed, it is subject to sale or disposal. In no case, though, would cargo be permitted to remain in port warehouses, which are not meant to be used for storage.

When I first took over the commercial port operation, I didn't realize that the military and AID had no joint operating agreement. I was quickly made aware of this fact and I went out of my way to keep the AID advisers informed about everything we did and why. Shortly thereafter, the State Department, Defense Department, and Vietnamese government worked out an agreement. One of my first jobs was to prepare a port tariff, to obtain Vietnamese government approval for the document, then to put it into effect. I soon found out this was not to be done easily. When we confronted the various U.S. agents who worked the ships in the port, they laughed. They knew there should be a tariff, but the lack of one saved them money. They did not want us to prepare one.

Fortunately for me, Mr. Schultz, one of the longshoremen sent over by Gleason to advise AID, was not just a warehouse man. He had a lot of experience with commercial port operations. We immediately got along. In contrast, the other port advisers and officials were often hostile at first, fearing that I was a threat to their jobs.

Schultz and I immediately obtained copies of tariffs from other ports in the area, such as Singapore and Hong Kong, to use as samples. We made the tariff as simple as we could possibly make it. (Actually, Mr. Schultz did most of the detailed tariff preparation.) We did not include many of the complicated legal clauses normally found in such documents. We laid out only the most basic rules and fees to permit ships to come in, to be worked, and to depart. It covered the rules necessary for commercial stevedore companies, importers, exporters, transship transportation, warehouse operations and the like. After we finished preparing our draft tariff, we were faced with the difficult job of finding the proper Vietnamese government authority to approve the tariff and then to enforce it.

I attempted, without success, to get the Vietnamese port commander to take over the job. AID didn't seem to be much help. Finally, I got help through General Westmoreland who enlisted the American ambassador, Mr. Ellsworth Bunker. The Vietnamese government assigned a Vietnamese major as the new port commander.

Maj. Pho-Quoc Chu, the port director of the Saigon commercial port, clearly a favorite of the government authorities, could call upon them for help. Although he lacked prior port experience, he was a very forceful young man and immediately realized the importance of his job and the steps that he had to take. He worked very closely with us from then on, which greatly improved our joint operations.

While the U.S. helped the South Vietnamese defend their country, we tried to stabilize Vietnam's economy. Our major scheme, the commercial import program noted earlier, provided credit for Vietnamese civilian importers. CIP procedures required documenting specific incoming CIP commodities and verifying payment or nonpayment of tariffs and other fees. Unfortunately, the Vietnamese government did not always agree with our methods. Neither did the large importers, who had the money and lots of political clout. We discovered that when both the government and the importers wanted to drag their feet, they were experts at it. We were beset by a wide range of problems including politics, graft, payoffs, Viet Cong activities, and laziness. Technical know-how had little to do with our actual accomplishments.

The CIP had a built-in conflict. The AID program was pushing in millions of dollars worth of goods in order to satisfy consumers, to lower prices, and stabilize the economy. The large importers wanted to keep prices high in order to make more money. It was difficult to dictate the correct solution. Americans took the attitude that, since we were fighting their war and supporting their economy, the South Vietnamese citizens should not object to us pushing them around. This was a false assumption. The Vietnamese government and their citizens did object.

The port became the logical focal point for all of these political problems. Finding solutions was extremely frustrating. Also, because the port was so pivotal in solving these problems, it developed a high profile. Nearly all visitors to Vietnam ended up there. Briefing visitors, discussing the situation with them, and showing them how the operation worked was very time consuming, but necessary. In most cases, this investment of time worked to our advantage.

In August 1967, the Army chief of staff, General Harold K. Johnson, then my old boss, General Meyer, visited us. The commander in chief of the U.S. Army, Pacific (CINCUSARPAC), General John K. Waters, visited several times, as did his replacement, General Dwight E. Beach.

In October, Secretary of Defense McNamara, accompanied by the chairman of the Joint Chiefs of Staff, General Earle G. Wheeler, visited Vietnam. I attended the meeting General Westmoreland hosted for these visitors and discussed the port situation. During my detailed presentation I asked Secretary McNamara to explain our situation to Premier Nguyen Cao Ky and emphasize our need for his help and assistance. After the meeting, both McNamara and General Wheeler wanted to visit the port. At the conclusion of their two-hour visit, both were extremely complimentary on the job we were doing. As always, many times during the visit General Westmoreland emphasized to the secretary of defense his support of our efforts.

Shortly after the McNamara visit, Premier Ky visited the port with several of his ministers, including his key rival, Minister of Economy and Finance Au Truong Thanh. Minister Thanh was the main supporter of the big importers. I thought that either he would replace the prime minister or be shot. Minister Thanh was replaced instead.

Premier Ky and his party spent more than two hours with us at the port, mostly for briefings and discussions. Ky was smart and extremely conceited, and I realized one should not get in his way. He was very friendly with me, but I'm sure General Westmoreland had made sure of that.

While the port remained a hot spot, we attracted many other visitors including the secretary of the Army, Stanley R. Resor, and the under secretary of the Navy. The vice chief of staff of the Army,

General Creighton W. Abrams, also spent a great deal of time in the port during his visit, joining Westmoreland as his deputy and later replacing him.

In October 1966, Generals Eifler and Engler assigned an additional port unit to help supervise the commercial operation, in response to our earlier request. A transportation terminal command (type A), under the command of Col. Cary A. Kennedy, arrived in Vietnam from Fort Eustis, Virginia, in October 1966. Their organization, consisting of thirty-eight officers and 101 enlisted men, increased our port complement to 250 officers, 1,500 to 2,000 enlisted men, around 2,000 civilian employees, and many hundred contract workers. Our annual budget was near $60 million.

When Colonel Kennedy started working closely with Major Chu and the AID representatives, especially Mr. Schultz, commercial operations began to improve tremendously. Because of Cary's very aggressive nature, many times I would have to smooth out hurt feelings up and down the line. Many times, complaints would come from General Westmoreland or General Eifler, but I worked it out. I thought it better for Cary to err on the aggressive side rather than require that I constantly push him into action.

Although I didn't often ask for General Westmoreland's help, on some occasions I had no other recourse. During the early part of my tour, when the port problems were at their height, Westmoreland would frequently call me on Friday evenings around seven o'clock and ask me to come up to MACV headquarters and bring him up to speed. I couldn't have asked for a better and more helpful commander. Any time I had a problem with D. G. MacDonald, the AID chief, I would ask General Westmoreland to intercede. He always did, going directly to Mr. MacDonald or through Ambassador Bunker. Any time this happened, I would alert General Eifler, so that he and General Engler would not be surprised. They never objected to my reliance on General Westmoreland.

To expedite the flow of commercial goods, we had to clear the paperwork with the Vietnamese government officials and commercial interests, such as importers and ship's agents. I assigned one of my best officers, Maj. Ted Rosenberg, as liaison officer and expediter. In addition, he was responsible for berthing incoming ships alongside the piers or in the river.

The perfect liaison officer, Major Rosenberg was smart, knew how to work smoothly with all types of people, and did whatever was necessary to accomplish the job. I soon learned that I no longer had to worry about commercial traffic or many of the other AID jobs. Ted took over, kept me informed of his actions and came to me for help only if the mission was beyond his or Colonel Kennedy's capability.

In spite of all this, we still did not move commercial cargo out of the port in the style we wanted. Apparently, an awful lot of the AID commercial items had not been ordered by importers and had not moved. After getting the okay from my bosses, I informed Mr. MacDonald at AID that I had to get the commercial cargo out of the port; if they didn't move it, I would. This was not pleasant news to AID.

I located a storage area in an abandoned stadium called Petris Key, which could be fairly well secured by AID and the Vietnamese government. It was fenced in and the field had a good hard stand. I moved all the unclaimed commercial AID items to Petris Key, stationed security guards in the area and reminded all concerned where the goods were stored. Unfortunately, those items that were still usable when we moved them didn't remain usable long when left out in the weather.

Before the war, rice had been the largest export (*not* import) item for Vietnam. In those days the rice moved from the fields to the warehouses along the canals, then by barge to the Saigon River for loading onto deep-draft ships. Rice provided a large portion of the cash flow for the Vietnamese economy. The war reversed all that. Vietnam had to import rice provided by U.S. grant aid.

A lot of grant aid cargo, such as rice and fertilizer, now filled at least half of the ships lying off Vung Tau. The Army was blamed for the failure to move these ships through the port. These bulk materials also filled most of the contract barges drifting up and down the river canals waiting to be unloaded. Most of this type cargo had been transshipped from deep-draft ships into the barges, which in turn were moved up the canals to storage warehouses for unloading and storage until the cargo was disposed of.

The size of the bag used for inbound shipments caused a problem for us in the port. Rice had traditionally been moved in twenty-kilogram sacks (about forty pounds). The Vietnamese laborers could carry these on their backs into the warehouse, then out of the warehouse onto the barge for movement to ship side. The bags were then loaded aboard ship by ship's tackle. Rice and fertilizer were moving in the opposite direction, from deep-draft shipping in the Saigon harbor into barges, then up the canals to the old rice warehouses. We planned to have Vietnamese labor unload the bags on their backs from barge to warehouse.

An energetic purchasing agent in AID found that he could purchase rice and fertilizer in 80-pound bags cheaper than in 40-pound bags. These 80-pound bags were much too heavy for the Vietnamese laborers to carry on their backs. We had to substitute cranes and forklifts for the Vietnamese laborers. Moving cranes up narrow roadways to these warehouses was a real challenge. If there were no adequate roads, we moved the cranes by barge. If wharf space at the warehouse was not adequate for the crane to work, we had to work the crane over from our barges, which tied up a lot of our equipment.

In addition to using the contract barges to move the rice and fertilizer, we also attempted to move it to the warehouses in trucks. Often before the truck driver reached the warehouse, his truck would be surrounded by 50 to 100 little children, who prevented the truck from moving. While he was immobilized, Vietnamese men would make off with the cargo. U.S. Army guards were not the answer, because we could not shoot at little children. We solved this problem by persuading AID and the Vietnamese government to find safer destinations to which the rice could be delivered.

The Saigon port operation was clearly different from anything else we had confronted. The United States did finally get the operation under control so the commercial port eventually took over the operation. This happened some time after I left the Saigon port and had returned to the States.

On the military side, part of our mission was to support Vietnamese military forces in the Delta through the small ports of My Tho and Can Tho. We accomplished this with the help of our U.S. military advisers. The scope of these activities enlarged dramatically when the 9th U.S. Infantry Division and our newly created and trained Riverine Forces arrived in Vietnam in late 1966. Since one of the brigades and its supporting units was to be stationed in the Delta, a new campsite named Dong Tam was built on a river canal. It was built along the canal bank on what had previously been tidal land, covered by water during high tide and exposed at low tide. This was a challenge for our engineers, whom we supported by providing water transportation and port operations from Saigon.

I assigned troops down there on a permanent basis. It was a most interesting operation. The brigade commander was Brig. Gen. (later Lt. Gen.) William B. Fulton. I would helicopter down at least twice a week to check the operation and to coordinate with Bill Fulton. After they finally finished the campsite, we continued to provide water and port transportation support. I also provided Bill an LCM company, his main form of transport up and down the various canals. Bill installed artillery pieces and mortars on some of the LCMs, thus creating gunboats to assist him in attacking the enemy. The LCM company commander, Capt. William ("Gus") Pagonis, later became a lieutenant general and supervised our logistical operations for DESERT SHIELD.

One more problem, an internal one, needs to be highlighted again. As mentioned earlier, during this period the Army was changing from the technical service system to a functional supply system. The Army had not really completed a plan to accomplish this. Consequently, we still operated the old system within the newly created organizations. It did not work well but, with a lot of hard work done by aggressive people, we ultimately got the job done.

During this time, we had some ten to fifteen transportation colonels in various key transportation staff and command jobs throughout the Saigon area. They commanded the transportation units, held transportation staff jobs on the MACV and U.S. Army, Vietnam (USARV), staffs, and had some general staff jobs. As I worked with these colonels, all of whom I knew, I became aware of one distracting trait. Each often criticized the others and they disagreed with one another about policies and procedures. All of this disagreement took place in plain view of other senior members of the various staffs. It put the whole Transportation Corps in a bad light. This was not the first time I had observed this trait in the Transportation Corps and I knew it was wrong.

In an attempt to eliminate this public bickering, I invited all the Transportation Corps colonels to join me for a dinner party at one of Saigon's local restaurants. They all accepted and it was such a success that we had dinner together every Sunday evening. Before long, we were all good friends having a great time, sharing all kinds of information and seeking advice. It worked to the advantage of each of us. Before these dinner parties, most of the group had not associated with the others at all. After, we spoke to the outside world about transportation with the same voice. We accomplished much more as a result.

At this point, I will present a brief review of the physical Saigon port and its operation from 1 June 1966 through our projections for June 1968. On 1 June 1966, the mission of the 4th Transportation Command was to receive, discharge, and clear to its first destination all military cargo that supported the III and IV Corps Tactical Zones. Data indicates that we handled 218,000 short tons in May 1966: 190,000 short tons of general cargo and 28,000 short tons of ammunition, including cargoes unloaded at Vung Tau. The 4th Transportation Command used five deep-draft berths in the Saigon port—three in the M&M area and two in the commercial end of the port. They occasionally also used river berths. Ammunition was discharged in the river at Nha Be and ship-to-shore operations were conducted at Vung Tau—several kilometers to the south.

Because of the somewhat confused operations, incoming cargo continued to build up. Ten to twelve ships with military cargo waited off Vung Tau at Cape St. Jacques for berthing space in Saigon. The materiel handling equipment could not cope with the backlog in the port and discharge vessels at a reasonably efficient rate. Trucks were barely able to clear the port, but the depots were not geared to handle cargo at the rate it was being received.

On 1 June 1966, the commercial sector of the port consisted of two deep-draft berths, the same ones used by the Army, with three berths used to discharge barges. Twenty-two buoy berths were available in the river. The dock area was only long enough to handle five U.S. flag-type ships.

The Saigon port authority's mission, formalized in May 1966, was to assign facilities and to coordinate their use by commercial agencies and stevedore contractors. No accurate records exist to reveal the port tonnage volumes at that time; our best estimate is that they handled about 140,000 to 150,000 short tons, including AID cargo.

Operations in the commercial port were cumbersome, without a single agency or individual with the authority to direct and control the operations of the port. The docks, warehouses, and cranes were decayed and antiquated. The port faced increased commercial imports and a completely inadequate wholesale marketing system. Very little operational and management information was available.

By 1 June 1967, military operations in the Saigon port proper were carried out using the three deep-draft berths in the M&M area, one berth in the commercial port, and one in the fish market area. (*See Map 3.*) The U.S. had completed building the fish market berth in October 1966. The Army also used three buoy berths to discharge bulk AID cargo. Two berths were returned to the commercial port in May; the fish market berth was returned on 1 July.

Newport had seven barge wharves, two LST slots, and three deep-draft berths. A fourth deep-draft berth became available on 10 July. Ammunition operations had been shifted from Nha Be to Cat Lai, the base camp of the 11th Terminal Service Battalion, which was responsible for ammo operations. Cat Lai was closer to the barge discharge sites up the river at Cogido, Buu Long, Thanh Tuy Ha, and Binh Trieu. South of the Saigon complex at Vung Tau, operations expanded to meet increasing delta support requirements. The construction of a DeLong pier, which could berth two deep-draft vessels, greatly improved efficiency. This pier became operational on 1 July 1967.

Between June and December 1966, the port at Saigon underwent many changes in organization, distribution of functions and authority, and method of operation. On 5 July 1966, the mission of the 4th Transportation Command expanded with AID support requirements. Our revised mission statement gave us responsibility for the receipt, discharge, and clearance to first destination of all military cargo coming through the port of Saigon, the back-load of retrograde military cargo, and harbor security which included security of vessels at all discharge areas in Saigon, Newport, Cat Lai, Vung Tau, and the Delta.

In addition we would receive, discharge, and deliver to first destination all AID-financed commodities consigned to the Vietnamese government and advise and assist the port authority in the operation of the commercial port.

With these enlarged responsibilities and our gradually improving capabilities, the 4th Transportation Command steadily expanded its volume of operation. In May 1967 we handled approximately 393,000 short tons: 355,000 short tons of general cargo, of which 99,000 short tons were AID, and 256,000 short tons were military (38,000 short tons were ammunition). This was an increase of 175,000 short tons over the preceding May. Generally, during 1967 we had no serious problems with the military operations in Saigon port. With experience, more resources and improvements, the military operation had been rendered relatively routine. We were able to concentrate on management refinements to improve the efficiency of the operation.

By this time the commercial sector of the port required all deep-draft berths for deep-draft vessels. This included the use of all intransit sheds alongside the deep-draft berths as well. In 1966 the commercial sector had only three barge discharge berths dedicated for its sole use.

The port authority, which had received the assistance and advice of the 125th Transportation Command since October 1966, now functioned quite well. It had taken on a broader and more meaningful mission and now regulated all users of the port. Although its operators had a long way to go before they became totally efficient, they had set definite objectives and made real progress.

The port authority had become a self-sustaining element of the government, responsible for effective port management. It was well aware of its vital role in sustaining the economy of Vietnam. In May 1967, a low tonnage month, the commercial port handled 171,500 short tons of which 164,000 were imports and 7,500 were exports. The commercial import program had caused this reduction of tonnage. Although this reduction was to be replaced with Vietnam government-financed imports, AID did not expect imports to reach the previous level.

As a result of the joint efforts of the port authority and the 125th Transportation Command, commercial operations in the Saigon port greatly improved. Port inventory, including cargo in transit sheds, barges, and ships being worked or at Cape St. Jacques, showed a favorable trend downward. In the past, the Saigon port had been a storage area for the retailers. At one time the port had been covered with cargo which importers could not afford, did not want, could not find, or preferred to hold back to raise prices. This inventory had fallen from

342,000 short tons in December 1966 to 89,000 short tons in May 1967. The inventory reduction had been accompanied, or perhaps caused, by the favorable inverse relationship of the tonnage discharged to the tonnage cleared. A reduction was also apparent in the number of barges under load.

In addition to these desirable trends, several other factors led us to believe that the port authority had made good progress. First, its control had become firmly established. Although this may have seemed relatively insignificant to some, it was an outstanding accomplishment. The port rehabilitation program was well under way and modern operational and management practices had been implemented. Increased cargo clearance and market absorption indicated that the port was becoming increasingly capable of favorably influencing the Vietnamese economy. Facilities were being used with ever-increasing efficiency and effectiveness. The port authority now had established controls, standards, penalties, and an administrative system to enforce port policy and the port tariff. Finally, the port had developed a management information system that allowed assessment of its performance in meeting objectives and that served as a solid premise for planning and control.

Our plans also called for continued development of the Saigon port to work toward the development of a wholesale distribution system. To this end, we encouraged the port authority to add comptroller functions to its organization and to introduce improved financial management systems. We assisted in formulating long-range plans to modify operations to match an improving economy and for improvements to the physical plant.

We also continued to seek implementation of labor reforms to improve the lot of the port workers. These included increased pay, better working conditions, safety, health, and overall fairness of employment consistent with good business practices. We developed training programs for management personnel, which included visits to U.S. ports by Saigon port executives to observe and study modern port practices. Finally, we encouraged promotional activities to regenerate the export trade which we hoped would rebuild the reputation of the Saigon port and produce a healthy volume of shipping traffic.

During 1968, Newport became the hub of military terminal operations in the Saigon port complex. Military operations in the M&M area continued in Saigon port to support the current troop level and AID cargo. Operations and missions at Cat Lai and Vung Tau continued.

The military mission in the Saigon port did not change substantially during 1967. We continued to be responsible for terminal operations in southern Vietnam, which included support of the Mekong

Delta. The AID mission did change. Now that the commercial port was under better control, we returned some operating responsibilities for AID-sponsored cargo to the Vietnamese. The 4th Transportation Command stopped handling fertilizer and recommended that the Vietnamese move bulk foodstuffs like rice, flour, and bulgur wheat. These commodities were relatively easy to handle and the import programs for them had been firmly established. The assistance and advisory mission continued, although by 1 July 1968 there had been a reduction in the pier-level portion of this mission.

Tonnage requirements for AID imports continued at current levels although there had been a substantial reduction in the military handling of AID-sponsored cargo. The U.S. Army was expected to handle about 275,000 short tons of military cargo and about 25,000 short tons of AID cargo per month. Ammunition was expected to total about 50,000 short tons per month, based on the current trends. About 40,000–50,000 short tons of ammunition were handled during the five-month period preceding May 1967. Vung Tau was expected to handle an additional 60,000 short tons. The reduction in net tonnage handled was obviously caused by the shift of AID bulk tonnages to the port authority along with facilities then used in the commercial port by the military.

The progressive trends initiated in the Saigon port continued in 1968. The general stability achieved in military operations continued throughout the commercial sector. Military and commercial terminal operations had not achieved perfection, but the situation had improved. There was still a long way to go to reach maximum efficiency. For example, the high volume of data created by this terminal operation was still being processed manually. An automatic data processing system had been planned for the military terminal operation by December 1967, and studies were being made to expand it to the commercial port.

As I look back on my years in Saigon, certain things stand out. The first is the importance of good organization, a clear doctrine, and good people. As we finally put together a good commercial port operation with the 125th Transportation Command, the commercial port improved greatly. Major Rosenberg, my main liaison in all of these activities, did much of the work.

An important part of port doctrine was the installation of a workable port tariff for all to follow. This helped make the Saigon port a modern, workable port, although by today's standards that technology has become obsolete. We modernized both the commercial and the military ports by using our operation center with its control boards and radio communication throughout the working areas.

Eventually, we had the most modern materiel handling and container handling equipment available at that time. Our harbor craft, landing craft, and cranes, along with the various contractor support, brought Saigon up to modern standards. However, supply personnel and depots remained below standard.

At the conclusion of my tour, as I prepared to leave the 4th Transportation Command, my greatest satisfaction came from the noticeable change in the morale of our troops. When I arrived, morale was at its lowest possible point. Everyone had told the 4th how poorly they were performing and what a mess they had made of the port, although none of it was their fault. When I left, the mood could not have been higher. They were the best, and they knew it. I truly hated to leave the 4th, as I had hated to leave the 53d Truck Battalion in Europe. But someone else had to be given a chance to learn all the extremely valuable lessons one can learn only from commanding troops in the field.

CHAPTER 10

Logistics in Washington

Upon my return to the Pentagon from Vietnam in 1967, I was assigned to the Office of the Deputy Chief of Staff for Logistics (DCSLOG) as director of transportation. Although this position was authorized for a brigadier general and I was still a colonel, a general officers' board was sitting at the time to select officers for the next brigadier general list. This assignment appeared to be a good sign for me. General Engler, the USARV commander when I arrived in Vietnam and for most of my tour at the 4th Transportation Command, was the DCSLOG. He and General Eifler had given me a superior efficiency report in Vietnam. When the brigadier general list was published a few months later I found out I had been selected. I was high on the list because of my seniority as a colonel, and was promoted to brigadier general on 17 August 1967.

At the time my family was still living in Falls Church, Virginia. As I began my three-year tour in the Pentagon, my three oldest children continued at the same high school, and were even able to graduate from this same high school, a very unusual privilege for a career military family.

As the new director of transportation I had a ready-made list of things I wanted to do, based on my field experience in transportation. I had learned about the many problems from the bottom up. I not only had to know the programs and their problems and to be able to suggest solutions, I also immediately faced the bigger problem of being able to sell my solutions to senior people. It's very easy to think you know the answers and to blame someone else for not buying your recommendations. Over the years I've noticed that my ability to articulate and to sell has not been my strongest trait. I've often wished that I had the ability of such salesmen as General Ferdinand J. Chesarek and General William E. DePuy. General DePuy could sell anything to anybody, at the drop of a hat. It is a valuable asset that I fear I have always lacked.

With so many projects on my action list, an agenda for the Office of the Director of Transportation developed. I put the movement of household goods at the top of my list. For some time, I had observed this process from the outside and came to the conclusion that the system needed lots of improvement. The Department of Defense and the Army spend millions of dollars every year to move household goods. It seemed to me that the carriers received a great deal of profit they didn't deserve. To familiarize myself with the organizations and their procedures, I visited several major installations on the East Coast.

In the Army, household goods are usually a family's most important possessions and in some cases, their only material possessions. When a young soldier and his wife change stations and move their household goods, they are at the mercy of the moving company.

Regulations clearly state who has what responsibilities. Unfortunately, though, in most cases the young soldier does not know or understand his or her responsibilities and those of the carrier. Most commanders showed interest only when their own personal household goods were being moved, but were not concerned about the movement of their soldiers' goods. For some reason, this logistics function did not engage their attention.

The local transportation officer at the station has inspectors available to spot check the carriers. Because of the lack of enough inspectors, however, inspections were usually inadequate. This was the case during 1967–1968 when I made my survey. As I traveled from post to post and checked with the various post transportation offices and their managers, it did not appear to me that movement of household goods received sufficient command attention. When I discussed this with the post commanders, I pointed out that security of household goods had much to do with the morale of their soldiers and that the commanders should be personally interested in this most uninteresting subject.

I was not the only general officer concerned about movement of household goods. The commanders of the Military Traffic Management and Terminal Service (MTMTS) had also given high priority to movement of household goods, which has improved this service a great deal over the years. Installation commanders should also give higher priority to the matter.

I also gave priority to improving Army general staff attention to MTMTS. Even though most of the general staff officers knew that MTMTS was a major subordinate command, they did not realize the importance of its services. This became very apparent to me even when I sat on a promotion board or participated on a school or command selection board.

This lack of understanding resulted from the organizational links through which MTMTS operated. Even though MTMTS was directly under the command of the Army chief of staff and the vice chief of staff of the Army, it was also under the technical supervision of the assistant secretary of the Army and the assistant secretary of defense for installations and logistics. MTMTS reported many of its actions through the civilian technical path rather than the command chain. The Army staff was inadvertently bypassed and MTMTS missed the opportunity to bring many of its achievements to the attention of the Army staff. I proposed to the vice chief of staff that the director of transportation be introduced into the chain of command, so that MTMTS matters could be staffed through the interested staff offices. It did not happen.

As director of transportation, I also devoted a great deal of attention to the U.S. Army Transportation Center at Fort Eustis, Virginia. I emphasized the need for additional instruction at the Transportation School and regularly encouraged the major units to adopt movement planning and movement control and to practice intransit asset visibility based on the required transportation documentation. Everyone had to understand the importance of these transportation functions.

I accomplished this through discussions with the commanding general of Fort Eustis and during every speaking engagement in the field. The manuals and directives we prepared or reviewed always emphasized these subjects. I also stressed that a good transportation officer must have a good understanding of the other logistics functions, such as supply and maintenance.

The Transportation Corps is responsible for items moved out to the field as well as returned items, from the time they are picked up from the customer until they are delivered back to the customer. The principle of intransit asset visibility means maintaining 100 percent visibility for the entire period. The items must be returned to the customer with proper documentation so that they can be identified and issued. If this accountability is not preserved the entire supply system can break down as it did in Korea, in Vietnam, and again in Operations DESERT SHIELD and DESERT STORM. Automation and modern communications can improve visibility, but automation must be used properly. All transportation officers must be thoroughly familiar with transportation management, movement planning and control, and traffic management. They must be able to use these skills whenever necessary.

The cost of transportation has rarely been addressed, probably because no mechanism exists to call attention to transportation costs. The requisitioner who creates the cost is not responsible for paying the transportation bill. He may not realize that, by imposing a strict required delivery date, he can increase the transportation costs from under $10.00 to over $500.00. If the unit ordering supplies was to be billed for transportation, lean stock levels would be easier to achieve and inventory in motion might become more feasible.

To obtain a consensus among all senior transportation officers on the importance of these concepts and the meaning of the terms and to solicit their help in stressing them Army-wide, I asked all the transportation generals in and around the Washington area to meet periodically. They all agreed to meet monthly to promote these transportation goals. All transportation general officers on active duty, not very many at that time, attended the meetings. I resumed this practice later when I commanded the Transportation Center at Fort Eustis, Virginia, and it has continued annually at Fort Eustis.

I was not able to use my spot in the DCSLOG office to promote these transportation principles Army-wide for very long. Within a few months after I became the director of transportation of the Department of the Army, the Department of Defense realized that sooner or later American troops would leave Vietnam and that retrograde planning would be required to accomplish this in an orderly manner. The Defense Department directed the services to initiate retrograde planning, with the Army having the principal staff responsibility.

General Engler, the DCSLOG, was assigned the principal staff responsibility for the Army. He in turn assigned me as the Army project officer for T-day, or termination day. In mid-1968 a peaceful agreement seemed imminent. Each general staff office was directed to appoint a T-day planning officer to assist me. We soon met to establish our responsibilities and objectives. Next, we drafted a Department of the Army directive that outlined future actions by the staff and by all of the appropriate Army commands.

As we reviewed the history of the U.S. Army's record in retrograde planning and movement it became obvious that the Army performed weakly in each of these areas, from battlefield retrograde to theater retrograde. The Department of Defense had initiated this staff planning to correct past mistakes and to improve this very important and costly operation.

Retrograde planning consumed the rest of my time as director of transportation. A separate element of the DCSLOG staff was established to coordinate with the staff as well as with special staff elements in all the CONUS and Pacific commands. They developed plans to rapidly remove troops, equipment, and supplies from Vietnam. Although in the end American troops left Vietnam in gradual increments over a four-year period, we were at least prepared for a more immediate withdrawal to support any peace agreement.

The operation required many steps beginning with determining what should be withdrawn, how to prepare it for retrograde, how to package and document it, where to send it, and whether to rebuild, repair, or scrap it. We wanted to retrograde the maximum amount of reusable equipment and supplies to the Army's system. On the other hand, we would have to leave behind a certain amount of supplies and equipment to support the South Vietnamese armed forces. Planning required constant trips to storage sites, as well as coordinating and cooperating with many units.

In the final analysis, our retrograde from Vietnam worked better than it had ever worked before. At first we thought there were about five million tons in Vietnam that we probably ought to retrograde, but getting it to its destination in the necessary condition was difficult. This project required a lot of time, but it was an interesting job and I learned from it.

In 1968, during one of my trips to Vietnam to coordinate the details of the retrograde plan, the major general promotion list was published. My name was on it. The list had been published just a few months after I had been promoted to brigadier general. As I was well down on this list, I did not pin on the second star for over a year. By that time, we had pretty well finished preparing the initial retrograde plan, which provided broad guidance to all Army commands involved in the Vietnam operation. The detailed planning and actual implementation was just about to occur. It would continue for several years and would prove to be extremely difficult. I would remain deeply involved in retrograde as I moved from one assignment to another.

As discussed in Chapter 8, the Army logistics system had undergone major organizational changes in the early sixties as the result of Secretary of Defense McNamara's Project 80; however, before these changes could be completed and before the Army logistics system could be changed, we became deeply involved in the Vietnam War. The hybrid Army logistics system struggled through this period, from 1962 to 1967.

On 26 March 1965, aware of the difficulties and that the Army's logistics system had problems during the Vietnam War, the Army chief of staff directed that the DCSLOG, with the assistance of the other principal staff officers, develop an outline plan for a comprehensive study of the Army's logistics system. The study plan was approved on 16 June 1965. On 27 August, Army chief of staff memorandum CSM-65-407 established the board of inquiry into the Army logistics system.

Lt. Gen. Frederick J. Brown served as chairman, reporting directly to the Army vice chief of staff. Maj. Gen. Horace F. Bigelow, an assistant DCSLOG at the time, was named vice chairman. The chief of staff's memorandum initially authorized sixteen full-time professionals and ten administrative personnel. Consultants both inside and outside of the Army were authorized. General Brown's overall task was to analyze the current Army logistics system to determine what changes and modifications would make it more responsive to materiel readiness requirements at company level and to recommend appropriate corrective actions.

The ensuing Brown Board report reviewed the evolution of the Army logistics system since World War II. It focused first on the relationship between the Army and the Department of Defense, including DOD's philosophy, the various reorganizations within DOD and the services, and the effects these changes had on the Army logistics system. It then discussed in great detail logistics operations and their control, evaluating their effectiveness with the current tools of systems analysis and computer models. This resulted in the most thorough, comprehensive, and detailed examination of the Army's logistics system ever made.

The Brown Board pointed out that the Army does not learn by reviewing history and the lessons it teaches, but continues to repeat the same mistakes. This is especially true in logistics, where the techniques, technology, and methods constantly change, but the basic missions remain the same. Another principal gap exists in the area of planning and doctrine. The study specifically indicated that the Office of the Chief of Military History provides a valuable service in compiling and analyzing historical data and that the Army should use its services a great deal more.

The board recommended putting someone in charge of logistics. They did not suggest the creation of a command, like the Army Service Forces of World War II, but proposed giving the DCSLOG the authority to manage the Army's logistics system. The board recommended how this could be done and made a strong case for why it should be done. Many of the recommendations were designed to return to the Army the kinds of centralized direction previously exercised by the chiefs of the Technical Services, but without the problems.

The report discussed personnel, doctrine, and systems. The board recommended that a new office be created in DCSLOG with the authority to supervise these areas Army-wide. As a result, the Army chief of staff later expanded the Office of the DCSLOG by adding an assistant DCSLOG for personnel, doctrine, and systems (PDS) with the staff necessary to meet the recommendations of the Brown Board study.

The study also recommended establishing a separate agency outside of the Washington, D.C., area to assist the ADCSLOG (PDS). The study further recommended that the personnel currently performing PDS roles in other agencies be transferred with the functions to the new agency, to be named the Logistic Doctrine, Systems Readiness Agency (LDSRA).

Coincidental with this organization change, the DCSLOG, Lt. Gen. Joseph M. Heiser, Jr., assigned me to be the first ADCSLOG (PDS). As soon as we were able to establish both our new office in the Pentagon and the new agency at New Cumberland, Pennsylvania, we developed a program based upon the many Brown Board study recommendations.

We first attacked the development of automated systems for supply, maintenance, transportation, as well as other logistics areas for Army units worldwide. The agency would accomplish most of the detailed work, with our office in Washington giving assistance in staffing and coordinating with the Combat Developments Command and the Army Materiel Command. AMC was responsible for development of automated systems on the wholesale supply side.

The Brown Board study was very specific in recommending our responsibility for coordinating personnel and training with the deputy chief of staff for personnel, the assistant chief of staff for force development, the Continental Army Command, and the Combat Developments Command.

The board further recommended that the Army publish a new regulation spelling out in detail the responsibilities and functions of the deputy chief of staff for logistics. The implementation instructions with the study filled six separate volumes: Volume 1, *Summary and Guide to Implementation*; Volume 2, *Asset Management*; Volume 3, *Acquisition Management*; Volume 4, *General Management of Logistics*; Volume 5, *Personnel, Training, and Organization*; and Volume 6, *Logistics Systems*.

Although the Brown Board considered its instructions in Volume 4 to be comprehensive, one shortcoming in its coverage of transportation was discovered too late to correct. The transportation omission related to overall strategic support of the Army and internal transportation within and between deployed forces. Thus the Brown Board study did not cover the role of transportation, a deficiency which frequently occurs, because the Army was unable to articulate its requirements for strategic movement. This was especially true in the case of fixing the magnitude of, and obtaining commitments for, the total requirements for strategic transportation, so that comprehensive, realistic and coherent planning and programming could be accomplished.

In ADCSLOG (PDS) and our agency at New Cumberland, we developed a detailed program to address all the study recommendations which the chief of staff had approved. The program specified the actions to be performed, as well as by whom and over what time period. We initially briefed the status of these program details to the DCSLOG, to the vice chief of staff of the Army, to the chief of staff of the Army, and to the secretary of the Army every week. At first, they all showed great interest. They had already approved the bulk of the recommended actions, and had informed the general staff and the major commands. After a while, we changed our briefings to every month and, after six or eight months, we briefed only the DCSLOG and his staff. The Army soon lost interest; as a result, very few of the recommended and approved actions were implemented completely. The Army would do well to review and update this fine study.

During this period, General Heiser held periodic meetings with the director of the Defense Division of the General Accounting Office. I would attend these meetings along with the key defense-oriented personnel in GAO. One month we would visit the GAO offices and the next month they would come to the Pentagon. During these meetings, we would brief GAO on the major logistics actions underway in the Army, especially actions to implement the Brown Board recommendations. GAO would in turn brief us on all reviews they were conducting that related to Army logistics.

We were always honest and straightforward in our discussions and briefings, as was the GAO. As a result, the GAO would learn where to go and who to see to obtain the most accurate, detailed information. Likewise, we were never surprised by a GAO review or by their reports. We found this exchange to be mutually helpful. This cooperation continued throughout General Heiser's term as the DCSLOG.

During my short tour as the ADCSLOG (PDS), our office and our agency in New Cumberland laid new groundwork by initiating actions to automate the Army logistics systems: supply, maintenance, transportation, et cetera. Much of the initial work required that the logistics functions be defined in sufficient detail so they could be programmed into computer language to produce the necessary automated management tools.

My year and a half as the ADCSLOG (PDS) completed my three-year tour on the DA staff, 1968–1971. When the job of DCSLOG at USARPAC became available, General Heiser offered it to me. I accepted this new opportunity with enthusiasm. I knew my family would enjoy living in Hawaii.

CHAPTER 11

Logistics in the Pacific

Looking back on the job of DCSLOG, USARPAC, I have wondered about the need for and the validity of the command itself. Over the years numerous reports have made the case for unified commands such as the Pacific Command and the European Command. When General Abrams commanded the MACV, he developed a great dislike for the unified Pacific Command and its three component commands, feeling they contributed little to the operation of the separate commands in Japan, Korea, and Vietnam. When he returned as chief of staff of the Army, he eliminated USARPAC.

I am thoroughly convinced, had he not died prematurely and had he remained chief of staff of the Army for his full four years, General Abrams would have accomplished a great deal more to eliminate CINCPAC itself. He felt very strongly that the Hawaiian commands were nothing but stumbling blocks to accomplishment in the Pacific. Out of necessity, as MACV commander, General Abrams had dealt directly with the Joint Chiefs of Staff, the Office of the Secretary of Defense, and in many cases the president's office itself, rather than going through CINCPAC and the components.

As I worked into my job as USARPAC DCSLOG, I realized that we really had very little responsibility over the logistics system in the Pacific. In fact, except for ammunition, our biggest job was to stay out of the way and avoid interfering with logistics support to Okinawa, Japan, Korea, and Vietnam. Requisitions for TO&E-authorized items were the only routine requests routed through USARPAC. Our only role was to check that the item had been, in fact, authorized for the unit—a very simple process.

Ammunition shipments, however, were a different matter. Our large ammunition office controlled the levels of ammo at all locations in the Pacific. We maintained accurate measures of ammunition levels and the condition of the ammunition by using our field ammunition inspectors and by reviewing the ammunition reports submitted by the commands. We also maintained visibility over all ammunition enroute from the U.S. to its many destinations. If necessary, we could divert ammunition shipments to alternate destinations.

After the enemy had destroyed considerable ammunition stockpiles in Vietnam, our Army decided to use storage in transit as much as possible rather than storing large quantities of ammunition on the ground. Another name for this concept is *inventory in motion*. By knowing exactly what ammunition was enroute, what ship it was on, and its destination, we possessed a flexibility that made the vulnerable ammunition dump passé. General Heiser's books, *Logistic Support* and *A Soldier Supporting Soldiers*, illustrate our application of this approach.[1]

Mr. Vincent P. Huggard, the deputy assistant secretary of the Army for installations and logistics, directed and supervised the entire ammunitions control operation. Vince had participated in ammunition operations during all of his career and ammunition remained his specialty as he was promoted up the civilian career ladder. Huggard became known as "Mr. Ammo." Highly respected throughout the Army, DOD, and on Capitol Hill, Vince reviewed all the ammunition requirements computations and presented them along with the budget to DOD and to Congress. All concerned thought so highly of him that they seldom questioned his requirement projections.

Mr. Huggard held close rein over ammunition operations during the entire Vietnam War. An important tool in ammunition control was the conduct of biannual planning meetings at USARPAC. At these meetings all requisitions for ammo were reviewed and were either approved and forwarded to the appropriate sources in the U.S., or they were changed as Vince saw fit. Ammunition shipments under way or being prepared for shipment were also reviewed. The Hawaii planning meeting devoted considerable time to reviewing ammunition expenditure rates in Vietnam as well as future ammo requirements.

At the close of each six-month meeting, participants prepared a detailed plan for ammunition for the next period. We followed the guidance in these plans as closely as possible. Our Ammunition Division in USARPAC supervised their application in the Pacific theater. Mr. Bob Surhiem, a key player in the ammunition operation, worked closely with Vince Huggard. As the civilian transportation officer at the U.S. Army Munitions Command, Bob had been experienced in ammunition movement for many years. During the semiannual ammunition meetings in Hawaii, he would develop the transportation movement plans for the next six months. Upon Huggard's approval, Surhiem would make sure that they were followed.

USARPAC also provided considerable grant aid and military sales to our allied armies in the Pacific. Although CINCPAC had responsibility for military assistance and sales under DOD, USARPAC

---

[1] Joseph M. Heiser, Jr., *Logistic Support* (Washington, D.C.: U.S. Army Center of Military History, 1991).

Heiser, *A Soldier Supporting Soldiers*.

reviewed the Army portions of these programs. It became obvious to me that we should know a lot more about the armies of our allies in the Pacific: we needed to know how they were organized, how they provided support, the levels of their normal requirements, and many other factors so that we could evaluate their requirements more effectively before submitting them to DOD.

We began meeting with the equivalents of our DCSLOG in each of our allied armies: Korea, Japan, Taiwan, Singapore, and Thailand. At first we did this informally in one-on-one meetings, but as interest grew we decided to meet together to discuss our mutual problems and interests. A different country sponsored each successive meeting, which provided us with a rare opportunity to become familiar with each country's organization, operation, personnel, and problems. These meetings became so successful that soon after I left USARPAC, the director of logistics, CINCPAC, took over and continued them.

USARPAC also had planning and operations responsibility for retrograde, the return of supplies and equipment from a command to CONUS. We coordinated the actions required to retrograde major end items between the theater's subordinate commands, such as Vietnam, Korea, Japan, Okinawa, Taiwan, the Department of the Army, and the Army Materiel Command. Our responsibility included the retrograde of end items to be rebuilt at our facilities in Japan and Taiwan. The cost of rebuilding these items at our offshore facilities was cheaper than in CONUS, and we could also avoid large transportation costs. AMC's inventory control points directly managed most of the repair parts and secondary items. General Heiser covers this process very thoroughly in *A Soldier Supporting Soldiers*.[2]

My tour of duty at USARPAC was supposed to last three years. In January 1972, after only a year and a half in Hawaii, I went back to Vietnam to be the director of logistics, J4, at MACV. Because my family enjoyed Hawaii very much, we moved off Fort Shafter and into a condominium in Honolulu, where they remained while I was in Vietnam.

Having previously been assigned to the joint staff, I had some experience with interservice staff problems and responsibilities. I knew that logistics is primarily a service, not a joint, responsibility. I had also learned what logistics areas fell in the joint arena. Even if one sometimes has to step on toes, it usually pays to tread lightly. Cooperation pays off in the long run.

I truly believe in logistics as a separate responsibility of each service because each service has a different mission, different equipment, and entirely different problems. Usually each service performs its mission under entirely different conditions. Although some support

---

[2] Heiser, *A Soldier Supporting Soldiers*.

may be provided more efficiently and more economically by a cross-service organization such as the Defense Supply Agency, economics should not be the main determinant. There really isn't anything economical about providing defense. The money must be spent to defend the country.

However, some logistics functions are truly cross-service, such as transportation. We must jointly share this function because we only have one transportation system to support the three services and our civilian economy. Each service cannot have its own air, land, or sea system. Although the Air Force sometimes thinks it has priority for air transport and the Navy feels it owns all sea-going transportation, such monopolies cannot be allowed. Transportation must be provided based on priority of need.

Joint control of transportation, although important, is not absolutely necessary. It is far more important to jointly allocate and control the requirements for movement, particularly when a shortage of transportation exists as during an all-out war like World War II. We never experienced a shortage of transportation during the Vietnam War. Movement control could have allowed more efficient and effective use of transportation, but that is never the overriding issue for combat support.

Although a joint transportation movement control agency existed at MACV under the control of J4, we really didn't control movement. Each service had enough transportation so that each had its own movement control organization.

When I returned to Vietnam, the services were implementing retrograde plans at a very fast pace. The USARV devoted a great deal of effort to the biggest job, Army retrograde. Between 1969 and 1972, USARV retrieved and shipped out some two million short tons of reusable Army materiel, valued at approximately $5 billion, which the Army would use again somewhere else.

By this time, the handwriting was on the wall: the days left for U.S. forces to remain in Vietnam were numbered. In addition to continuously retrograding materiel, USARV was also redeploying forces. These monumental tasks became USARV's main missions. As a result some equipment was damaged, some asset visibility was lost, some careless packing took place, and some dirty parts were shipped. But on the whole, USARV did a good job.

Major item distribution instructions had been issued and were controlled by the U.S. Army, Pacific. USARV had also published regulations and procedures for handling this same materiel. The destinations of special project stocks; nonstandard equipment; repair parts; communication equipment; post, camp, and station equipment; and many other items created a significant problem for USARV. It taxed USARV's processing and management capabilities to the maximum.

Not everything went as planned because of the rapid movement of units, the constant turnover of personnel, the need to use an increasing number of Vietnamese personnel rather than U.S. military, and the rapid reduction in the number of adequately trained U.S. supervisors to oversee the Vietnamese. Nevertheless, Army logistics leaders realized at the time the importance of documenting this withdrawal of forces with lessons learned because it had never before been done properly. Each withdrawing unit prepared detailed after-action reports (AARs) for the Army to use in any future withdrawals.

In Vietnam, the most truly combined mission in which I participated was working with the Vietnamese and other allied forces. At least 90 percent of my time as J4 was devoted to working with Lt. Gen. Dong Van Khuyen, the director of logistics of the Vietnamese armed forces and commander of the Joint Logistics Command. (Although the term "joint" was used, the Army dominated the group because Army troops made up the majority of the armed forces.) I regarded General Khuyen as honest, intelligent, and professional in all respects, and spent considerable time working with him and other Vietnamese logisticians. Although they were doing a good job, they needed to make improvements and changes before they could assume complete responsibility for logistics support after all U.S. forces departed Vietnam.

General Khuyen agreed with my assessment. I suggested that we bring a small team of U.S. experts to Vietnam to work with a team of Vietnamese counterparts, appointed by Khuyen, to determine the changes and additions required by the Vietnamese Armed Forces Support System. Following my request to the DA for such help, a small team headed by Col. Herman W. Sheriff from the Army's DCSLOG, Supply and Maintenance Directorate, soon arrived. His team consisted of several other experts from the Army DCSLOG staff and from AMC, joined by a group of Vietnamese logisticians. The team ran Pathfinder 1, a complete review of the Vietnamese support system.

Throughout the project, Khuyen and I met weekly—sometimes twice a week—for updates on the status of the plans. We would often provide guidance as we thought necessary. After Pathfinder 1 had been completed, Pathfinder 2 was established to draw up the detailed procedures to implement the recommendations of Pathfinder 1. A Vietnamese colonel headed each Pathfinder team with Colonel Sheriff as deputy chief. The plans the team developed were, in fact, Vietnamese plans which the Vietnamese believed they could carry out. Colonel Sheriff and his two teams acted as advisers.

The Vietnamese and U.S. experts specialized in supply, maintenance, and logistics plans. The team also included an American automated data processing hardware specialist and a strategic communications specialist. The team visited over ninety different activities scattered throughout South Vietnam, from combat units and the direct and general support units to the Logistics Command headquarters and the Office of the Chief of Technical Services. The final plan embraced every aspect of the Vietnamese armed forces logistics system. Although the supply system was in fact being automated at the start of Pathfinder 1, automation later expanded to all levels of the Vietnamese forces. After General Khuyen and I approved Pathfinder 1 and 2, implementation began in the middle of 1972.

The American forces had no depot rebuild facilities in Vietnam, a lack that created a big problem when we pulled out. All American rebuild of retrograde units had been performed in either Japan or Taiwan; in some cases, the hardware had been shipped back to the United States. To accommodate the Vietnamese, we established a rebuild facility on the outskirts of Saigon. With tremendous help from AMC and their experts, we equipped this facility with the necessary shop equipment, machine tools, hand tools, and training manuals. AMC, with help from contractors, began an extensive program to train personnel to operate the facility. This very ambitious project provided General Khuyen and the Vietnamese forces with a necessary capability.

As the time approached for U.S. forces to pull out, we also needed to ensure that the Vietnamese forces had the equipment and supplies authorized for them. Distracted by the pressures of a demanding war, we had not spent much time or effort to check the South Vietnamese authorizations against our records in the United States which indicated what supplies we had provided to them. I was shocked when I saw the reports submitted by the advisory teams we had assigned to study this subject. American logisticians had never reconciled what DOD thought it had issued to the Vietnamese armed forces and what these forces recorded that they had received.

When DOD shipped equipment and supplies to the Vietnamese army, we assumed without checking that the goods were received. Before I could ask DOD to issue the additional supplies and equipment that we owed the Vietnamese army, I had to reconcile our records with those of the Vietnamese. General Khuyen and I then assigned all of our personnel to inventory teams. They began the tedious process of inventorying equipment and supplies in the hands of all South Vietnamese military units throughout the country. This huge effort required a great deal of time and most of our logistics personnel for the rest of 1972. As our teams moved around the country, General Khuyen and I spent a great deal of time on the road visiting as many sites and units as we possibly could.

At the same time, a major logistics problem with the South Korean forces came to light. The two Korean divisions in South Vietnam were stationed north of the Cam Ranh Bay area and were supported out of Cam Ranh Bay. Soon after my arrival in Vietnam, I visited the Koreans. To my surprise, I discovered that most of their combat equipment was nonoperational. When I inspected the artillery, I found that the guns were immaculate and had been maintained in excellent condition. The only problem was that they couldn't fire. Each was missing a vital component or repair part and, in many cases, the barrels had been worn out and required replacement.

When I asked why they had not replaced the worn parts, they told me that USARV had stopped filling their requisitions. I returned to Saigon via Long Binh and USARV headquarters to discuss this with Lt. Gen. William J. McCaffrey, the commander of USARV. He told me that they no longer honored Korean requisitions. For some time the Koreans, who knew our system better than our own units did, had been obtaining equipment and parts illegally from the Cam Ranh Bay depot. As a result, he had ordered Cam Ranh Bay to stop supporting the Koreans completely.

When I informed General Abrams about this condition, he merely told me to correct it. I had to send inventory teams to the Korean divisions to determine their shortages and had the Koreans submit emergency requisitions to obtain the parts. We monitored these transactions closely and informed DA, USARPAC, and AMC on a regular basis. We wanted to rectify these shortages as quickly as possible because we had been told that the Koreans would soon be moved out of country. Since they were to turn over all their gear, including TO&E equipment, to the Vietnamese forces, we wanted it all to be in operable condition. We would use the materiel from the Korean divisions to replace the shortages we had discovered during our joint U.S./Vietnamese inventories.

This transfer of equipment presented another problem, the poor relationship between the Koreans and the Vietnamese. They frequently got into fights and often would not speak to each other. We had to send more American inventory teams up to the Korean area along with the Vietnamese receiving teams. U.S. logisticians would accept the equipment and supplies from the Koreans and prepare receipts for it; then they would turn around and issue it to the Vietnamese forces. My team was aware of the absurdity of what they were asked to do, but they performed this slow and tedious procedure successfully.

I spent most of my time during the last six months of my tour following up on our joint inventories. We finally developed records for the Vietnamese armed forces which we both agreed upon and which OSD could use to ensure that the Vietnamese armed forces had the equipment and supplies authorized for them. Unfortunately, I later learned from Maj. Gen. John E. Murray, my replacement, that the U.S. did not finish the resupply and apparently had not intended to do so, even while we were making our inventory.

We soon learned that a cease-fire agreement between the North Vietnamese and the U.S. was imminent. The agreement included specific limits on the size and type of organization that could remain in South Vietnam to assist the South Vietnamese. This organization would be known as the Defense Attaché Office, having only about fifty personnel.

The office, headed up by a U.S. general officer known as the Defense Attaché, would consist mainly of civilians with a few military members. The Defense Attaché and his deputy would be the only U.S. general officers left in Vietnam. I was to be the new Defense Attaché and was told to start immediately to develop the authorized organization by filling the spaces as soon as possible. We would very soon replace MACV and all other U.S. personnel in South Vietnam. We were given precise directions about our mission, our operational limits, and with whom we could work. My new group was to take over the command after the departure of General Frederick C. Weyand, commander of MACV, and his staff.

I requested mostly key civilian personnel and a couple of military to man the Defense Attaché office. Before I could complete the roster I was informed that General Murray, who had been J4, CINCPAC, was replacing me and that I was being reassigned to Fort Eustis, Virginia, as the commanding general of the Transportation Center. I was elated to get out of Vietnam, anticipating the inevitable upcoming problems, and I was very pleased with my assignment to Fort Eustis.

General Murray, of whom I thought highly and whom I had known and worked with for years, arrived in late December 1972 and took over what was to become a very difficult and unhappy experience. I returned to Hawaii, packed the family, and returned to Fort Eustis, Virginia.

CHAPTER 12

Running Fort Eustis

It was certainly satisfying to be named commanding general of the Transportation Center and commandant of the Transportation School, which meant returning to Fort Eustis, Virginia, the home of the Transportation Corps. My family was excited too. Our oldest daughter and our youngest son had both been born at Fort Eustis. This was to be our third tour there; the post and the local community were home to us. From a practical standpoint many of our friends in the area were by then community leaders who could be counted on to help with community relations.

My first assignment to Fort Eustis had occurred after World War II, in January 1947, as a result of my transfer from the Engineer Amphibious Command and my integration into the Transportation Corps of the Regular Army. Our second tour to Fort Eustis followed the Korean War, and coincided with another reduction in Army strength.

As we returned for the third time, following another war, major changes were again taking place in the Army's organization, doctrine, training, and equipment. As the result of my recent experiences in Vietnam, I had many ideas about these changes and what they implied for the Transportation Corps' relationship with the rest of the Army. I had closely observed the misunderstandings that had occurred within the Army about the mission and the importance of transportation. I had seen confusion on the part of transporters as well.

Overall, the Army had deteriorated badly during the Vietnam War. All of the Army's assets—personnel, equipment, and research—had been poured into the war effort for ten years. This diversion had been at the expense of the rest of the Army. As I returned to the Transportation Center, I knew I would be faced with many of the same problems we had experienced in 1947 and 1956. Only this time, I would be responsible to ensure that the necessary changes were made.

I looked forward to the challenge. My job would no longer include being chief of transportation because Project 80 had eliminated all the chiefs of the Technical Services. (This position would not be revived for several years.) But even without the title or authority, I would have many of the same responsibilities of the chief.

I also recalled the Brown Board study and its recommendation that the Army logistics system regain many of the responsibilities and troop support roles previously held by the chiefs of the Technical Services, without resurrecting the duplication and procrastination that had existed before Project 80. The Transportation Center, particularly the Transportation School, was responsible for many of these functions.

This mission was especially important during the period following our Vietnam experiences. We would no longer have responsibility for research and development or for managing the appropriated funding and, of course, would not have the authority that accompanied these responsibilities. This role had been taken away and had not been returned. The center controlled most of the transportation TO&E units remaining in the active force and was responsible for ensuring their state of readiness in case of an emergency.

Upon my arrival at Fort Eustis, I found out that the Army was undergoing another major reorganization. As we had discovered during the Vietnam War, the Army organization had not worked well. The Combat Developments Command, which was supposed to develop new organizations and new doctrines for the Army component commands to implement, had not worked. The major component commanders could not wait for all this development to occur before changing from a technical service system to a functional system. As a result, each major component commander had developed his own logistics system. Because each system was different, the branch centers and schools could not prepare individuals and units properly for assignment to each unique command. The variety of systems also created problems when dealing with AMC and its wholesale supply system.

At that time, the Army consisted of three major commands: the Combat Developments Command, the Continental Army Command, and the Army Materiel Command. As mentioned, CDC was responsible for the development of concepts, doctrine, TO&E, and equipment. CONARC commanded all the CONUS installations, units, and schools, and implemented CDC's output. AMC was responsible for research and development in coordination with CDC, and for providing wholesale logistics support to the Army.

Because this organization had not worked well, the Army was reorganizing. Two or three new major Army commands were renamed and their responsibilities rearranged. The Training and Doctrine Command (TRADOC) and the Forces Command (FORSCOM) replaced CDC and CONARC, while AMC remained the same. TRADOC was responsible for preparation of organizational TO&Es and for concepts, doctrine, and training. It exercised these responsibilities through the branch centers and the schools it commanded. To assist in managing these responsibilities, TRADOC established three intermediate centers:

the Combat Arms Center at Fort Leavenworth, Kansas, to oversee the combat arms schools; the Logistics Center at Fort Lee, Virginia, to oversee the logistics schools; and the Administrative Center at Fort Benjamin Harrison, Indiana, to oversee the personnel, finance, and administrative schools. The Transportation School worked with the other logistics schools under the staff supervision of the Logistics Center.

FORSCOM commanded CONUS installations and the forces not under TRADOC. FORSCOM was also responsible for Reserve and National Guard training and for individual and unit training throughout CONUS. AMC remained responsible for the wholesale logistics system including research, development, and procurement of weapons in coordination with TRADOC.

When I arrived at Fort Eustis, the reorganization was just beginning. As commander of the Transportation School and Center, I coordinated with the commanders of the Logistics, Quartermaster, Ordnance, and Missile and Munitions Centers.

The Communications Center and School and the Engineer Center and School were combat support organizations rather than combat service support like transportation. Therefore, they were separate from the Logistics Center and the Combat Arms Center. They worked with the Logistics Center for logistics, but they also worked with the Combat Arms Center on matters of combat support. They were directly under the command of TRADOC.

For the next two and a half years, we devoted a great deal of our time and effort to developing the very vital training and doctrine. As new concepts and doctrines were developed and approved by TRADOC, we added them to our school and unit training curricula. It was necessary to produce a tremendous number of new training manuals and publications. All had to be rewritten and published, a very time-consuming process.

Based upon my previous experiences in transportation and logistics during World War II, Korea, and Vietnam, I of course put a great deal of emphasis on those areas which I knew were in great need. For example, I concentrated on proper transportation documentation; asset visibility, particularly in transit; movement planning; and movement control. Although these were all transportation responsibilities, not all were well understood or appreciated by most transporters. These concepts had all been introduced in the Transportation School immediately after World War II and had been taught for some time thereafter. Gradually, they had been dropped as other matters brought up by the combat side of the Army crowded them out. Our performance in Vietnam had been in part reflected in this change in curriculum. I reintroduced them into both the school courses and unit training.

Upon returning to the Transportation Center, I found an even greater challenge—the shift to an all-volunteer Army. We had to change from depending upon the draft for our soldiers to a system in which enlistees wanted to join the Army or, in our case, wanted to join the Transportation Corps. I soon decided that we probably had an advantage over most other branches, especially the combat arms branches. One asset we enjoyed was active support from the transportation industry, which had supported the Transportation Corps since its inception.

The relationship between the railroads and the Army had been long standing. During the period of rail expansion during the 19th century, Army engineers not only assisted but also provided major guidance to the railroads as they established rail lines throughout the United States. (Protecting engineers scouting for suitable railroad roadbeds had led General George Custer to his demise.) Our government encouraged this effort because of the advantages that rail transportation provided. The Transportation Corps has always maintained a very close relationship with the railroads and arranged for commercial transportation for the Army.

Starting before World War II, nearly all of the class A railroads had affiliated with the Army and had sponsored Army reserve rail units. The railroads had organized these units, made up of company employees. The railroads contributed much time and funds to support them. The units were organized along regular military lines, but as specialized railroad companies: operating battalions were made up of companies to operate the rail lines and equipment maintenance companies to maintain the rail equipment. Also, shop battalions provided heavy maintenance for rolling stock and locomotives, as well as senior headquarters units to manage these support units.

Many of these units had been called to active duty during World War II and provided the backbone when we took over, rebuilt, and operated the destroyed rail facilities in Iran, France, Germany, and elsewhere. These rail units, called Army affiliated units, had operated these foreign rail systems, eventually turning them back to the commercial carriers. This worked very well.

In Iran, the rail units provided transportation from the Persian Gulf up through very difficult terrain into Russia to aid our military support of the Russian forces in World War II. The affiliated units actually on active duty performed similar chores in Korea during that war.

When President Truman took over the railroads from 1948–1952, he did so by calling to active duty senior members of the military railway affiliation program, the Military Railway Service. These executives took off their president or vice president hats and put on their military uniforms to run the railroads through their own companies under President Truman. It worked well with few difficulties. Unfortunately, as the use of rail transportation declined in this country, the Army lost interest in the affiliation program. The units have now disappeared. Still, the railroads and the Transportation Corps have a close association as we have with all modes of transportation.

As we began to develop the all-volunteer program, it occurred to me that the Army could offer a very attractive career path for young enlisted men interested in working in transportation. They could join the Army, be trained in the field of their choice and, after leaving the service, enter commercial transportation. Industry supported this idea and was delighted to work with the U.S. Army. Once again, we attempted to sell the Army on affiliation programs with industry before we asked the transportation industry to support it. Our request fell on deaf ears—the Army was not interested.

When I commanded Fort Eustis, the aircraft industry constantly sought aircraft mechanics. The Army seemed to provide an excellent path for a young person interested in an aviation maintenance career. The young man could enlist and, after his basic training, come to Fort Eustis for his military occupational specialty (MOS) training and later his advanced MOS training in aviation maintenance. He would then be assigned to one of our aviation units.

If he desired to leave the Army after he completed his enlistment, he would be prepared to join a commercial airline as an aircraft maintenance specialist. If he wanted to obtain a college degree in aircraft engineering, he could join one of the Army's many off-time higher education programs at the Army's expense and obtain a degree. We arranged such a program with St. Leo College, which specializes in aviation. St. Leo's provided this off-time, after-hours program to soldiers of Fort Eustis who wanted it.

We arranged similar programs with industry in other fields of transportation. One time, we were invited to participate in the Daytona 500 stock car race. I was asked to wave the starting and finishing flags. The Daytona race committee invited as many of our automotive maintenance repair students as feasible to join race car crews and observe the preparation of the car before the race and the other support during and after the race. Our enlisted mechanic students really enjoyed this opportunity. It did much for our student morale. As a result of these career incentives, we began to meet our volunteer enlistment quotas. I believe it worked very well. I still believe the Army should consider affiliation programs for all combat service support units.

We also began updating the TO&Es of our transportation units. The terminal service (port operations) company had the most urgent need for restructuring. Its TO&E had not been changed materially since its original preparation before the Korean War. With an associ-ate in the Office of the Chief of Transportation, Maj. "Dunny" Dunn, I had prepared many of the first TO&Es for terminal service units based mostly on our World War II experience. This standard had not substantially changed since then.

The terminal service unit TO&E required review and update because of the development of the container for ocean freight. We needed to add some additional skills to the unit and we particularly needed to make major changes in the authorized cargo handling equipment. The terminal service operation had changed from han-dling break bulk cargo manually, with some assistance from small, commercial forklifts, to unloading and moving mostly containerized cargo, using large container handling equipment.

As containerized freight came into use, we had first used small, short-masted forklifts to assist in loading and unloading the contain-ers. Now we required large, rough-terrain forklifts and heavy-lift cranes to discharge containers from ship to shore, from barges and landing craft, and to move the containers to their destinations. We estimated that unloading and moving 20- and 40-foot containers across beaches and through undeveloped areas would require large, rubber-tired cranes with an outreach of 60 to 80 feet, capable of han-dling 250 tons. We could reduce the size of the gangs because of the additional cargo handling equipment, but we certainly had to upgrade the capability of our cargo checkers.

When my estimate of the size of the crane required was questioned and our ability to develop one was doubted, I always said that it's not *if* we can do it, but *how* can we do it: we are now in the age of container-ization. This problem was not solved easily, but today most of our ter-minal service companies have their own large, rough-terrain forklifts and 250-ton, rubber-tired cranes that can operate over beaches and through undeveloped areas.

I also attempted to sell the Army leadership on a combat, amphibious, over-the-beach capability for the Army like that devel-oped during World War II by the engineer amphibious units. Today our transportation boat units and terminal service units provide the nearest capability. Current doctrine is premised on operating only through friendly areas and over friendly beaches. Such units would, of course, lack the combat engineer capability that is organic to engineer amphibious units. But this could be handled.

I knew the Army could not afford active service units with this capability, but I did believe we should publish Transportation Corps doctrine and literature that could be called upon if and when needed. The combat engineer requirement could be added easily whenever it was required. The relationship could be much the same as that which engineer port construction units now provide to transportation ports. I also felt that some peacetime amphibious training would be helpful. My idea did not sell. Army leaders did not believe the Army would ever again be called upon to perform this mission. Instead, they were prepared to rely on the Marine Corps to make the combat over-the-beach landings, after which Army units could come ashore as required.

One look at the size and capability of the Marine Corps today would indicate that it could not provide this support. The same conditions existed before World War II. Once the war started, the Army leadership soon learned that they could not rely on the Marine Corps alone. At the peak of World War II, the Marine Corps had six divisions with amphibious capability. The Army, meanwhile, was landing from 80 to 100 divisions all over the world. The same doctrine exists today: the Army depends upon the Marine Corps for all combat landings. Today, the Marine Corps has only one division with amphibious capability. Navy transports can carry only one Army division as well.

I'm sure the Army would be faced with serious conflicts about roles and missions from the other services if it attempted to organize and train amphibious units. But, I believe it would be advisable for the Transportation Center to locate those doctrine and training manuals used in World War II and to maintain updated files in the school at Fort Eustis. The Cold War is over for now, but with small problems emerging throughout the world, it does not seem far-fetched to think that we might need this capability again.

Upon my return to Fort Eustis, I noticed that our harbor craft, landing craft, and coastal shipping vessels were still of World War II vintage. The introduction of air-cushion vehicles posed problems. Six such craft had been used in Vietnam: the Navy had operated three in the Da Nang area, and the 4th Transportation Company operated three in the Delta. Army transportation had been deeply involved in air-cushion vehicle R&D before Vietnam. At that time we had still been using aircraft-type construction for this type of equipment in one of the most difficult environments in the world. I was extremely skeptical of trying to use air-cushion vehicles over beaches until the state of the art had been greatly improved. To justify this position, one has only to review the maintenance records of the air-cushion vehicles currently assigned to Fort Story, Virginia, a satellite of Fort Eustis.

Most of our transportation TO&E units at Fort Eustis did not belong to TRADOC, even though they were located at a TRADOC installation. They belonged to FORSCOM because of the mission for which they had been organized and trained. Most were actually a part of the Army's XVIII Airborne Corps' fast deployment forces, under its operational control in many respects. So we looked to the XVIII

Corps for much of the command and control. As members of the fast deployment forces, they were required to maintain a very high state of readiness and periodically they were put on the alert. During these exercises, the entire post helped to check out the units to be sure they met the deployment requirements—an excellent training procedure.

Working with the Logistics Center and the three other logistics schools to prepare doctrine and training required a great deal of attention. It required many meetings and some traveling, but the task was interesting and helpful for all of us. Occasionally, we would meet with the Combat Arms Center to coordinate logistics doctrine with combat doctrine at Fort Monroe under the direct supervision of the TRADOC commander, General DePuy.

Working with the local community surrounding Fort Eustis, another important task, consumed a great deal of my time and effort. I believed then, and still do, in the importance of maintaining a good relationship with our civilian community. In the final analysis, we in the military work for them. They are our bosses and the ones who provide all the assets we so badly need.

I was on very good terms with our local congressman, Thomas Downing of the first district in Virginia. We met frequently, both socially and for business. Tom frequently came to me to ask for assistance on community projects. Tom never asked me to do something I did not believe was proper or legal. If Tom had to take a stand that was not to our liking, he would always tell me beforehand, and I would understand.

We assisted the community in cleaning up the area by moving out junked vehicles. This activity helped the peninsula, Gloucester County, and the southern part of the Delmarva peninsula. The cleanup provided good equipment training for our terminal service companies and for our transportation truck companies. The units understood what they were doing, and they received not only training but a great deal of satisfaction supporting the projects. The citizens of the communities where we worked were always friendly and would go out of their way to assist, often providing food and soft drinks during our work.

When I assumed command of Fort Eustis in January 1973, my wife and I also embarked on a program to improve the appearance of the post. When we first saw Fort Eustis in 1947, it was a dreadful sight. During the last couple of years of World War II, the fort had been used as an Italian POW camp. The barracks and most of the buildings, World War I and II temporary structures, had been painted black and were enclosed by barbed wire. Although the land is completely flat and will always be, it was also desolate looking without shrubs and trees. Although the appearance of the buildings at the fort improved some over the years, by the time we returned for our third tour the landscape was still very bleak.

My wife and I initiated several projects to relieve this demoralizing prospect. We obtained funds to accomplish considerable landscaping, including planting a great many small trees. My wife also began a memorial tree planting program. The officers and noncommissioned officers wives clubs helped her to solicit $25.00 donations for trees tagged with the donor's name. Georgia convinced me that we badly needed a professionally designed landscape plan before we started to plant trees and shrubs.

With the assistance of the post engineer and his post agronomist, Mr. Tony Rizzio, a proposal was prepared and a contractor was hired to carry out a basic landscape plan. The results have continued to inspire all subsequent base commanders to continue implementing the landscaping plan. Not all the trees came from appropriated funds— Georgia's memorial tree fund generated many plantings in remote areas of the post and, through the efforts of her volunteers, generated a great deal of interest by most post personnel.

In recounting one's life and career, it is natural to concentrate on one's official life and official duties, overlooking the contributions one's family made. As I look back on my career, I feel I should highlight the role a family can play in an officer's career, especially the contributions made to the Army by the many Army wives who have volunteered their time and services to activities on the post and in the civilian community.

The Army makes unusual demands on wives and mothers. My wife raised our five children almost entirely on her own. During most of my career, the Army became involved in a war every five or six years, from World War II through the Vietnam War. I was overseas in World War II, the Korean War, and Vietnam for a total of over seven years. Even when stateside and living with the family, I would spend many overtime hours in the office or away on travel. None of this seemed to adversely affect Georgia's excellent job carrying out the difficult family responsibilities.

One frequently hears the comment that Army life, with its constant moving and changing schools, adversely affects the children. It is frequently cited as the reason for problems with family or children. In our case, and for many other military families we know, this aspect of Army life has added benefits. Our children have been broadened by their travels and have made many friends, including some overseas. Army families tend to be very close knit and often seem to devote a lot of time enjoying each other's company.

My wife, like many Army wives, has always approached new assignments as new opportunities for her and our children to gain knowledge. This was especially true whenever we traveled outside the United States. Georgia always looked to the future rather than the past. She accepted any hardships she had undergone as part of the price for having new opportunities. Our children have absorbed this attitude and it is apparent in all their actions.

Wives of officers have the opportunity to take part in Army community life. Georgia was a real professional at recruiting and supervising volunteers. She enlisted volunteers from officers and enlisted wives as well as from civilians both on and off the post. The volunteer jobs allowed us to undertake projects for which funds were never available to hire help. A commander in today's Army must rely on volunteers.

Military wives volunteered and accomplished many useful programs for which we had no funds. For example, as many as eighty wives helped to operate our post information and support center. The center supported numerous voluntary projects such as orientation classes for newly assigned enlisted men and their wives on the various post facilities and activities. They explained the advantages of using the commissary, post exchange, and local theaters. They helped young families find living quarters off post, if necessary, and provided information on where to shop. It was amazing how many young soldiers and their young wives, often with small children, would arrive with little or no knowledge about how to open a checking account or even how to write a check, let alone where to go for health care for themselves and their families.

The wives also provided volunteers for the American Red Cross, the post hospital, and many other services on the post. They contribute a great deal to community life on a military installation and, of course, all without pay.

Georgia had become very much involved with this volunteer work, starting during our early assignments at Fort Eustis. She became very good friends with the wives of the senior officers on the post which gave me social access to these officers that I would not otherwise have had.

When I took command of the 53d Truck Battalion in Germany, our battalion area, especially the headquarters area, was very unattractive. To remedy this, Georgia and several other volunteer wives landscaped and planted the area. Their very noticeable improvements led to an amazing number of compliments from officers and enlisted personnel in the battalion.

As my career progressed, Georgia continued her activity in garden clubs, both on and off military posts. As a member, Georgia met and often became good friends with civilian community leaders. Through her contacts, we both developed good friends in the community long before I could have through military contacts alone. This had been especially true during our various assignments at Fort Eustis. Because of her efforts, when we arrived back at Fort Eustis and I took command in 1973, we received an extremely cordial welcome from leaders in Newport News, Williamsburg, Yorktown, and Gloucester County.

Georgia is very talented at gardening, landscaping, flower arranging, and many other art forms. She augmented her natural talents with college courses. One needs only to compare Fort Eustis when we saw it in the 1940s devoid of trees and its appearance when we departed in 1976. Today, mainly due to Georgia and her volunteers, it is a beautiful, tree-covered post. Her contribution is well known by most members of Fort Eustis and the surrounding civilian communities.

As our children grew older, they also contributed much to both our on- and off-post life. Through their friends, we met several civilians we would otherwise never have known. Some became our best friends in retirement.

DeLong pier with overhead tramway during training on James River, circa 1957.

Colonel Fuson, Commander, 55th Transportation Battalion, receives a safety briefing at 501st Transportation Company.

Sunday night meeting of Transportation Corps colonels, Saigon; *below*, Gate 1, Headquarters, 4th Transportation Command, Saigon.

Colonel Fuson surveys operations at Saigon port; *below*, aerial view of Saigon port.

Operation LEXINGTON, LCU unloading, 1966; *below*, 1099th Transportation Company LCM in Saigon port, 1966.

Colonel Fuson escorts General Beach, CINCUSARPAC, during water tour of Saigon port; *below*, Secretary of Defense McNamara meets with Ellsworth Bunker, U.S. Ambassador, and General Westmoreland in Saigon, 1967.

Colonel Fuson briefs General Westmoreland during tour of port of Saigon, 1967.

Brigadier General Fuson visits U.S. Army Transportation Command, Japan, 1968; *below*, USARPAC retrograde operations: M–48s await loading, circa 1971.

USARPAC retrograde operations: Da Nang port and PDO lot, circa 1971.

General Fuson promoting boating safety as Commander, Fort Eustis, 1974; *below*, Mrs. Fuson landscaping at Fort Eustis, circa 1975.

General Fuson, DCSLOG, speaking to the American Logistics Association meeting.

CHAPTER 13

Army Deputy Chief of Staff for Logistics

After serving as commanding general of Fort Eustis from 1973–1975, I heard that I might be reassigned to Department of the Army as the deputy chief of staff for logistics. I really wasn't ready to leave Fort Eustis; we hadn't finished all the projects we had underway. But one can never pass up the opportunity for a bigger job and a promotion. The rumors soon proved to be true, and I was interviewed by the Army chief of staff, General Weyand, the secretary of the Army, the deputy secretary of defense, and the secretary of defense. After the interviews, I learned that the Senate had cleared my confirmation for promotion to lieutenant general and that I was to report for duty in Washington.

Leaving Eustis in the hands of Maj. Gen. Alton G. Post, my wife and I moved to Quarters Five at Fort Myer, Virginia. On the top of a hill overlooking Washington, D.C., this was the most dramatic setting we had ever occupied.

My several years on the DCSLOG staff gave me an understanding of the job and increased my pleasure in the assignment. My experience in logistics at all levels in the field would help me in this new assignment. Because I had never been assigned to the Army Materiel Command, I was still inexperienced in the wholesale logistics system. But I also knew that in the DCSLOG job I would spend a great deal more time with the retail system.

I failed to anticipate the amount of frustration I would encounter in the job. During my previous assignments as the director of transportation and then as the assistant DCSLOG for personnel, doctrine, and systems, I had been free from frustration.

During my previous tour, the Office of the DCSLOG consisted of over 1,000 personnel, with another 500 in what is now called the Logistics Evaluation Agency (LEA). At that time the DCSLOG managed three large jobs: procurement, the Army's worldwide real estate, and the Army's operations and maintenance function. For each of these, the DCSLOG prepared the budgets, testified before Congress, and had a great deal to do with controlling expenditures of money throughout the Army. In Washington, if you prepare the budget and have some control over how the money is spent, you have clout. With this clout you attract the attention of the major commands as you go about your business as DCSLOG. Without this kind of clout, you have absolutely no audience.

While I was in USARPAC, the DCSLOG had lost these major responsibilities and the personnel that went with them. When I returned to DCSLOG, its strength was around 400. The LEA had also been reduced in personnel and responsibilities.

One of the first things I did was to review Volume 1, the summary volume, of the Brown Board study. As I had suspected, the Army had gone in a direction opposite to that recommended by the study. Instead of placing one person in charge of the Army logistics system and centralizing management, the Army had decentralized more and scattered logistics functions and responsibilities throughout the staff.

This redirection was the result of another study carried out by Undersecretary of the Army Herman R. Staudt. I understood at the time that the change had occurred because Secretary of Defense James R. Schlesinger had a strong dislike for the Army Materiel Command. I never learned the basis for his strong feelings, but before my interview with Schlesinger for promotion, General Weyand had coached me to listen carefully as the secretary berated AMC and to keep my mouth shut. Having worked for General Weyand in Vietnam in MACV as his J4, I knew him well and had the greatest respect for his advice.

During my interview, Secretary Schlesinger spent about thirty minutes elaborating on all the faults of AMC, and he wanted to know what I was going to do about it. Fortunately he never gave me an opportunity to respond, because at that time I didn't have the slightest idea about the problems at AMC nor if I could do anything about them. As it turned out, I had absolutely no authority over the Army Materiel Command, nor did it ask for my advice or assistance, or even my cooperation.

The reorganization had occurred during the tour of my predecessor, Lt. Gen. Fred Kornet. Fred had spent his entire time fighting the reorganization without success. When I first met with General Weyand, he told me about Kornet's struggle, but since the decision had been made, he didn't want me to reopen it. I agreed not to.

When faced with a logistics problem that I could not solve, I would go to General Weyand or his vice chief, General Walter T. Kerwin, Jr. They were both supportive, but because they were busy with other problems I could not spend much time worrying them with logistics matters. Also, many of my problems were the result of the organizational changes.

During 1975, the U.S. military had just pulled out of Vietnam and was in the process of reorganizing for the future. Because the services had devoted so much time and so many resources to Vietnam for ten years, the rest of the forces had suffered. The imbalance had to be rectified.

The challenges of the mid-1970s were multiple. First, the Army and the other services had to rely on the all-volunteer force for the first time. The military could no longer depend on the draft. This new system appeared fraught with uncertainties. I had already had some successes in this area, with the Transportation Corps all-volunteer program, while commanding Fort Eustis.

Second, during the ten years of Vietnam, much of our training had been neglected. The Army was now working hard to upgrade and update all of its training. The new technology required that all curricula be updated.

Third, the importance and the needs of the individual soldier and his family had also been neglected. Command and leadership at all levels had to be reviewed, upgraded, and improved.

The Army had to move away from the crisis management attitude developed during the Vietnam War. All of these problems and many more had to be addressed during this post-Vietnam period when the Army was also undergoing severe budget constraints. This was the environment I faced as DCSLOG.

I had identified many actions that I wanted to initiate to get the Army logistics system back together to operate as a single, integrated system that would support the soldier in the field. These actions were not possible because many senior Army leaders did not want to see the Army logistics system centralized as it had been under the Technical Services. They still remembered the amount of authority each Technical Service chief possessed, as well as his personal congressional support and his friends in the military-industrial complex. The Army leaders also remembered the parochialism that existed in the old system.

Yet, as Army equipment becomes more and more complex (as is rapidly happening today) logistics expertise becomes even more important. Both the Brown Board and the more recent Joint Logistics Review Board (the Besson Board) recommended that the Army put someone in charge of its logistics system so that the system could perform more effectively, more efficiently, and more economically. During my tour as DCSLOG I briefed everyone, from the secretary of the Army on down, on this premise. I lectured the students in all the service schools, but without success. Apparently I did not have the ability to articulate this concept and its importance to the Army.

I did not feel strongly that the DCSLOG should be in charge of the logistics system, as the Brown Board had recommended. It could very well have been the commanding general of the Army Materiel

Command, if he was given enough help and authority, but some one person had to be in charge. In the final analysis, AMC had the real expertise in logistics. This had certainly become evident during the Vietnam War. AMC provided the expert assistance in Vietnam, Taiwan, Japan, and Okinawa, using both their direct hire civilians and their contract personnel.

The Army also faced another particularly disturbing dilemma. We were told that we had to reduce the number of support troops in the active force and rely on Reserve and National Guard support units instead. Several senior Army leaders used the term reduction of "tooth to tail," meaning the reduction of service support troops while maintaining the strength of the combat troops. Senator Sam Nunn initiated the legislation that created this shift, known as the Nunn Amendment. The number of active support troops continued to reduce for some time thereafter as more and more active duty support troops were replaced with Reserve and National Guard troops.

Soon after I became DCSLOG, we updated our annual program and spelled out the various actions the staff and I thought we should continue to pursue. We attempted to briefly describe the goal of each project and the period of time it should require for completion. At monthly program reviews the staff was briefed on the status of each project and, if needed, provided additional guidance. These meetings allowed everyone to know what logistics activities were taking place in DCSLOG and in the Army. We used the Logistics Master Plan, which General Heiser initiated in 1972, to demonstrate how each program contributed to our overall objectives.

In my opinion, one of the more important projects was formalizing integrated logistics support (ILS) and publishing the Army regulations governing ILS. Many considered that paying attention to eventual logistics support during the development process was unnecessary and, in fact, a hindrance to development of combat weapons.

The objective of ILS programs is to influence the design of materiel systems hardware and software to ensure that personnel will be able to operate, maintain, and support the system. ILS also promotes advanced training, so that the weapon can be maintained by the time it has been produced, and sees that any special tools and the necessary test, measurement, and diagnostic equipment (TMDE) is available when the weapon is operational. It ensures that training manuals are prepared in time for personnel training and that packaging, handling, transportability, standardization, interoperability, and other such requirements, affecting the logistics supportability and life cycle costs of the equipment, are considered.

ILS requires that all these facets of a weapon be reviewed at every stage of its development to improve operational readiness and reduce operating costs. The goal of ILS is to provide equipment that soldiers can effectively and efficiently maintain in the field. Although DOD had directed the services to implement ILS sometime earlier, the research and development community of the Army had not been enthusiastic.

The Logistics Evaluation Agency in New Cumberland, Pennsylvania, spent a great deal of time and resources maintaining close oversight on all R&D projects to ensure that ILS was being considered. They briefed me periodically, along with my staff, on these developments so we could voice any concerns as each new system was briefed up through the staff for final approval or rejection. The only problem was that our comments and objections were usually voices in the wilderness. My vote, only one among ten or twelve other principal staff members, seldom made any difference.

The general approach of most of the key personnel, especially contractors, was to develop the weapon system first and correct any logistics deficiencies later. Write the training publications and worry about life-cycle costs later. Because of this attitude, many weapon systems were developed, tested, and fielded with major deficiencies that should have been corrected during development.

The promoters of the division air defense (DIVAD) system became such strong advocates of the weapon, as frequently occurs, that they continued to push DIVAD in the face of all sorts of performance problems. It was a terrible shame that finally it required that the secretary of defense step in to stop development in spite of all the tests that DIVAD had failed.

During this period, we also attempted to standardize the TMDE for all newly developed weapons systems so that the same test equipment could be used at all echelons of maintenance for more than one piece of equipment. A standardized TMDE would simplify the supply system and be more cost effective. But here again, contractors for weapon systems were permitted to develop or procure unique TMDE for each new weapon system, rather than use a standard system already available, if it would do the job. Army policies on standardized test equipment had little or no effect on the R&D community and they were permitted to proceed.

This practice was the reason I felt strongly that procurement and production should be separated from R&D as they previously had been under DCSLOG. This would allow for disinterested experts to overview the R&D project and its advocates during the development phase. This oversight had been the responsibility of DCSLOG, working with the assistant secretary of the Army for installations and logistics, before the Staudt Study in 1973 and 1974.

When General Heiser was the DCSLOG and I was his Assistant DCSLOG for Personnel Doctrine and Systems, he initiated periodic meetings of the Logistics System Policy Council. The meetings were first held in Washington, but after the Logistics Center was established at Fort Lee, Virginia, the meetings were moved there. As DCSLOG I continued to hold the meetings, attended by the director of the Logistics Center, the directors of the four logistics center commands, and the DCSLOGs from each major Army command. We would hold briefings on current topics in logistics and discuss problems of concern to the council members. The meetings were always informative and helpful.

As DCSLOG, General Heiser had also initiated quarterly meetings with the General Accounting Office. These meetings had stopped during my absence from DCSLOG, but I renewed them. The key personnel in the GAO concerned with Army logistics were still in their jobs, and I was well acquainted with them. We would brief GAO on our major logistics concerns and ask for their comments. They would, in turn, brief us on all GAO reviews or audits under way that concerned Army logistics and update us on the status of such projects.

These meetings prepared us for publication of their formal reports, and we knew when they would arrive at the Department of Defense and the Army. By the time the report was published, we had initiated corrective action. In many cases, our comments while their reports and reviews were in progress prevented errors or misconceptions from being published.

While I was DCSLOG, the Army continued to have problems with its automated systems. We had a separate Logistics Systems Division that worked closely with the LEA and all the major commands to develop and implement some sixteen separate Department of the Army Standard Automated Logistics Systems. Our automation group tasked various agencies for support, managed policy, and coordinated the interfaces and standardization actions required. The sixteen logistics systems were in various stages of development and implementation Army-wide.

One obstacle that had existed while I was ADCSLOG (PDS) persisted after I became DCSLOG—my inability to convince the expert logistics functional staff, both those in my office as well as those in the field, that they had to take an active part in the design of automated systems. The logistics experts continued to let data processing personnel design systems without their input. As a result, the created software products did not provide the type of information and reports that the functional logistics people needed to manage logistics properly. The information system experts designed systems to serve their own purposes and not necessarily to help the logistics functional people.

A few years ago, General Heiser and I returned to ODCSLOG as consultants to GAO and asked to be updated on their automated supply, maintenance, and transportation systems. The briefing room was full of action officers. As the briefing progressed, Heiser and I continually asked functional type questions without receiving any functional type answers. Finally, I stopped the briefing to ask if any functional personnel—people who actually did the work—from supply, maintenance, or transportation divisions were in the room. Not a hand went up. All of the action officers were from the information staff. This type of costly failure has much to do with the asset visibility inaccuracies that exist throughout the Army's supply system.

Foreign military sales and grant aid were very important at the time. Over the years the emphasis has shifted from grant aid to military sales. We were supporting many countries, especially in the Middle East, that had the cash to buy the weapons they wanted. Now that the Vietnam War was over and we were drastically cutting back on our forces and equipment, our industrial base was being reduced. The military sales to foreign countries provided an excellent means of maintaining our industrial base, which was to our advantage.

We also supported our North Atlantic Treaty Organization (NATO) allies with military sales. We worked closely with the Germans on cooperative logistics and tried to expand cooperative logistics to all NATO countries, an extremely difficult task. Domestically, none of the services wants to depend on another service for logistics support; each feels the other really does not understand its special problems. Similarly, each country in NATO feels strongly that logistics is a national responsibility. No country wants to depend on another country for this support. In addition, each wants to support its own industrial base to the maximum.

Our NATO allies frequently used the term "two-way street." This meant that each country should be able and authorized to contribute equally. Unfortunately, the U.S. industry, with its political clout, insisted that every weapon system in the U.S. military forces be American-made, even though Germany or another NATO country had a similar system already available that was just as good. U.S. industry had become used to this in the years after World War II when we were the only country capable of developing weapons. Now that our allies could also produce equipment, they wanted their share of the market. For this reason, they did not see the United States participating fairly; they believed it was a one-way street. They were correct.

Each NATO country with forces deployed in Europe planned to independently provide logistics support to its forces. As noted earlier, the fact that all had to share the one transportation system presented a problem. The commercial rail, highway, and waterway systems of

France, Germany, and the Benelux countries would have to support all troop movements. But each NATO country planned to use this one system separately, rather than cooperatively. They all recognized the problem and NATO created many boards, committees, and planning groups to work on it. If a war came, someone had to be in charge of movement planning and movement control. But such a control management system, including all NATO countries, was never established.

At one time our staff, working with the transportation community in NATO, developed a centrally managed system that was accepted by the top military planners in NATO. For the first time, we would have a unified NATO transportation movement planning and control system. It looked as though we might be taking the first step in overcoming one of the long-term problems of NATO logistics management.

Our plan was agreed to all the way across Europe until it reached the German government, which killed the project. German leaders saw the plan as an American ploy to obtain financial support from the other countries rather than each country providing its equal share. Later, in 1977, General Heiser would recommend a similar transportation movement control plan, described in his chapter on logistics, as part of the NATO long-term defense plan.[1]

During this period, the NATO procedures for host nation support were being developed. Host nation support had been based upon bilateral agreements between each NATO country and the nation in which its troops were stationed or through which its troops would move. The host nation provided transportation and other logistics support functions on a reimbursable basis.

We faced another major problem as a result of the Vietnam War. For many years, we had operated bases all over the Pacific to support Vietnam. This support created large stocks of supplies and equipment, especially ammunition, in Okinawa, Japan, Korea, and Thailand. Our war plans in the Pacific had changed drastically; consequently, we did not have a justification for much of this ammunition. Other ammunition in Japan and Korea had been left over from the Korean War, and some was no longer of the type our Army used. However, the South Korean and Japanese forces could still use much of the ammunition and they were extremely hesitant for us to remove it from their countries.

The Pacific Utilization and Redistribution Agency (PURA) had withdrawn a lot of excess supplies and distributed them worldwide, but there still remained a large surplus of ammunition. To continue to operate these Pacific facilities and to maintain the supplies, equipment, and ammunition was extremely expensive. Since we were trying to draw down and reduce our costs, this overhead had to be reduced.

---

[1] See Heiser, *A Soldier Supporting Soldiers*, Chapter 12.

Our major problem was that we did not have a firm basis for how much needed to be removed or where to store it. This excess included operating stocks, war reserve stocks, project stocks, and so forth.

Our mission in Thailand was changing completely. There we experienced major coordination problems with the Air Force and the Navy about ammunition. What was our future to be in Thailand? I discussed this with Lt. Gen. Edward C. Meyer, the deputy chief of staff for operations and plans (DCSOPS) at the time, who suggested that we perform a joint study to determine future missions in the Pacific and to redo our overall war plans. This would create a firm basis for estimating our personnel, equipment, and supply needs.

The study, called WESTPAC III, would set the posture for U.S. Army forces in the Pacific during fiscal years 1978–1982. In October 1975, the Army chief of staff provided guidance to DCSOPS and DCSLOG to initiate this in-depth review of logistics forces and supporting bases in the Pacific, our participation in Northeast Asia, and our ability to support the evolving Forward Defense Strategy in South Korea.

On 6 May 1976, the chief of staff approved the actions suggested in WESTPAC III. Realignment of forces occurred in Japan, South Korea, and Hawaii, while U.S. forces in Thailand were reduced based upon the Thailand government's demands for the complete withdrawal of U.S. forces except for the Joint U.S. Military Assistance Group.

After WESTPAC III, we began to relocate our stocks and to declare supplies, equipment, and many installations as surplus. The South Korean government felt strongly that we should not remove our ammunition from their country, even though it exceeded our needs. Apprehensive about the intentions of the North Koreans, the South Koreans wanted to hold all the ammunition they could.

After a trip to Korea to discuss this approach, we determined that the best and most economical solution to the problem was to have the Koreans take over the excess ammunition and operate the facilities under a joint ownership arrangement. We would leave only a few U.S. personnel to ensure that the Koreans lived up to the agreement. This was the most economical approach for us. It would cost a lot more to move it out of the country or dispose of it than to leave it. To the best of my knowledge, the Koreans still operate and maintain these facilities and the ammunition. We worked out a similar solution in Japan and Thailand, where we were in the process of giving up facilities and stocks for which we had no requirement.

I continued the same futile efforts to focus general staff attention on the Military Traffic Management Command (MTMC), formerly the Military Traffic Management and Terminal Service, that I had initiated during my earlier tour in the Office of the DCSLOG (described in Chapter 10).

After being DCSLOG for a little over two years, I rapidly approached my mandatory retirement date. With 35 years in the U.S. Army, I handed in my papers and retired—a very sad day in my life. But all good things come to an end.

CHAPTER 14

Retirement and the General Accounting Office

I spent the first six months of my retirement resting and traveling. My wife and I spent two months in Hawaii and moved our permanent home from Falls Church to Gloucester, Virginia. I began to explore the possibilities of consulting work.

I was offered several consulting jobs by the various study groups or think tanks in the Washington area, but these did not prove satisfactory. Often the main reason for asking my participation was to help them land defense business. I did not approve of this, had opposed the practice by retired officers while I was still on active duty, and certainly didn't want to follow the same course.

Retired General Heiser, who had been consulting for the U.S. General Accounting Office (GAO), asked me to assist the GAO as a consultant. Heiser had spent a lot of time doing this and enjoyed it, but he had become more and more involved with Defense Department/NATO tasks. In early 1978, I began consulting one or two days a week at the GAO. This consulting work allowed me to keep in touch with some of the same Army projects with which I had been involved for many years, working with many of the Army military and civilian logisticians. By keeping abreast of all the Army logistics reviews and audits being conducted in the General Accounting Office, I could help the Army by ensuring that the GAO action officers understood the Army areas they were reviewing and received accurate data.

I also encouraged the deputy chief of staff for logistics to meet periodically with the senior logistics personnel in GAO, as I had done in the past. This cooperation has always worked to our mutual advantage.

I continued this consultation with the General Accounting Office for eight years, and enjoyed every minute of it. The GAO personnel were very professional, honest, and extremely conscientious. But after eight years I found that I had lost touch with the Army's logistics operations and that someone more recently retired should take my place. I gave up my consultant job with GAO in late 1986.

During these years, I continued to review past and present audits and reports on the Army's logistics system made by the GAO, the Army Audit Agency, and the Office of the Secretary of Defense.

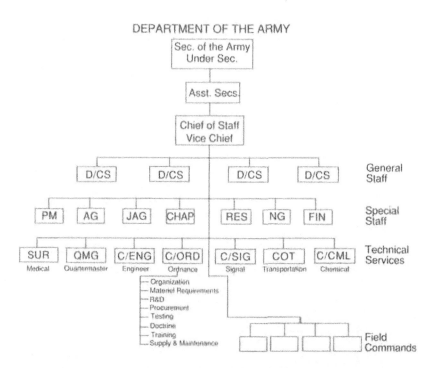

DEPARTMENT OF THE ARMY

Figure 1. Army Organization Before 1962 and Project 80

These reports continued to reiterate that the Army logistics system was neither organized nor managed effectively and efficiently for either peace or war. Certainly, the Army was not just ignoring these findings and recommendations, but rather, there must have been a more basic reason that the trend continued. Budget restraints contributed to the problem in peacetime, but lack of money was not the only cause. The same deficiencies had existed during the Vietnam War when money was not a factor.

In my opinion, the Army is not organized properly to solve its problems. If the U.S. were suddenly thrown into a major war, the Army support system would have to be reorganized as it was for both world wars, but next time I don't believe time would be available. What is the basis for this statement? To answer this question requires a short review of history.

In 1962 and 1972, two major Army reorganizations occurred that have had major effects on this issue: Project 80 in 1962–1963 and Project Steadfast in 1972–1973. Before 1962 the Army had been organized along technical service lines for logistics as indicated in *Figure 1.* The seven Technical Services (Ordnance, Quartermaster, Signal, Engineer, Chemical, Medical, and

Transportation) were each responsible for their own commodities and services worldwide.

The chief of Ordnance, for example, had responsibility for the major war-making items such as guns, tanks, trucks, and ammunition. He went before Congress to obtain the authorizations and appropriations for these commodities and their support. In coordination with industry, the chief of Ordnance directed research and development and procurement of his commodities. The Ordnance department procured, stocked, stored, and issued the commodities worldwide. The chief of Ordnance was responsible for supply and maintenance of these commodities worldwide. He was also responsible for the doctrine, manuals, and procedures that governed system operation. He managed Ordnance personnel and training worldwide.

The other chiefs performed the same functions for their commodities and services. Although they displayed their true expertise in their domestic base (military, civilians, and the large industrial base) they organized, trained, and deployed technical service units worldwide to support their systems in the field. They were responsible down to the forward edge of the division direct support units and, through this organization, coordinated with the combat units to assist them in their logistics mission. They operated and were responsible for this worldwide system, and they disciplined it.

As it did under the Technical Services, the Army's logistics system still consists of four levels of support—organizational, direct, general, and depot:

> • At the combat unit level, equipment operators and unit mechanics perform *organizational* supply and maintenance. This level consists of mostly preventive maintenance and supply support. The companies and battalions are equipped for this level and nothing more.
> • *Direct* support is performed at the division level and consists mostly of repairs by replacing components and supply support. The division is authorized only the skills, tools, TMDE, and repair parts to perform this level of repair.
> • *General* support can be performed at corps and the higher headquarters for which the authorized skills, tools, TMDE, and repair parts are available to actually repair end items and components.
> • *Depot level* support is performed at the wholesale level and is generally located in the United States. This level overhauls and rebuilds components and weapon systems. For some commodities, general and

depot level support have been combined and are performed by wholesale commodity commands either in
the theater or in CONUS.

Before 1962, the Technical Services performed direct, general,
and depot support. (*See Figure 2.*) The chief of each Technical
Service was completely in charge. As an administratively independent
agency, each Technical Service controlled its own organizations, procedures, personnel, intelligence, training, and planning. Each had its
own budget which, added together, accounted for well over half of the
Army's appropriations. The Technical Services operated installations
in many congressional districts, their principal sources of political
support. Their dissimilarities were as marked as their similarities.
They differed widely in their often archaic procedures which could
generate a prodigious amount of red tape and make it difficult for the
Department of the Army to control their operations and for industry to
do business with them.

The system also led to duplication and waste. Because it was
almost impossible for the Army to manage, to coordinate, or to control their varied functions without a unified service or materiel command such as that set up during both world wars, the Technical
Services were unpopular and had been for many years. The Army
wanted to change from a system of seven different supply and maintenance systems to one, single functional system—a standard supply
and maintenance system. (*See Figure 3.*)

In 1962, Secretary McNamara approved implementation of
Project 80, which caused many changes to the Army logistics system.
It reorganized Army logistics along functional lines rather than separate technical service disciplines. It removed personnel and training
responsibilities from the Technical Services and centralized them. It
created three major commands in the continental United States, as
indicated in *Figure 3*: one for training and forces management, one
for combat development, and one for wholesale logistics management. Project 80 ignored the retail logistics system management and
the necessary relationship between the producer and the consumer.

An additional factor could not have been foreseen by McNamara
or the Army. Immediately following this decision and before the
Army could adjust to this drastic change and begin to solve the many
problems it caused, the United States had become deeply involved in
the Vietnam War. All else was sidetracked.

Although OSD guidance had been broad, it had asked the Project
80 study group if the Technical Services were to be subordinate to a
service command or were to be replaced by a research and development or materiel command. The study group observed that in the past

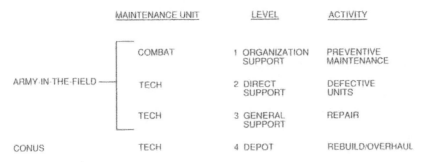

MAINTENANCE UNIT	LEVEL	ACTIVITY
COMBAT	1 ORGANIZATION SUPPORT	PREVENTIVE MAINTENANCE
TECH	2 DIRECT SUPPORT	DEFECTIVE UNITS
TECH	3 GENERAL SUPPORT	REPAIR
TECH	4 DEPOT	REBUILD/OVERHAUL

Figure 2. Technical Services Maintenance Operations

two world wars, the Army had to make major logistics organization changes at the last minute in order to successfully support the war efforts. The group further observed that the method used to coordinate support in both wars had been to make the Technical Services subordinate to a service-type command with both wholesale and retail logistics responsibility. This was not politically popular with the Technical Services and their supporters. It worked with some success but was abandoned after both wars.

The study group, apparently reflecting the strong dislike for the Technical Services and their methods of operation that permeated the Army and the Office of the Secretary of Defense, recommended against creating a service command to supervise the Technical Services. In fact, it advised the Army staff to get out of technical support operations because of the inevitable conflict between staff and command viewpoints.

The study group believed the Technical Service chiefs were too isolated. The group especially criticized the Technical Services' personnel policies, recommending broader career opportunities for both military and civilian personnel. Referring again to the Technical Services, the group pointed out that the increasing complexity of weapon systems required greater flexibility in the assignment of people with specialized talents. Furthermore, under the Technical Services organization, training was fragmented among too many agencies.

I find here a major lack of consistency in the study group's findings. On one hand, they link the need for better utilization of personnel and better training management to the need for more technical skills. They apparently hoped to solve this problem by creating generalists rather than specialists. They hoped to manage people better by centralization regardless of skills required, rather than allowing the Technical Services, with their specialized talents, to continue to manage and train technical people to perform highly technical jobs.

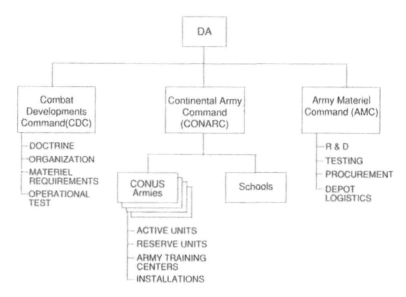

Figure 3. Department of the Army Organization After Project 80

As a result of Project 80, the U.S. Army reorganized its entire structure. With two exceptions the Technical Services were abolished. Their service support missions, functions, and responsibilities, along with similar missions and functions of the combat Army were reassigned to the U.S. Continental Army Command, whose missions and responsibilities were broadened. Some were reassigned to the Army Materiel Command or the Combat Developments Command, the two new commands. Others were assigned to the theater army commands. *Figure 3* displays the post-organization Army major commands and their primary functions.

CDC was responsible for determining materiel requirements based on how the Army was to fight and how it should support itself in the field. These support functions previously had been the responsibility of the Technical Services. CONARC, with its newly acquired service schools, was to translate the CDC concepts and doctrine into training manuals and procedures for both individuals and units and to provide the appropriate school training. Training was another responsibility formerly performed by technical service units. Finally, the wholesale, or producer, part of the Technical Services was regrouped under AMC. AMC was given responsibilities for the CONUS wholesale base only; at the time it had no retail responsibilities overseas or for the Army in the field. The theater commanders were responsible for operating their own systems, independent from the CONUS wholesale base.

Almost immediately the Army's logistics system switched from seven standard, well-disciplined systems worldwide, to functional organizations in each theater that were separated from their wholesale base. Overnight, a wall was placed between the wholesale CONUS base and each army in the field. The CONUS base continued to operate the wholesale system using its civil-military expertise, but the theater commanders had to maintain the complex equipment in the field with soldiers who had comparatively little training and expertise. This procedure was in accordance with doctrine and training supposedly developed by CDC and CONARC.

As the Army did away with the Technical Services, they did away with a great deal of waste and duplication, but unknowingly also lost something very important and essential. The Army in the field lost the much needed assistance of the industrial base. *There was no one in charge of the total system!* That's the way we fought the Vietnam War.

The one exception was aviation, new again to the Army and terribly important and expensive. Army aviation units had been among the first deployed to Vietnam in 1961 and initially had poor logistics support. As a result the aviation system soon reverted to the vertical-type support resembling the structure of the old Technical Services. The wholesaler, AMC, with its commodity command for aviation, was told to go into the field, to get into Vietnam with whatever part of the aviation support community was necessary, including the industrial base, and to design a supply, maintenance, and support system for aviation based upon requirements at the flight line.

The resulting vertical weapon support system did not bring with it the previously unpopular bureaucratic approach. Support personnel consisted of soldiers, a few direct-hire civilians, and much contractor support. This was necessary because the Army could only train soldiers to a certain proficiency level in order to get them to Vietnam for a year, the statutory tour length for the Vietnam War, then return them to the United States and discharge them.

In order to maintain the expensive helicopters, the Army had to use large numbers of contractor personnel with the real expertise in maintaining aviation equipment. In order to support aviation equipment in Vietnam, certain depot-type functions had to be performed in the theater. To support aviation, the Aviation Command procured a deep-draft ship, the *Corpus Christi Bay*, that carried required maintenance equipment on board. The necessary maintenance personnel, both military and civilian, were assigned to the ship and the ship was moved to Vietnam waters. The *Corpus Christi Bay* moved from the Cam Ranh Bay up the coast to whatever area required its support. Damaged aircraft requiring maintenance beyond the capability of the *Corpus Christi Bay* were moved offshore or back to the United States for repair.

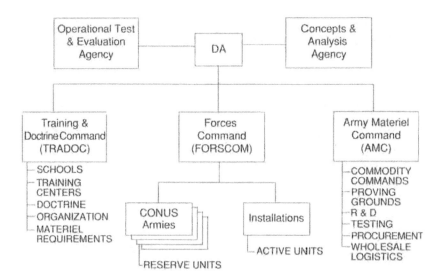

Figure 4. Organization for Department of the Army After Project Steadfast

Medical support performed well in Vietnam because the Surgeon General had been exempted from Project 80. The Army Medical Corps continued to function as a Technical Service; it organized, trained, and assigned its medical supply and maintenance personnel. It continued to operate a standard, well-disciplined system worldwide.

The Project 80 reorganization failed in many respects. It did not recognize the importance of managing the producer and consumer systems as one. It created not one logistics system worldwide, but many uncoordinated and uncontrolled subsystems with no one in charge of the total system. It failed to recognize the difficulty of managing and training logistics specialists. In the end, Project 80 created larger, more damaging problems that prevented sound logistics organization and management.

In 1973, Project Steadfast followed Project 80 and created another sweeping reorganization that continued to centralize the major Army functions. *Figure 4* shows the realignment of functions in the three major Army commands already reorganized ten years earlier. Steadfast renamed the Combat Developments Command the Training and Doctrine Command (TRADOC), with combat development and training functions. The Continental Army Command became the Forces Command (FORSCOM) to manage active and reserve forces in CONUS. AMC remained unchanged. Additionally, all medical activities in the United States were centralized under the U.S. Army Health Services Command; strategic communications were unified under the U.S. Army Strategic Communications Command; and all personnel functions were placed under the U.S. Army Military Personnel Center.

Conspicuously absent from Project Steadfast's consideration was the major logistics problem in the Army, which had existed since Project 80 and the rigorous surgery it had caused. Throughout the Project Steadfast study, it must have been assumed that centralizing logistics management was less important than centralizing concepts, doctrine, and training for the Army in the field under TRADOC.

Clearly, concepts, doctrine, and training for logistics at the organizational, direct, and general support levels must be coordinated closely with combat developers rather than with the depot or base level logistics developers. Nevertheless, the depot and other wholesale components must also be brought into the process. This point must be emphasized because it is the major difference in philosophy between the Army leadership and the logisticians; that is, whether to combine the total logistics system under one command or whether to break up the logistics elements between the CONUS-based wholesale and retail systems with logistics doctrine and management dispersed to the field.

Project Steadfast established a logistics center at Fort Lee to coordinate the technical service schools in the development of logistics doctrine for the Army in the field, but it provided for little coordination between Fort Lee's work and the doctrine that AMC was developing for the wholesale system. Retail logistics doctrine was then developed independently from the wholesale logistics doctrine. Somehow the DCSLOG was supposed to coordinate these requirements; however, being a three-star general, the DCSLOG had little or no leverage over the TRADOC, AMC, or theater armies commanded by four-star generals. The major problems with the current Army logistics system stem from this basic difference in philosophy between the Army leadership and the logisticians.

The Army leaders believe that the organizational, direct support, and general support levels of the field logistics system should be designed, developed, and implemented in the field with little or no coordination with the wholesale system. They believe this for two reasons: first, they apparently feel that the field logistician will better understand the user's problems, requirements, and environments; second, they fear that the logisticians, if they get together, will design and operate a system for their own benefit rather than for the benefit of the combat units. This is valid criticism!

How can the Army correct this organizational problem? The Army must put together a truly experienced blue-ribbon study group similar to the Brown Board to examine the various support systems by function, commodity, and service. The Army should then develop a total logistics system, both centrally managed and responsive to the users in the field. Someone must be in charge of every aspect, either by function, commodity, or service.

Personnel management is a more difficult problem to handle. Certainly the Army cannot afford or would not want to return to seven or eight different systems such as existed with the Technical Services; however, logistics managers must be more intimately involved in the management and training of logistics personnel. Here again, a study group is required to produce a solution.

CHAPTER 15

Persistent Transportation Logistics Problems

Reflecting on my more than thirty-five years experience in Army logistics, I find both strengths and weaknesses in the Army support system. Although logistics functions at both the strategic and the operational levels of war, its effect on tactics, although indirect, is also powerful. In many cases, transportation, a subdiscipline of logistics, can be key because it is this function, along with communications, that links the three levels of war together and often produces the success which strategy, operations, or tactics, however brilliantly conceived and executed, could not achieve alone.

Intransit Asset Visibility

Throughout my early years in transportation, at the Transportation School, in Pacific transportation units, in Europe, and during support of combat operations in Korea and Vietnam, I was taught and observed the importance of port and beach clearance of incoming supply items as a vital part of the operations of the overseas line of communication. This clearance was especially important during wartime while supporting combat units.

However, I do not ever remember being told of the importance of asset visibility in transit from origin to destination. I was never warned about the basic fundamental problem of moving goods in tens of thousands of unmarked boxes and transportation's responsibility to solve it, or at least to lessen its effects. Through experience alone, I learned of the need for paperwork to accompany shipping containers. I believe it is still not well understood by many logisticians and our Transportation Corps personnel.

During both Korea and Vietnam, thousands of tons of critical cargo representing millions of dollars was lost, destroyed, or misused. It was misplaced because of inadequate identification during transit or at theater reception areas. In each case, the port operator blamed the receiving customer for not knowing what he had received. The receiving customer blamed the port operator for delivering it to him without enough documentation for him to accurately receive it into his inventory and enter it into his files. As a result, thousands and thousands of critical supplies were never used.

I'll always remember listening to the advice of Col. Buck Bratcher, my number one teacher in stevedore operations during the Korean War. While we were unloading cargo and pushing it to the depots, I would ask him, "Shouldn't we do a better job of identifying this stuff before we shove it down their throat?" Bratcher would always say, "They ordered it. Give it to them. Let them worry about its identity." I think that describes the attitude of most transportation port operators I've known. I tended to agree more with the customer, the supply side. I think I did even as early as the Korean War, but I didn't really understand the system.

The transportation system must maintain complete, 100 percent accurate, asset visibility. When we initially pick up a shipment, we have the information. Some way or another, we have to maintain that relationship between the container and its contents throughout its entire period in transit. We must tell the customer what we are delivering, in enough detail so that he can do his job under terribly crowded and difficult combat situations.

In the early 1960s the Office of the Secretary of Defense established a uniform system for all the services to requisition, move, and store supplies and equipment. Supply procedures were covered in the Military Standard Requisition and Issue Procedures (MILSTRIP) and transportation procedures were covered in Military Standard Transportation and Movement Procedures (MILSTAMP). MILSTRIP covered worldwide supply but the original MILSTAMP covered procedures for movement to and from the theater, not within the theater. Had these systems been followed, many problems would have been solved. Unfortunately, MILSTRIP and MILSTAMP were too often ignored.

Again, it is almost impossible for one to visualize the amount of cargo that arrives during wartime and the speed at which it arrives. The enormous volume complicates the job tremendously, but it does not excuse the lack of proper asset visibility. This is especially important during the early days of combat operations.

The current state of the art in transportation, communications, and automation make it possible to solve the problem if everyone understands the system and follows the procedures and doctrine. Transportation personnel must understand their responsibilities and must be acutely aware of the customer's need for asset visibility in transit. It is being observed in the commercial shipment business today. Many examples exist to be followed.

Not too long ago, the American President Line was doing a great job of moving supplies from Japan to New York using ship, rail, and trucks. They maintained 100 percent asset visibility by item throughout the entire shipment cycle. The information available from the American President Line was so accurate that Macy's in New York could plan to receive an item on a Friday and put it on sale Saturday before it knew precisely what was going to come out of the shipping container. It *is* possible. It is very important that the Army get on with performing this kind of job.

Recent articles and reports on Operations DESERT SHIELD and DESERT STORM show that we still have an intransit visibility problem. The action in the desert demonstrated conclusively that transportation documentation and intransit asset visibility systems are not sufficiently responsive to the Army's information needs. Although a great deal of automation and communications improvements have been made in recent years, cargo documentation remains a difficult and often unwieldy procedure. In the attempt to push supplies and equipment to the Persian Gulf quickly, cargo descriptions, receiving unit addresses, and priorities were often incomplete. In many cases, entire containers arrived in theater without any documentation at all. Even after arrival, the theater distribution system was unable to maintain effective control. Equally significant, all of these problems occurred in a country with the most modern port handling and transportation facilities in the world.

Another factor which must always be taken into account is the time available to accomplish the tremendous transportation operation required to deploy a sizable military force. Most war plans call for mobilization and initial movements of troops, equipment, and supplies to be accomplished in ten days or less. But Iraq's defensive military strategy allowed the U.S. military to dictate when the war would commence and to prosecute the war on U.S. terms. The Army was able to transport personnel and equipment to Saudi Arabia and distribute these assets within the country over several months before hostilities began. Had hostilities started earlier, the Army's logistical problems would have intensified.

Basic Supply and Maintenance

While consulting for the General Accounting Office, I stayed in close touch with the key Army transportation officers, both on the DA staff and in the major commands. I observed that most transportation officers still do not have a good understanding of the total logistics field. Yet, every good transportation officer must know how basic supply and maintenance works. Much of this knowledge can be acquired while commanding a transportation company if the officer involves himself with the supply and maintenance of his own equipment.

As I look back on my assignments at the company and battalion levels, I must admit that I failed to become as familiar as I should have with the jobs of my supply sergeant and repair parts clerk, the prescribed load list (PLL) clerk. Neither did I get my hands dirty with the maintenance sergeant and his mechanics. I could have and should have done both. As a truck battalion commander in Germany, I had religiously observed early morning motor stables while every driver performed maintenance on his truck. But I did not really become as involved in the detailed procedures as I should have.

Actually, not until I became a major general, commander of the Transportation Center and commandant of the Transportation School, did I begin preaching this doctrine. At every opportunity, I would tell our young Transportation School students that before they could consider themselves to be good transportation officers, they must first become good basic supply and maintenance officers. I would attempt to explain this in detail, but it was difficult to get the message through. Yet before anyone can become an able logistician at any level of command or staff, he needs to begin at the bottom and thoroughly understand at least one commodity in complete detail, even if it is supply support for his own motor pool.

Transportation Management and Movement Control

Transportation officers must understand the meaning of three terms: transportation management, traffic management, and movement control. *Transportation management*, a very broad term, can apply to all types of transportation. It can mean the management of the overall transportation system, the management of any mode within the system, or the management of traffic moving through the system. *Traffic management*, a commercial term, refers to the rules, regulations, rate structures, routing, and service information governing movement of personnel and freight by commercial transportation. Each group of carriers and terminals has a traffic guide that indicates routes, rates, and special instructions. This is the basis upon which they charge and collect fees.

In the military, when we move personnel or cargo by commercial transportation, we follow the traffic guides of the carrier and, of course, consider both cost and getting the job done. In peacetime, cost is the main consideration. In wartime, we replace the term traffic management with the term *movement control*, particularly to and within the theater of operation. Traffic management and movement control both require detailed planning and programming of movement. But movement control must balance competing requirements against existing, often scarce, capabilities.

As mentioned earlier, the term movement control originated with the British in World War II and was developed to a very high state of effectiveness during the latter stages of the war. General Lee's European Communications Zone, the major logistics command in Europe, provided logistics support for all of our forces. Lee's staff prepared a monthly movement program which consolidated all movement requirements and allocated specific missions to the various modes of transportation. If you wanted something moved, you had to forecast its need on a monthly basis to ensure its subsequent movement. There were, of course, daily changes created by the tactical situation and other local needs. When changes were required, they had to be very specific and justified.

As I read history, General Lee observed movement control very closely. Since the war, the U.S. Army in Europe has tried to practice movement control but, because transportation is usually adequate in peacetime, the Army cannot really test its abilities in this area. There is no need to balance resources if transportation is plentiful.

Wartime operational plans require that wartime movement programs be developed. But because of the lack of understanding and appreciation for movement control at all levels, customers are not prepared to submit their detailed requirements for movement. Without such detailed requirements there can be no movement planning or programming. In time of war, movement control planning and programming would become mandatory whether trained for or not.

We attempted movement control in Vietnam in 1966. The Traffic Management Agency (TMA) was established at MACV. The 507th Movement Control Group had trained at Fort Eustis and moved to Vietnam to provide this service. It worked for the U.S. Military Assistance Command, Vietnam, under the direct supervision of the director of logistics, J4. Because adequate transportation was available in Vietnam, there was no need to give TMA the necessary authority to control transportation. As a result, each of the three services developed its own movement control agency to balance in-country movements. Planning and programming of movements does not apply to both traffic management and movement control. It is only applicable to movement control in wartime.

Some regard peacetime transportation planning for war a waste of time, in the hope that these rather tedious procedures can be avoided because industry can meet the need, except maybe in the theater of operation. That's totally wrong thinking. History indicates that in wartime, transportation is always in short supply everywhere. One only needs to review the history of this country during total war, as during World Wars I and II. Competition between the military and the civilian economy for transportation in this country was great and had to be controlled at the top. During total wars, the same control was needed in the theaters of operation.

As I discussed this subject with the General Accounting Office auditors, who constantly worked in the area of peacetime traffic management rather than movement control, I would ask them about the reactions they got when reviewing this subject with the services. They reflected the common belief that there would not be a shortage of transportation in wartime, so they should not worry about movement control and movement planning.

Most had little understanding of the vast difference between obtaining transportation in peacetime and wartime. In peacetime, the profit motive encourages cooperation in the transportation system. Because the customer wants to move his goods at the cheapest rate and carriers want the business, they cooperate. In peacetime, transportation is nearly always adequate as long as the price is right. In an emergency, all this changes. The customer no longer cares about dollars. His only thought is getting his supplies to the right place at the right time and in usable condition. He does not care about transportation utilization rates.

The transportation manager, on the other hand, is interested in the most effective and efficient way to manage the fixed assets of civilian and military carriers. There has never been enough transportation during an emergency and there never will be. Transportation is always the first shortage to occur. The transportation manager is judged completely on how well he manages this very scarce item. Consequently, a conflict of interest arises between the customer and the transporter, requiring an arbiter who can make command decisions at the highest level.

A review of the Army's history underlines this point. Historians record the daily conflicts in World War II between the chief of operations, General Lutes, and the chief of transportation, General Gross, in the U.S. Army Service Forces, that required them to appeal to the commanding general of the Army Service Forces, General Somervell, to decide movement priority. Within the Army, this was a command decision. When competition for transportation occurs in a joint forces operation, the problem of balancing requirements against capabilities becomes far more difficult and, in fact, much more difficult than it was in World War II. During World War II, everything that moved overseas was under the Army chief of staff, who delegated to an Army Service Forces officer the authority to make these kinds of decisions. Nothing like this exists today.

Before the Goldwater-Nichols Department of Defense Reorganization Act of 1986, strategic transportation decisions could only be made by the secretary of defense and the president. Goldwater-Nichols gave the chairman of the Joint Chiefs of Staff the authority to direct the armed forces, including the commanders of the unified and specified (theater-level) commands. The act also gave clear responsibilities to these commanders. Thus the commander of the joint United States Transportation Command, working with the commander of the Central Command (CENTCOM) during Operation DESERT SHIELD, performed the necessary movement planning and control for this transportation-intensive effort.

In peacetime we use the commercial carrier system to provide military transportation. Currently, three military transportation operating agencies, the Military Airlift Command, the Military Sealift Command, and the Military Traffic Management Command, provide or arrange for commercial air, land, or sea transportation. All these agencies are under the operational control of the joint Transportation Command.

In case of all-out war, transportation would not be adequate even for defense, let alone for the needs of the country's economy. Who would determine the priorities of movement between the civilian economy and the military? If there were more than one theater of operation, who would determine who or what was going to move within the civilian economy and within the military? We haven't had this problem since World War II, when a system was established to meet this need. At that time President Roosevelt established several high-level organizations, like the War Shipping Administration and the Munitions Assignments Board, which worked directly for him. They constantly reviewed and balanced requirements against capabilities, not only for transportation, but for all scarce resources.

The Reagan administration established a wartime planning agency as soon as it took over in 1981. President Reagan signed the letter that established the Emergency Mobilization Preparedness Board, manned by the heads or the deputy heads of eleven major governmental agencies, including the Department of Transportation. The board was organized into twelve working groups, all designed to control wartime mobilization planning, including transportation. The secretary of defense established a deputy secretary of defense for policy to coordinate DOD mobilization planning, a most difficult job. Initially, the late General Richard G. Stilwell was brought in full time to help the OSD deputy for policy. Stilwell devoted more than twelve hours a day attempting to do this job. It covered every area in which arguments about allocation of resources could occur.

The problem overwhelmed Stilwell, partly because of the way OSD and the joint staff are organized. Although logistics is the responsibility of each service, transportation is not. Each service cannot acquire its own transportation system. Our only transportation system is the commercial one in the U.S.

Of all logistics functions, transportation is the only truly joint system. Consequently, during mobilization and war preparations, someone must decide who gets priority for movement between the Army, the Navy, and the Air Force. Someone must decide which units go on Military Airlift Command (MAC) flights to Europe first. The system now requires that the Transportation Command decide, in coordination with the unified or specified combat commander. If more than one command were involved, there might be a problem. The JCS chairman during Operation DESERT SHIELD, General Colin L. Powell, displayed this kind of authority under the secretary of defense and the president. Nevertheless, this does not solve the priority problem between the military and the civilian economy.

Amphibious Doctrine

Current joint doctrine and war plans visualize the administrative deployment of Army troops in support of contingency plans. That is, Army units would be moved by surface and air to the objective area and be loaded/unloaded by predeployed support units. The scenario is thought of in terms of the way troops are handled during our Redeployment of Forces to Germany (REFORGER) exercises in Europe today. If a combat landing were required, joint plans call for any landings to be made by Navy/Marine Corps amphibious forces. This mind set is similar to existing plans when we began World War II. It was visualized then, as now, that if the Army units had to be combat landed, they would follow Marine Corps amphibious landings.

By 1942 it was evident that this approach would not be satisfactory. The services operated under different conditions with different missions, which required different concepts, doctrine, and know-how. Soon after Pearl Harbor the Army staff realized that if the Army was to carry the war to the Germans, the Japanese, and the Italians, then amphibious operations were absolutely essential.

The Marine Corps is traditionally manned, equipped, and trained to go ashore, fight, and occupy a beachhead area for at most thirty to forty days. The marines then backload and return to the near shore for reequipping and retraining. The mission of the Army, on the other hand, in the past and probably into the future, has been to land in an objective area, and thereafter build a line of communication on shore to support land forces as they move inland until the enemy land forces have been defeated. The missions are different and the required support is different.

There have been a few exceptions. One occurred when the 3d Marine Amphibious Force was required to land in the Da Nang area in South Vietnam, to establish a base, and to remain in support of operations, all of which was normally the job of the Army. In this case, the marines were not equipped, trained, or capable of establishing a communications zone to support their combat and support units. The Navy was forced to develop a logistics organization to support the Marine

Corps in the Da Nang area, but this was an exception and a departure from normal doctrine.

In any future war, because of the relative size of the Marine Corps, the Army would have to make amphibious landings as it did in World War II. The need for landings would also likely occur if we became involved in two contingency operations in different parts of the world which, as I understand it, is the basis for requirements in our war planning today.

Currently the Army has no capability, no concept, no doctrine, no training, no unit equipment, and no organization to carry out these difficult amphibious operations in combat. The organizations nearest to having such a capability are the Transportation Corps' logistics over-the-shore units, equipped and trained to unload and move cargo. But they are not organized, equipped, or trained to develop lodgment (beachhead) areas with all the engineering requirements that go with such actions. Plans do not exist to marry them up with combat units for assistance in combat unit landings and their subsequent deployment and unloading over unfriendly beaches in combat. Nor do plans include the even more difficult task of assisting to develop lodgment areas and providing logistics support under combat conditions until normal resupply can be established.

I understand the Army has neither the funds nor the desire to add this capability. It has not been approved as joint doctrine. But if war were to occur, in all probability the Transportation Corps would be called upon to duplicate the actions of the engineer amphibious units in World War II. Therefore, it would be wise for the Transportation Corps, either in its museum or in its school, to acquire all historical information on the Engineer Amphibious Command and its engineer boat and shore regiments of World War II.

They should build a library of manuals, doctrine, organizational information, training literature, and training records. It would certainly be wise to update the information to match the current automated Army supply, maintenance, and transportation doctrine. I'm sure the Army does not believe the need exists; however, filing all the relevant information in the museum and school would make it available should the need ever arise. Looking back on my firsthand experience with the difficulties in learning how to accomplish this mission in World War II, I know that it would be a slow, costly, and difficult job to reinvent such capabilities in the future.

Retrograde Planning

This area must receive more attention as part of all Army planning and needs much more emphasis in our school system. The Army has always carried out retrograde operations poorly. The only exception was in Vietnam. During this war, an economy-minded OSD directed that all services perform detailed retrograde planning during the gradual U.S. disengagement from Vietnam. As a result, a great deal of equipment and supplies were recovered and placed back into the supply system or used for other authorized purposes. This planning saved many millions of dollars.

Although we recommended early on that the Army initiate retrograde planning and retrograde actions at the beginning of DESERT SHIELD, at first our recommendations were not followed.

Early Deployment of Support Personnel

It is also vital to deploy sufficient support units (especially transportation and supply personnel) early, with the combat force. This would enable the support system to immediately begin to organize the support operation and provide sufficient support when and where needed.

During my experience, especially in Korea and Vietnam, this was not done and the support system had a difficult time playing catch-up once the necessary personnel arrived. The Army generally deploys support personnel only after support breaks down and force commanders realize a break-down has occurred. Although I was not involved in the latest Gulf War, all reports indicate that support personnel were again deployed only after the system had bogged down. For any operation, the need for support personnel should be realized from the beginning of plans.

Distribution

In today's high-tech world, as the Army relies more and more on automation, instant communication, and new forms of transportation, the word *distribution* is beginning to seem more appropriate than *logistics* to describe support to the Army in the field. We have already discussed various problems in distribution including transportation management, asset visibility, retrograde planning, total system command and control, inventory in motion, and funding for second destination transportation.

A change in the funding process could conceivably have more effect on correcting the problems than any other approach. If the customer had to justify his budget for transportation, he would have to take a personal interest in inventory in motion, i.e., total requirements, assets on hand, future requirements, items requisitioned, items in the pipeline, total asset visibility of items in transit, expected time of arrival, and least cost of transportation. Through inventory in motion the customer could manage distribution far more effectively and efficiently, and for much less cost. The response of Army leadership to this recommendation will probably be that such a system would place too heavy a burden on the already overloaded combat commanders.

But this same workload problem exists for management of the total logistics "distribution" system. When the Army decided in 1962 to eliminate the Technical Services and become functional, it decided that the Army chain of command could, and would, manage the logistics system rather than have the Technical Services do it. But proper management of the cost of the system is a vital part of the job that Army leadership assumed in 1962. Because of this lack of attention on system management by the Army leadership, the secretary of defense has increasingly centralized management of many logistics functions at the OSD level, such as the Defense Logistics Agency, the Defense Commissary Agency, post exchanges, and medical support. Others on the horizon are also slated for centralization.

Leadership

Much has been written over the years about leadership. Why? Because it is so important to all human relationships, especially in the military, and yet it is so difficult to define. Most articles describe leadership through example rather than attempting a definition.

I will always remember a speech on leadership given by Dr. Douglas Southhall Freeman shortly after World War II. At the time and for many years after, Dr. Freeman had been the editor of a Richmond, Virginia, newspaper. He also was an outstanding historian who had written *Lee's Lieutenants*, *George Washington*, and other volumes. After being introduced, Freeman stood alone in the center of the stage for an entire hour. He used no training aids and he never moved. Nevertheless, he kept us sitting on the edge of our seats for the entire hour. I do not recall ever hearing a more impressive talk.

Dr. Freeman discussed leadership, his favorite subject. He did so by recounting the actions of various Confederate commanders during Civil War battles. As he described the commanders' conversations with each other, their problems, their actions, and their orders to their troops, they came alive and we listeners felt that we were actually there witnessing the scene. Freeman conveyed his ideas on leadership by describing how each good commander handled his troops, the enemy, and the battle. We left with a deep appreciation of humility, selflessness, character, courage, and integrity, but never really understood how these leadership qualities had been developed.

In 1917, Maj. C. A. Bach wrote one of the best articles on how to develop leadership. Bach had enlisted in the 13th Minnesota Infantry of the National Guard and served as a sergeant with the regiment in the Philippines. Promoted to lieutenant in the 36th U.S. Volunteer Infantry, he transferred to the Regular Army as a first lieutenant in the 7th Cavalry. In an address delivered to the graduating officers of the Second Training Camp at Fort Sheridan, Bach analyzed how to be a leader. His remarks were printed verbatim in the Waco, Texas, *Daily Times Herald* on 27 January 1918. In November 1942, Senator Henrik Shipstead of Minnesota inserted the remarks in the *Congressional Record* and they were printed as Congressional Document 289.

The speech, which appears as an appendix to this book, continues to be regarded as the best composition on leadership ever recorded. In essence, Bach urged his charges to "know your men, know your business, [and] know yourself," explained the differences between an "officer" and a "leader," and provided the formula by which a young lieutenant could transform himself from one to the other.

APPENDIX

Leadership

by

Major C. A. Bach (1918)

In a short time each of you will control the lives of a certain number of other men. You will have in your charge loyal but untrained citizens, who look to you for instruction and guidance. Your word will be their law. Your most casual remark will be remembered. Your mannerism will be aped. Your clothing, your carriage, your vocabulary, your manner of command will be imitated. When you join your organization you will find there a willing body of men who ask from you nothing more than the qualities that will command their respect, their loyalty, and their obedience. They are perfectly ready and eager to follow you so long as you can convince them that you have those qualities. When the time comes that they are satisfied you do not possess them you might as well kiss yourself goodbye. Your usefulness in that organization is at an end.

From the standpoint of society, the world may be divided into leaders and followers. The professions have their leaders, the financial world has its leaders. We have religious leaders, and political leaders, and society leaders. In all this leadership it is difficult, if not impossible, to separate from the element of pure leadership that selfish element of personal gain or advantage to the individual without which such leadership would lose its value. It is in the military service only where men freely sacrifice their lives for a faith, where men are willing to suffer and die for the right or the prevention of a great wrong, that we can hope to realize leadership in its most exalted and disinterested sense. Therefore, when I say leadership, I mean military leadership.

In a few days the great mass of you men will receive commissions as officers. These commissions will not make you leaders, they will merely make you officers. They will place you in a position where you can become leaders if you possess the proper attributes. But you must make good—not so much with the men over you as with the men under you. Men must and will follow into battle officers who are not leaders, but the driving power behind these men is not enthusiasm but discipline. They go with doubt and trembling, and with an awful fear tugging at their heartstrings that prompts the unspoken question, "What will he do next?" Such men obey the letter of their orders but no more. Of devotion to their commander, of exalted enthusiasm which scorns personal risk, of their self-sacrifice to ensure his personal safety, they know nothing. Their legs carry them forward because their brain and their training tell them they must go. Their spirit does not go with them.

Great results are not achieved by cold, passive, unresponsive soldiers. They don't go very far and they stop as soon as they can. Leadership not only demands but receives the willing, unhesitating, unfaltering obedience and loyalty of other men; and a devotion that will cause them, when the time comes, to follow their uncrowned king to hell and back again if necessary.

You will ask yourselves: "Of just what, then, does leadership consist? What must I do to become a leader? What are the attributes of leadership, and how can I cultivate them?"

Leadership is a composite of a number of qualities. Among the most important I would list self-confidence, moral ascendancy, self-sacrifice, paternalism, fairness, initiative, decision, dignity, courage. Let me discuss these with you in detail.

Self-confidence results, first, from exact knowledge; second, the ability to impart that knowledge; and, third, the feeling of superiority over others that naturally follows. All these give the officer poise. To lead, you must know—you may bluff all your men some of the time, but you can't do it all the time. Men will not have confidence in an officer unless he knows his business, and he must know it from the ground up. The officer should know more about paper work than his first sergeant and company clerk put together; he should know more about messing than his mess sergeant; more about diseases of the horse than his troop farrier. He should be at least as good a shot as any man in his company. If the officer does not know, and demonstrates the fact that he does not know, it is entirely human for the soldier to say to himself, "To hell with him. He doesn't know as much about this as I do," and calmly disregard the instructions received. There is no substitute for accurate knowledge. Become so well informed that men will hunt you up to ask questions—that your brother officers will say to one another, "Ask Smith—he knows."

And not only should each officer know thoroughly the duties of his own grade, but he should study those of the two grades next above him. A twofold benefit attaches to this. He prepares himself for duties which may fall to his lot at any time during battle; he further gains a broader view point which enables him to appreciate the necessity for the issuance of orders and join more intelligently in their execution.

Not only must the officer know, but he must be able to put what he knows into grammatical, interesting, forceful English. He must learn to stand on his feet and speak without embarrassment. I am told that in British training camps student officers are required to deliver ten-minute talks on any subject they may choose. That is excellent practice. For to speak clearly one must think clearly, and clear, logical thinking expresses itself in definite, positive orders.

While self-confidence is the result of knowing more than your men, moral ascendancy over them is based upon your belief that you are the better man. To gain and maintain this ascendancy you must have self-control, physical vitality and endurance, and moral force. You must have yourself so well in hand that, even though in battle you be scared stiff, you will never show fear. For if you by so much as a hurried movement or a trembling of the hand, or a change of expression, or a hasty order hastily revoked, indicate your mental condition it will be reflected in your men in a far greater degree.

In garrison or camp many instances will arise to try your temper and wreck the sweetness of your disposition. If at such times you "fly off the handle" you have no business to be in charge of men. For men in anger say and do things that they almost invariably regret afterward. An officer should never apologize to his men; also an officer should never be guilty of an act for which his sense of justice tells him he should apologize.

Another element in gaining moral ascendancy lies in the possession of enough physical vitality and endurance to withstand the hardships to which you and your men are subjected and a dauntless spirit that enables you not only to accept them cheerfully but to minimize their magnitude. Make light of your troubles, belittle your trials, and you will help vitally to build up within your organization an esprit whose value in time of stress cannot be measured.

Moral force is the third element in gaining moral ascendancy. To exert moral force you must live clean, you must have sufficient brain power to see the right and the will to do right. Be an example to your men. An officer can be a power for good or a power for evil. Don't preach to them—that will be worse than useless. Live the kind of life you would have them lead, and you will be surprised to see the number that will imitate you. A loud-mouthed, profane captain who is careless of his personal appearance will have a load-mouthed, profane, dirty company. Remember what I tell you. Your company will be the reflection of yourself. If you have a rotten company it will be because you are a rotten captain.

Self-sacrifice is essential to leadership. You will give, give all the time. You will give of yourself physically, for the longest hours, the hardest work and the greatest responsibility is the lot of the captain.

He is the first man up in the morning and the last man in at night. He works while others sleep.

You will give of yourself mentally, in sympathy and appreciation for the troubles of men in your charge. This one's mother has died, and that one has lost all his savings in a bank failure. They may desire help, but more than anything else they desire sympathy. Don't make the mistake of turning such men down with the statement that you have troubles of your own, for every time that you do you knock a stone out of the foundation of your house. Your men are your foundation, and your house leadership will tumble about your ears unless its rests securely upon them.

Finally, you will give of your slender financial resources. You will frequently spend your money to conserve the health and well-being of your men or to assist them when in trouble. Generally you get your money back. Very infrequently you must charge it to profit and loss.

When I say that paternalism is essential to leadership I use the term in its better sense. I do not now refer to that form of paternalism which robs men of initiative, self-reliance, and self-respect. I refer to the paternalism that manifests itself in a watchful care for the comfort and welfare of those in your charge.

Soldiers are much like children. You must see that they have shelter, food, and clothing, the best that your utmost efforts can provide. You must be far more solicitous of their comfort than of your own. You must see that they have food to eat before you think of your own; that they have each as good a bed as can be provided before you consider where you will sleep. You must look after their health. You must conserve their strength by not demanding needless exertion or useless labor.

And by doing all these things you are breathing life into what would be otherwise a mere machine. You are creating a soul in your organization that will make the mass respond to you as though it were one man. And that is esprit.

And when your organization has this esprit you will wake up some morning and discover that the tables have been turned; that instead of your constantly looking out for them they have, without even a hint from you, taken up the task of looking out for you. You will find that a detail is always there to see that your tent, if you have one, is promptly pitched; that the most and the cleanest bedding is brought to your tent; that from some mysterious source two eggs have been added to your supper when no one else has any; that an extra man is helping your men give your horse a supergrooming; that your wishes are anticipated; that every man is Johnny-on-the-spot. And then you have arrived.

Fairness is another element without which leadership can neither be built up nor maintained. There must be first that fairness which treats all men justly. I do not say alike, for you cannot treat all men alike—that would be assuming that all men are cut from the same piece: that there is no such thing as individuality or a personal equation.

You cannot treat all men alike: a punishment that would be dismissed by one man with a shrug of the shoulders is mental anguish for another. A company commander who for a given offense has a standard punishment that applies to all is either too indolent or too stupid to study the personality of his men. In his case justice is certainly blind.

Study your men as carefully as a surgeon studies a difficult case. And when you are sure of your diagnosis apply the remedy. And remember that you apply the remedy to effect a cure, not merely to see the victim squirm. It may be necessary to cut deep, but when you are satisfied as to your diagnosis don't be divided from your purpose by any false sympathy for the patient.

Hand in hand with fairness in awarding punishment walks fairness in giving credit. Everybody hates a human hog. When one of your men has accomplished an especially creditable piece of work, see that he gets the proper reward. Turn heaven and earth upside down to get it for him. Don't try to take it away from him and hog it for yourself. You may do this and get away with it, but you have lost the respect and loyalty of your men. Sooner or later your brother officers will hear of it and shun you like a leper. In war there is glory enough for all. Give the man under you his due. The man who always takes and never gives is not a leader. He is a parasite.

There is another kind of fairness—that which will prevent an officer from abusing the privileges of his rank. When you exact respect from soldiers be sure you treat them with equal respect. Build up their manhood and self-respect. Don't try to pull it down.

For an officer to be overbearing and insulting in the treatment of enlisted men is the act of a coward. He ties the man to a tree with the ropes of discipline and then strikes him in the face, knowing full well that the man cannot strike back. Consideration, courtesy, and respect from officers toward enlisted men are not incompatible with discipline. They are parts of our discipline. Without initiative and decision no man can expect to lead.

In maneuvers you will frequently see when an emergency arises, certain men calmly give instant orders which later, on analysis, prove to be, if not exactly the right thing, very nearly the right thing to have done. You will see other men in emergency become badly rattled: their brains refuse to work, or they give a hasty order, revoke it: give another, revoke that: in short, show every indication of being in a blue funk.

Regarding the first man you may say: "That man is a genius. He hasn't had time to reason this thing out. He acts intuitively." Forget it.

"Genius is merely the capacity for taking infinite pains." The man who is ready is the man who has prepared himself. He has studied beforehand the possible situation that might arise, he has made tentative plans covering such situations. When he is confronted by the emergency he is ready to meet it.

He must have sufficient mental alertness to appreciate the problem that confronts him and the power of quick reasoning to determine what changes are necessary in his already formulated plan. He must also make the decision to order the execution and stick to his orders.

Any reasonable order in an emergency is better than no order. The situation is there. Meet it. It is better to do something and to do the wrong thing than to hesitate, hunt around for the right thing to do and wind up by doing nothing at all. And, having decided on a line of action, stick to it. Don't vacillate. Men have no confidence in an officer who doesn't know his own mind.

Occasionally you will be called upon to meet a situation which no reasonable human being could anticipate. If you have prepared yourself to meet other emergencies which you could anticipate the mental training you have thereby gained will enable you to act promptly and with calmness.

You must frequently act without orders from a higher authority. Time will not permit you to wait for them. Here again enters the importance of studying the work of officers above you. If you have a comprehensive grasp of the entire situation and can form an idea of the general plan of your superiors, that and your previous emergency training will enable you to determine that the responsibility is yours and to issue the necessary orders without delay.

The element of personal dignity is important in military leadership. Be the friend of your men, but do not become their intimate. Your men should stand in awe of you—not fear. If your men presume to become familiar it is your fault, not theirs. Your actions have encouraged them to do so. And, above all things, don't cheapen yourself by courting their friendship or currying their favor. They will despise you for it. If you are worthy of their loyalty and respect and devotion they will surely give all these without asking. If you are not, nothing that you can do will win them.

And then I would mention courage. Moral courage you need as well as physical courage—that kind of moral courage which enables you to adhere without faltering to a determined course of action which your judgement has indicated as the one best suited to secure the desired results. Every time you change your orders without obvious reason you weaken your authority and impair the confidence of your men. Have the moral courage to stand by your order and see it through.

Moral courage further demands that you assume the responsibility for your own acts. If your subordinates have loyally carried out your orders and the movement you directed is a failure, the failure is yours, not theirs. Yours would have been the honor had it been successful. Take the blame if it results in disaster. Don't try to shift to a subordinate and make him the goat. That is a cowardly act.

Furthermore, you will need moral courage to determine the fate of those under you. You will frequently be called upon for recommendations for the promotion or demotion of officers and noncommissioned officers in your immediate command. Keep clearly in mind your personal integrity and the duty you owe your country. Do not let yourself be deflected from a strict sense of justice by feeling of personal friendship. If your own brother is your second lieutenant, and you find him unfit to hold his commission, eliminate him. If you don't, your lack of moral courage may result in the loss of valuable lives.

If, on the other hand, you are called upon for a recommendation concerning a man whom, for personal reasons you thoroughly dislike, do not fail to do him full justice. Remember that your aim is the general good, not the satisfaction of an individual grudge.

I am taking it for granted that you have physical courage. I need not tell you how necessary that is. Courage is more than bravery. Bravery is fearlessness—the absence of fear. The merest dolt may be brave, because he lacks the mentality to appreciate his danger; he doesn't know enough to be afraid.

Courage, however, is a firmness of spirit, that moral backbone, which, while fully appreciating the danger involved, nevertheless goes on with the undertaking. Bravery is physical; courage is mental and moral. You may be cold all over; your hands may tremble; your legs may quake; your knees may be ready to give way—that is fear. If nevertheless, you go forward; if in spite of this physical defection you continue to lead your men against the enemy, you have courage. The physical manifestations of fear will pass away. You may never experience them but once. They are the "buck fever" of the hunter who tries to shoot his first deer. You must not give way to them.

A number of years ago, while taking a course in demolitions, the class of which I was a member was handling dynamite. The instructor said regarding its manipulation: "I must caution you gentlemen to be careful in the use of these explosives. One man has but one accident." And so I would caution you. If you give way to the fear that will doubtless beset you in your first action, if you show the white feather, if you let your men go forward while you hunt a shell crater, you will never again have the opportunity of leading those men.

Use judgement in calling on your men for display of physical courage or bravery. Don't ask any man to go where you would not go

yourself. If your common sense tells you that the place is too dangerous for you to venture into, then it is too dangerous for him. You know
his life is as valuable to him as yours is to you.

Occasionally some of your men must be exposed to danger which
you cannot share. A message must be taken across a fire-swept zone.
You call for volunteers. If your men know you and know that you are
"right," you will never lack volunteers, for they know your heart is in
your work, that you are giving your country the best you have, that
you would willingly carry the message yourself if you could. Your
example and enthusiasm will have inspired them.

And, lastly, if you aspire to leadership, I would urge you to study
men. Get under their skins and find out what is inside. Some men are
quite different from what they appear to be on the surface. Determine
the workings of their minds.

Much of Robert E. Lee's success as a leader may be ascribed to
his ability as a psychologist. He knew most of his opponents from
West Point days, knew the workings of their minds, and he believed
that they would do certain things under certain circumstances. In nearly every case he was able to anticipate their movements and block the
execution.

You do not know your opponent in this war in the same way. But
you can know your own men. You can study each to determine where-
in lies his strength and his weakness: which man can be relied upon to
the last gasp and which cannot.

Know your men, know your business, know yourself.

BIBLIOGRAPHY

Besson, General Frank S., Chairman. A Report by the Joint Logistics Review Board, Transportation and Management Control.

Brown, Lt. Gen. Frederic J., Chairman. *Report by the Department of the Army Board of Inquiry on the Army Logistics System*. March 1967.

Cannon, M. Hamlin. *Leyte: The Return to the Philippines*. Washington, D.C.: U.S. Army Center of Military History, 1987.

Division of Responsibility in Wartime Between National Commanders and Major and Subordinate Allied Committees, NATO Military Committee Document 36/2. NATO Headquarters: Approved by the Heads of State on 30–31 May 1978.

Epley, William W. *Roles and Missions of the United States Army*. Washington, D.C.: U.S. Army Center of Military History, 1991.

Heiser, Lt. Gen. Joseph M., Jr. *A Soldier Supporting Soldiers*. Washington, D.C.: U.S. Army Center of Military History, 1992.

Heiser, Lt. Gen. Joseph M., Jr. *Logistic Support*. Washington, D.C.: U.S. Army Center of Military History, 1991.

Hewes, James E., Jr. *From Root to McNamara: Army Organization and Administration, 1900–1963*. Washington, D.C.: U.S. Army Center of Military History, 1983.

Huston, James A., *The Sinews of War: Army Logistics, 1775–1953*. Washington, D.C.: U.S. Army Center of Military History, 1988.

Miller, John, jr. *CARTWHEEL: The Reduction of Rabaul*. Washington, D.C.: U.S. Army Center of Military History, 1990.

Milner, Samuel. *Victory in Papua*. Washington, D.C.: U.S. Army Center of Military History, 1989.

Smith, Robert Ross. *The Approach to the Philippines*. Washington,

D.C.: U.S. Army Center of Military History, 1984.

Smith, Robert Ross. *Triumph in the Philippines*. Washington, D.C.:
U.S. Army Center of Military History, 1991.

U.S. Army. *History of the Second Engineer Special Brigade*.
Harrisburg, PA: The Telegraph Press, 1946.

U.S. Army Lines of Communication in Europe, 1945–1967.
Headquarters, U.S. Army, Europe, and Seventh Army, Office of
the Deputy Chief of Staff for Logistics (Operations), 1968.

INDEX

Made in the USA
Monee, IL
25 March 2022